EXPORT Made Simple

The Made Simple series
has been created
primarily for self-education
but can equally well
be used as
an aid to group study.
However complex the subject,
the reader is taken
step by step,
clearly and methodically,
through the course. Each volume
has been prepared by experts,
using throughout the
Made Simple technique of teaching.
Consequently the gaining
of knowledge now becomes
an experience to be enjoyed.

In the same series

Accounting
Acting and Stagecraft
Additional Mathematics
Advertising
Anthropology
Applied Economics
Applied Mathematics
Applied Mechanics
Art Appreciation
Art of Speaking
Art of Writing
Biology
Book-keeping
British Constitution
Calculus
Chemistry
Childcare
Commerce
Commercial Law
Company Administration
Computer Programming
Cookery
Cost and Management Accounting
Data Processing
Dressmaking
Economic History
Economic and Social Geography
Economics
Electricity
Electronic Computers
Electronics
English
Export
French
Geology
German
Human Anatomy
Italian
Journalism
Latin
Law
Management
Marketing
Mathematics
Modern Electronics
Modern European History
New Mathematics
Office Practice
Organic Chemistry
Philosophy
Photography
Physical Geography
Physics
Pottery
Psychology
Rapid Reading
Russian
Salesmanship
Soft Furnishing
Spanish
Statistics
Transport and Distribution
Typing
Woodwork

EXPORT Made Simple

Henry Deschampsneufs, B.A. (Oxon), M.I.Ex.

Made Simple Books
W. H. ALLEN London
A Howard & Wyndham Company

Printed and bound in Great Britain
by Butler & Tanner Ltd,
Frome and London
for the publishers W. H. Allen & Company Ltd,
44 Hill Street, London W1X 8LB

ISBN 0 491 01908 4 casebound
ISBN 0 491 01918 1 paperbound

Preface

In the Liston Report, the British Overseas Trade Board declared that the commercial strategy of the country must not fail for lack of suitably motivated, educated and trained people to engage in export trade at all levels. This view is shared by almost every government in the world.

The purpose of this book is to show how export can be handled in a truly professional way. It aims to help you to become a highly professional exporter.

To accomplish this three things are necessary. First, international trade is made up of both exports and imports, since one country's exports are another's imports. You must be aware, therefore, of the extent and operation of international trade if you wish to take part in it by exporting.

Second, you must be well versed in the mechanics of export, or what is termed Export Practice, even if you are not actively engaged with it.

Third, you must be able to go out and get business from overseas in what is now a highly competitive world market place. Marketing is concerned with selling people what they want or need, rather than what a manufacturer or merchant wishes to sell them.

Hence this book is divided into three parts:

Part 1: International Trade. This deals with trade from both the world and national points of view, using Britain as an example of an exporting nation. It shows the importance of export to a company and the individual, and gives some indication of the opportunities in it for you.

Part 2: Export Practice. This covers pricing, quotations, orders, office organisation, transport, documentation, insurance, payment and finance, as well as the legal aspects of export practice.

Part 3: Export Marketing. This considers local environments, and shows how information about them may be obtained. It studies the product to be exported, and how it may best be distributed, sold and promoted. It deals with market selection, and the preparation and execution of marketing plans.

There has been a tendency in the past to consider Export Practice and Marketing as two separate subjects, whereas they are both an integral part of the whole export operation. Hence both are given more or less equal prominence in the book.

Only the essential information required by the everyday exporter has been included, so a comprehensive list of further reading has been provided. At the end of each chapter there are sets of Questions and Answers and Exercises by which you may test yourself on what you have learned, because this book has been designed particularly for self-study. It will also be of direct interest to students and lecturers taking the BOTB Foundation Course in Overseas Trade, Parts I and II of the Institute of Export Final Examinations, and the Diploma in Marketing of the Institute of Marketing. It will be invaluable for those taking management courses, such as Diplomas in Management Studies and Business Policy, which have an international marketing option, as well as anyone working in export shipping, marketing and merchanting or supplying services to exporters, such as banking, all forms of transport, insurance, distribution, research and promotion.

HENRY DESCHAMPSNEUFS

// Acknowledgements

My grateful thanks are due to:

My exporting friends all over the world, and especially my colleagues in the Institute of Export, who have taught me all I know about export—

My many students, who show so much interest in export—

My wife and daughters, who have supported me loyally in my export career—

Geoffrey Whitehead, who has helped greatly with the manuscript of this book.

H.D.

Contents

PART 1

INTERNATIONAL TRADE

1

WORLD TRADE

Exporting goods and services to people in other countries is one of the most fascinating and exciting commercial activities in the world. To put export in its proper perspective you must first understand something of the background to international trade, because this affects to some degree what you as an exporter may or may not do. The climate of international trade is largely responsible for the opportunities which may present themselves to you in other parts of the world. The conduct of international trade affects how you handle your own exports, while the profitability of your efforts will depend to some extent on the working of the international monetary systems.

It will also be necessary to examine international trade from a national point of view, because you have to act against your own country's background. This, however, will be considered in the next chapter. The two chapters in Part 1 should give you a picture of the scene into which you are entering, rather like a football team having a look at the pitch and its surroundings before the start of a match.

Without becoming too deeply involved with the mechanics of international trade, you should know how it operates and its extent in the world. You should know how monetary systems work, because they relate directly to the ability of overseas customers to buy from you. You should also be aware of how international organisations seek to regulate international trade, because this affects how and where your goods may be exported.

Hence this chapter has been divided into the following sections:

1. The operation of world trade
2. The international monetary systems
3. The international organisations

The Operation of World Trade

There are three areas where some knowledge of world trade will help you with your own export operations. One is the history of world trade; the second is the theory behind world trade; and the third is the extent of it today.

The History of World Trade

If you define world trade as the exchange of goods between people in different parts of the world, you will understand that this activity has been in existence for centuries. It began as soon as people started to visit each other's lands, saw what the local people's products were like, and decided they wanted them. This they accomplished by **bartering** their goods for those of the other people. As you might expect, the earliest forms of international trade were centered around the eastern end of the Mediterranean Sea. Britain has been involved from well before the birth of Christ, when the Phoenicians came to Cornwall to exchange their textiles for Cornish tin.

Yet the old idea of straight barter was being discarded as long ago as the sixth century B.C. in favour of an **exchange system** based on gold and silver, coins being bought and sold by weight and content. In Roman times coins of many nations were traded against each other, and this was the beginning of what today is called a system of **foreign exchange.**

The greatest boost to world trade was given in the sixteenth century, when merchant adventurers from Spain, Portugal, Holland and Britain sailed all over the world, buying raw materials and foodstuffs in exchange for produce from their own countries. In fact, the beginnings of the British merchant houses can be traced to this period, a tradition which still exists in the activities of the merchants, who are today responsible for about a third of all Britain's exports. Moreover, transport by sea and marine insurance practices also had their origins about this time.

As a result of this expansion of international trade, three widely held beliefs grew up:

1. That international trade was wholly in a country's interests, because what one country gained was at the expense of another. You may consider this a curiously static view of the world's resources.

2. That wealth consisted of gold and silver, and that these were more important than goods. Gold and silver could be used to buy the means of making war on other countries, whose conquests would lead to increased resources.

3. That a country should try to obtain a balance of exports over imports, since any deficiency would have to be paid for in gold or silver. The reserves of bullion accumulated by favourable balances meant, moreover, that in emergencies you were able to buy food and raw materials from other countries.

These 'mercantile' theories were, to some extent, demolished by Adam Smith in his book *The Wealth of Nations*, published in 1776. He preached the doctrine of **Free Trade**, both within a country and internationally. He held that the interaction of the laws of supply and demand tended to produce some equilibrium in trade. And since he was convinced that a policy of 'laisser faire' was better than any form of control, he disliked government interference with trade, because he said it would not work. By 'laisser faire' he meant 'let things work themselves out', without government controls.

International trade has continued to grow, but has been subject to many artificial restraints and restrictions, to the extent that it is difficult to establish the basic principles on which it exists.

The Theory of International Trade

In their simplest form, the reasons why trade takes place between people of different countries are:

(*a*) Different regions in the world have different resources. For example, uranium is found in Zaïre but not in Europe. Hence the people in Zaïre export their uranium to Europe, which in turn supplies Zaïre with goods which are not produced there.

(*b*) Some people are more efficient at doing certain things than others. You might say the Germans are more skilled in technical matters than the Indians, not because the Germans are intrinsically cleverer than the Indians, but because the opportunities have been greater for the Germans.

(*c*) In certain parts of the world there is a greater demand for goods than the local people can produce. Britain is such a country.

In general, therefore, it is held that people should specialise in what they do best. This is called the principle of **Comparative Advantage**. Hence you may say that people should concentrate in those areas of trade where they have the greatest comparative advantage over others, and should leave alone the activities where they have the greatest comparative disadvantage.

It is not, however, quite as simple as this, because countries and people do not always specialise in what they can do best, nor are the rewards for so doing always comparable. Moreover, there is not completely free trade in the world. When a country can produce goods which are extremely competitive, it tends to favour free trade, because it has most to gain. But when its goods are uncompetitive, and lack any comparative advantage, the country tends to become protectionist, and impose restrictions on trade with the rest of the world. Restrictions on international trade are generally imposed by nations:

(*a*) For strategic reasons
(*b*) To protect local industries and employment
(*c*) To preserve a balance of payments

Such restrictions almost inevitably reduce that country's own standards of living, and create situations where the principle of comparative advantage is not applied. Yet basically when you think in terms of your own export product or service, you should ask yourself what comparative advantage it has over other similar products in the world, because this is what will ultimately sell it.

The Extent of World Trade

Trade in the world has developed to such an extent that its annual total, expressed in monetary terms, is around £250,000 million. It includes almost every known kind of material and manufacture. It represents the fastest growing commercial activity in the world. Almost every country recognises that by participating in trade its own standards of living can be raised, which is as important for companies as it is for countries.

Some countries, like some companies, are more involved with international trade than others. The Netherlands, Belgium and West Germany, for example, export over a third of their total production, and import most of their raw materials.

The main trade in manufactured goods is between the more developed countries, because of their high involvement with international trade. The chief trading partners of the USA, for example, are Canada, Japan and West Germany. Yet international trade also benefits the developing countries of the world, who are the principal suppliers of raw materials, although their export is insufficient at present to counteract their rapidly growing populations, or the corruption in so many of their political systems.

Some idea of the extent and importance of world trade in our everyday lives may be gauged from an examination of the materials used in the production of a commonly known and used product like the Volkswagen 'Beetle'. These materials are imported from no less than 38 countries in Asia, Africa,

America and Europe. They total 12,000 tons a day, and range from steel, copper, zinc and manganese to cotton, wool, jute and plastics. The car itself is finally assembled in Germany, and is a good example of how international many of the products in common use today have become.

You will understand, therefore, that export is only one side of international trade, because your exports are always someone else's imports. Before you can export, someone must be able to import, and they can only do this if they have earned sufficient to pay for what you send them. Hence when you study international trade as it affects your own business, you must look at both the exports and the imports of any area where you believe there may be some possibility for your goods (this will be considered in more detail in Part 3 of this book).

The International Monetary Systems

Money is still the main medium of exchange used in international trade, although barter is also used when the supply of the right kind of money runs out, or the money is required for internal reasons. Virtually every country in the world has its own currency and since you, as an exporter, wish to be paid in your currency, this means your customer has to pay you in a currency which can easily be converted into yours.

As imports pay for exports, the result is known as the **balance of trade**, and any deficit will have to be made good by **borrowing**; by paying out of **reserves**; or by means of **invisible** earnings. The latter are payments for services, as opposed to goods, whose earnings are classed as **visibles**. You will recall that a balance of export earnings over import spendings has been the objective of countries for many years, although it has been found that ideally a country's earnings and spendings should about balance, otherwise, if some countries have all the money, no one can buy from them.

The international transactions of a country may be classified in three ways:

1. The **current account**, which includes the export earnings and import spendings on both goods and services.
2. **Investment and capital flows**, which cover official changes in the monetary balances held by the country.
3. The **official reserves** and holdings with the international monetary organisations, such as the International Monetary Fund (IMF).

Each country's currency will have a value in relation to the currencies of other countries, so that the **balance of payments**, which represents the balance of total trade, is settled by payments between the various currencies. So long as these are on fixed exchange rates, any deficit can be made good by the transfer of gold and other reserves. After the end of the Second World War the monetary authorities tried to maintain the value of different currencies by fixing official values for each, either in terms of the dollar or in relation to a specific amount of gold. This worked well for some 25 years, but eventually the system ran into difficulties, even though the IMF had been set up to act as a source of reserves. The dollar and sterling, which financed the greater part of world trade, and which were used as reserve currencies by most countries, found the task of financing world trade too great, and both were heavily devalued in the early seventies.

Hence there is now in existence a system of **floating exchange rates**, which fluctuate according to supply and demand. This means that the home economy of any country can be allowed to expand, and full employment be enjoyed, until such time as its exports become too expensive for other countries to buy them or demand that country's currency. In this case the currency will float down on the foreign exchange, until its exports become cheap enough for other countries to start buying them again. But for countries like Britain, which have to import vast quantities of raw materials, as sterling depreciates so imports become more expensive, and the balance of earnings over spending becomes more difficult to arrange.

The IMF now issues assets known as **SDR's, or Special Drawing Rights** (a form of asset allocated to countries on the basis of their IMF quotas). These are not freely negotiable like gold or foreign-backed reserves, and may only be used to settle genuine balance of payment needs. They are available to countries, but not to companies.

Traditionally money has been based on gold, but in recent years gold has been officially prevented from performing its task as a medium of exchange, or a store of value, so it no longer forms the basis for international trade. It is still, however, hoarded by certain countries such as France, the USSR and South Africa, as well as by some of the new oil-rich countries of the Middle East.

The ultimate aim is to form a world bank with some form of SDR's making a kind of world currency; it has already been suggested, for example, that oil should be paid for in SDR's and not in any national currency.

The current disease in the world today is **inflation**, which is simply an excess of purchasing power over the supply of goods available. This is no new disease, because when Spain discovered new sources of gold in the sixteenth century the price of almost everything in the world rose, as too much money chased too few goods. The same is true today, only it is paper money and not gold that is causing the difficulty. Inflation will not be cured until world supply more nearly matches world monetary demand. World trade has also grown faster than acceptable currencies to finance it, so it is probable that only by the use of SDR's, and their equivalent, can a real growth in world trade be achieved.

International Organisations

There are four principal world organisations which affect international trade.

UNCTAD/GATT

GATT stands for the **General Agreement on Tariffs and Trade**, such agreements being made principally between the developed nations. But attempts are being made to extend them through UNCTAD, the **United Nations Conference on Trade and Development**, to the 90 or so developing nations. The main task of UNCTAD/GATT is to encourage the development of free trade in the world through multilateral trading agreements; non-discrimination between trading nations; and by consultations taking place between countries before they impose trading restrictions on each other. There is now being introduced a tariff system favouring the export of manufactured goods from developing nations, whereby they can maintain high tariffs on imports, but export manufactures to developed nations on a low-rating tariff.

OECD

The **Organisation for Economic Cooperation and Development** (OECD) consists of 22 nations, including all the West European countries, along with Japan, Australia, New Zealand, Canada and the USA. It came into being as an attempt by Britain and America to rebuild Europe after the war. Its main aim is to prevent members discriminating against each other in trade, and, like UNCTAD/GATT, provides technical help to developing nations.

The IMF

The International Monetary Fund was formed in 1944 with the signing of the **Bretton Woods Agreement**. Its aim is to avoid the international currency problems so prevalent between the two world wars, which have become more acute since then. It comprises virtually all the Western countries, and, as you have seen, its main aim is to provide a huge reserve of currency in the form of SDR's and gold, as well as currency drawn from its members.

IBRD

The **International Bank for Reconstruction and Development** is generally known as the World Bank. Its main aim is to finance development projects in developing countries, such as the improvement of agriculture, the control of the populations and the training of local labour.

In addition to these international organisations, the complexities of international trade have been increased by the formation of mutual trading blocs. These include the **Planned Economies** (the name now given to Comecon, or Council for Mutual Economic Aid, countries behind the Iron Curtain); the **European Economic Community** (EEC); the **European Free Trade Association** (EFTA); and a number of other free trade areas in South America, Central America, the Caribbean and Africa. These will be dealt with in more detail in Chapter 10, but their main intention is to increase trade between members.

Another complication has been the growth of the **multinational companies**, with interests on a vast scale all over the world. A good example is International Business Machines, or IBM. Much of the instability of the foreign exchange market has been blamed on the activities of these companies, but so far as one can see the effect of the transfer of their holdings from one currency to another has been minimal. However, these companies have huge assets, in some cases greater than those of a small country, and tend to use their powers for their own benefit rather than acting in the best interests of international trade.

Such then is the background to world trade, against which export has to be considered. International trade is a vast subject, and you are advised to study it in depth if you wish to understand fully the market place in which your goods will be sold. This is rapidly becoming a world market place, thanks to mass communications, because people everywhere are informed of what is produced and are persuaded to buy. Your problem as an exporter is to ensure that your product is fully recognised in this world market place, and at the same time to see that it is easily obtainable wherever a demand for it occurs.

Revision

Cover the page with a sheet of paper and uncover one question at a time.

Answers	*Questions*
	1. Define International Trade.
1. The exchange of products between one country and another.	2. What did the mercantilists believe?
2. That international trade was wholly in a country's interests, and that gold and silver were wealth.	3. What principles did Adam Smith preach?
3. Free Trade and 'laisser faire'.	4. Name a West European country greatly dependent on international trade.
4. Belgium, Holland, West Germany.	5. What is the total annual amount of world trade today?
5. About £250,000 million pounds.	6. What is meant by the Balance of Payments?
6. The surplus of export earnings over import spendings.	7. What does SDR stand for?
7. Special Drawing Rights.	8. What is IBRD?
8. The World Bank.	9. What is another name for the Comecon countries?
9. The Planned Economies.	10. Where can uranium be found?
10. Zaïre.	

Exercises

1. What do you think are the main reasons why international trade takes place?
2. Explain what is meant by the principle of Comparative Advantage.
3. Why is it said that one person's exports are another's imports?
4. What is the International Monetary Fund designed to do?
5. How do a country's Balance of Payments get settled?

2

WORLD TRADE AT A NATIONAL LEVEL

Having looked at world trade on a global level, we must next consider it at a national level. Countries have traditionally been classified as individual export markets, but as you will see in Part 3, an export market is merely a group of foreign people who may be induced to buy your export product or service. Such a group is often called a **demand market**, which will seldom be confined to an individual country.

But since countries often act in various ways to protect their national sovereignties, by imposing restrictions on the international trade in which they engage, you need to examine world trade at a national level, because this both provides a background to any company's export possibilities and often dictates the methods of trading you need to adopt in various parts of the world.

If you can assess a country's trade performance, you will be in a better position to decide how important it is to your own company's exports, while the richer a country the more likely it is that any group of people in it can afford to buy your product. At the same time, in order to bring export down to both a company and individual level, you must examine the importance of export to a company, as well as look at the opportunities that exist for any individual who makes it a career.

Hence this chapter has been divided into the following sections:

1. A country's trade performance
2. Groups of countries in international trade
3. The importance of export to a company
4. Job opportunities in export

A Country's Trade Performance

You may assess this under seven main headings that form the background to any evaluation of the world's markets. Other considerations will be dealt with in Part 3, but for the present you must consider national boundaries because they still affect the conduct of world trade.

The Gross National Product (GNP)

The **GNP** of a country is the sum total of all the incomes accruing to the factors of production such as land, labour, capital, etc. GNP can also be considered as the income which accrues from any form of a country's economic activity. This is sometimes referred to as the **Gross Domestic Product** (GDP), although there are usually statistical differences between the two sets of figures. They can be calculated in three ways:

1. As the value added in production
2. As the incomes paid as rewards to factors in production
3. As the expenditure on purchases

GNP or GDP is an excellent indication of a country's standing in the world market place. Britain's stands now at some £50,000 million, but seems unlikely to grow at more than 1–2 per cent p.a. Other countries are achieving a much higher rate of growth, even a country like Turkey expecting something in the region of 7 per cent, although 1 per cent for Britain may be greater than 7 per cent for Turkey. Yet if you relate GNP to population, Britain is way down the world list in about fourteenth place, and below such countries as the USA, Sweden, Canada, West Germany and Japan.

Degree of Industrialisation

As you have seen, the greater a country's industrialisation, the greater its wealth. In the case of Britain, however, a decline in her share of international trade in manufactured goods presents a worrying position. This share used to be about 16 per cent, but has now fallen to under 10 per cent. The world leader is West Germany, with over 20 per cent, while Japan's share has risen to over 14 per cent.

While a degree of industrialisation is necessary for any country wishing to improve its standard of living, it does not follow that to compete directly with the industrialised countries is the only solution. Where labour, for example, is freely available it might be put to use in producing hand-made articles, which in an age of mass production are increasingly hard to obtain and often prohibitive in cost. Simple industrial products such as a lathe produced in a developing country would not only help imports, but probably find a ready market in neighbouring countries.

Natural Resources

In the past a country's **natural resources** have played a major part in determining that country's wealth. But this is not always the case today, since a country like Belgium has become rich by providing an **'added value'** to the materials it imports. There are certain natural resources many countries could develop, provided they also attempt to add some value to them before exporting them. One example is food, forecast as the world's next crisis product. Many of the poorer countries could grow more food, and if they could also process that food to make it acceptable to the importing countries, they would be able to earn far more than by merely exporting the food in its original state. Even a root like manioc can easily be turned into a fertiliser.

Tourism arises from the use of natural resources like sunny climates, mountain scenery and long coastlines. These have been turned to advantage by countries like Spain, which now earns most of her foreign currency from tourism. Many other countries have yet to take advantage of their tourist possibilities, in an age when people are continually seeking new places to visit.

Exports

The **direction** of a country's exports is important, especially as a government can assist in channelling these in certain directions. Britain, for example, used to send 40 per cent of her exports to the Commonwealth, whereas the figure is now under 15 per cent. Her exports to the rest of the world, excluding Europe, have fallen from 37 to 30 per cent, but Europe now takes nearly half of all British exports. Hence there is a great deal to be said for a country establishing common trading partners. At the same time a country's exports should go to as many parts of the world as possible, in order to avoid hard times if certain countries are doing badly.

The **kind of exports** of a country is important, because in general the wider the range, the less likelihood of difficulties. Spain's dependence on tourism and the Middle East's reliance on oil place them both in vulnerable positions should anything happen to affect these industries. In this respect Britain is better off, because the 70 per cent of her exports represented by manufactured goods covers a wide range of products. A further 13 per cent is in chemicals, and 10 per cent in food, drink and tobacco.

Imports

About 50 per cent of Britain's total imports are in manufactured or semi-manufactured goods, so that the greater part of her total trade is in this field, which shows that Britain, like other industrialised nations, imports and exports similar kinds of goods. As you might expect, Britain imports considerable quantities of raw materials, amounting to about 15 per cent of her total imports. A further 10 per cent can be added for oil, and most of the remaining 25 per cent is accounted for by food, drink and tobacco.

An additional problem for Britain has been that while the EEC has offered immense possibilities for British exports, it has also given Community exporters increased opportunities in Britain, which they have taken advantage of more successfully than the reverse.

You may well ask at this stage if some **restriction of imports** would be in British interests, but the problem is that there would probably be retaliatory action, making exports harder to sell. Many countries do restrict imports, however, and you will find that your opportunities in export will be affected by any country's attitude towards its import trade.

Balance of Payments

If you add up a country's imports and exports, you will arrive at its balance of payments situation. In Britain in 1975 visible exports amounted to £18,500 million. To this must be added earnings from invisibles of about £1,500 million, making a total of £20,000 million. Imports, however, amounted to £22,000 million, leaving an adverse balance of about £2,000 million. This was doubled in 1977, and when a country's balance of payments is in imbalance over a period of years it is said to be in a state of **fundamental disequilibrium.**

Where a deficit has to be made good this may be done: (*a*) by borrowing from other countries; (*b*) by devaluing the exchange rate of its currency; (*c*) by selling reserves of gold or foreign currency. While these measures help overcome an adverse balance of payments, loans from abroad will be expensive and mean invisible losses in years to come; a devaluation in the exchange rate will lower the standard of living which can only be restored by harder work; and selling reserves will be serious unless they can later be replaced.

Investment

At the root of a country's ability to play a major role in international trade lies its willingness to invest in both the means of production and in people. Britain has for far too long failed to invest sufficiently in either, preferring to spend her available resources far more on providing social benefits, which at the present time she can hardly afford. You can see the difference a willingness to invest in export makes when you compare the performance of countries like Japan and West Germany, which, after being defeated in the Second World War, decided the only way back to prosperity was to go all out for as much international trade as possible. Even a small country like Hong Kong has encouraged the entrepreneurial spirit which is so characteristic of export success. Much can be learned of a country's future prospects by examining its investment policy as applied to international trade.

Groups of Countries in International Trade

Having made an assessment of a country's trade performance, you will have made a start towards evaluating it in relation to your own export possibilities. By comparing the performance of different countries, you should be able to classify them according to their importance in international trade. Such a classification may be made in a number of ways, of which two are of practical value.

1. You should consider how far any individual country is able to take part in international trade. In this respect you might divide the countries of the world into four main groups as follows:

(*a*) Those countries which traditionally have become **industrialised**, and which are major exporters and importers of manufactured goods, as well as probable importers of raw materials. You might include in this group the countries of Western Europe, the USA, Japan and Canada, along with Britain. These countries have a high proportion of their total world trade with each other.

(*b*) Those **partially industrialised** countries which export both raw materials and some manufactured goods, whose export earnings have been helped by good demand and high prices for their raw materials in particular. Such a group would include Australia, South Africa and New Zealand, along with major Latin American countries such as Venezuela, Brazil and the Argentine, and certain African countries such as Kenya and Zambia, although the latter are weak in manufactures.

(*c*) The basically **non-industrialised countries** which are oil producers, comprising many of the Middle East countries like Iran, Saudi Arabia and Iraq, along with Indonesia, Borneo and Nigeria. They are now rich from their oil revenues, but have to import almost all their manufactured goods requirements.

(*d*) The **non-industrialised** countries who are without oil or any major source of raw materials, which represent the poor markets of the world. Such a group might include many of the smaller African states, the Central American republics apart from the banana countries, and of course certain of the countries in the East, like India, with an inability to feed themselves.

It is impossible to place every country accurately into any of these groups, while their composition is constantly changing. But if you export manufactures of some kind, clearly your best prospects will lie in the first two groups, with some prospects in the third, depending on how far industrialisation is taking place; Iran might be a better place than Kuwait, for example, in this respect.

But even so, such a classification does not take into account an equally important factor in international trade, the ability and willingness to engage in international trade.

2. Under this heading you might consider three groups according to their involvement with trade in the world:

(*a*) Countries which are prepared to participate as fully as possible in both import and export business. This would include the countries in the first group above, but it would not include all those in the second group, because some of them are pursuing a policy of attempting to be self-sufficient in manufactures, such as Brazil, the Argentine and, in certain categories, South Africa.

(*b*) Countries which will only participate in world trade by importing essential requirements. This group would include all the Planned Economies, most of the Latin American countries, and countries in the East which are politically motivated in the same way as those of the Planned Economies, such as Sri Lanka, Burma, China and Vietnam.

(*c*) Countries which are willing to participate in world trade but which lack the means of doing so, which roughly corresponds to the fourth group in the first classification.

You can see from this classification that in the second group your opportunities will only lie in supplying the means of production, which means a different method of trading on your part.

Such is the national background to international trade as seen through the eyes of the 150 or so countries which make up the world market place. But it is, as you will see in Chapter 10, only a background, because it does not enable you to specify with any degree of accuracy the potential markets overseas for your goods. It only enables you to be aware of the constraints placed on export by nations, and thus be able to avoid those parts of the world where the constraints are too strong to be overcome.

The Importance of Export to a Company

In the past many British companies have either overlooked export trade because the domestic market has been able to satisfy the company's output, or they have had easy exports largely owing to the protection afforded by preferential Commonwealth tariffs. Since neither of these factors now applies, only those companies which have in the past taken export trade seriously find themselves in a strong position. The disappointing balance of payments situation is mainly due to this shortsighted attitude by British industry towards export, some 85 per cent of all export trade from Britain being in the hand of a little over 1,000 companies. Moreover, the lack of professionalism so often seen in export may be traced to a reluctance of many British companies to have it handled by well-trained and well-paid staff.

But export is as important to a company as it is to a country, and you may identify six areas where this applies.

Spreading the risk

While a domestic market prospers a company can afford to ignore export. But as soon as demand at home declines, the company which relies on it alone will suffer. Since it is unlikely that every market in the world will suffer equally at the same time, a company which has a soundly based export trade is more likely to weather the storm. Experience shows that companies with healthy export sales almost always do better than those which rely purely on their domestic market, which has been proved conclusively in Britain in 1975/6.

Improved profits

There is a myth that exports are less profitable than domestic business, this having been encouraged by the practice of **marginal pricing** (see page 23). As you will see later, this is not the best way to export, because provided the export pricing policy of a company is soundly based, export can contribute as much, if not more, to the company's revenue as domestic business.

Economies of scale

Since export calls for increased production, there are nearly always economies of scale to be made when production is increased to cater for increased export business. This is particularly the case when research and development costs are considered, because in many instances the extent of the domestic market is too small to enable them to be recouped profitably.

Opportunities for growth

While it is not always true that growth in itself is a good thing, the opportunities provided by a healthy export business enable a company to grow in a way that is denied to companies restricted to their domestic market. As a simple example, a fish merchant in London has increased the size and profitability of his business by exporting kippers to Europe. Deservedly he won a Queen's Award to Industry for his enterprise.

Europe

As you have seen, membership of the EEC has not so far been to Britain's advantage because of a failure to exploit the increased possibilities. But no British company can avoid being concerned with other Community markets, which means some involvement with export.

Social responsibility

Most companies realise that today they have some social responsibility towards the community in which they operate. If the well-being of the community requires a healthy export trade, then any company which ignores export is acting irresponsibly, and deserves any retribution it may be given. Moreover, export enables a company to offer considerable job satisfaction to its employees, because it is a satisfying and rewarding occupation. This is an area of immense importance for the future, because unless a company can be seen to be acting in the interests of the community, it is unlikely to be allowed to continue.

Job Opportunities in Export

A basic knowledge of export opens up innumerable opportunities for an export career. There are four main options for the young man or woman wishing to work in export.

1. *You can join the export department of a manufacturing company.* You should first choose a company which makes a product of interest to you. If you are mechanically minded, stick to companies producing industrial products. If you prefer dealing with people on a large scale, then choose a company in the consumer field, say in food, pharmaceuticals or household appliances. This will enable you to combine a career in export with a field of activity which interests you, as well as allowing you to use any particular additional skills you may possess.

2. *You can work for an export merchant.* If you have no particular interest in any one kind of product, the activities of a merchant, who buys and re-sells products of all kinds for world markets, may be of interest to you. As you have seen, merchants are still responsible for a high proportion of international trade. You should get in touch with the British Export Houses Association if this type of export work appeals to you.

3. *You can export services instead of goods.* There are many types of services which can be exported, ranging from architecture, engineering and property development to services in the construction industry. Consultants are continually in demand in overseas countries, in specific industries, many agricultural areas, and in management training. You should get in touch with your local professional organisation if the idea of exporting your services appeals to you.

4. *You can work in services used by exporters.* Export requires the services of shipping, banking, insurance, packing, financial and advertising experts, as well as people skilled in handling research and design, the registration of patents and trade marks, and a whole area of legal matters. Two useful bodies to contact are the Institute of Freight Forwarders and the Society of Shipping Executives (for advice on shipping in its broadest meaning as a career), while there are Institutes covering all the remaining services which will be pleased to help anyone anxious to make a career in their particular field.

The Institute of Export in London runs an employment bureau, while there are employment agencies concerned with both shipping and marketing staff in export. The Institute of Marketing is increasingly turning its attention to export, as are bodies like the British Institute of Management and the Institute of Directors. There are equivalent bodies in other countries, such as SAFTO in South Africa, and the Institutes of Export in Australia, New Zealand and Canada, affiliated to the Institute of Export in London.

For those of you who are still considering whether or not to take up an export career, you may care to remember that if you are aiming at a top position in industry, such posts are increasingly being offered to those who have both domestic and international experience. So even if you do not wish to make export your main business interest, you will need to know something about it if you aspire to reach the senior ranks of a company.

Revision

Cover the page with a sheet of paper and uncover one question at a time.

Answers	*Questions*
	1. What is meant by fundamental disequilibrium?
1. When a country's balance of payments is in permanent imbalance.	2. Which country leads the world in the export of manufactured goods?
2. West Germany.	3. What proportion of British exports now goes to Europe?
3. More than 50 per cent.	4. What does GNP stand for?
4. Gross National Product.	5. What are 'invisible' exports?
5. Exports of services, as opposed to goods.	6. What is an economy of scale?
6. A reduction in costs achieved by a larger operation.	7. What is forecast as the world's next crisis product?
7. Food.	8. What does an export merchant do?
8. Buys and re-sells goods for export.	9. What kinds of services are used by exporters?
9. Shipping, banking, insurance, packing, advertising, research.	10. What was the extent of Britain's adverse Balance of Payments in 1975?
10. Some £2,000 million.	

Exercises

1. What kind of job satisfaction might you expect from a career in export?
2. Why do you think Britain's exports are insufficient to pay for her imports?
3. How would you group the countries of the world in terms of international trade?
4. How do you think a company can benefit from exporting?
5. Discuss the main aspects of trade which affect a country's ability to grow rich.

PART 2

EXPORT PRACTICE

From the moment an enquiry is received by a supplier, and even before then, when the details of any product or service available to buyers in other countries are made known, there is a well tried system of export practice that must be used by any company in the export business. Such a system is explained in some detail in this part of the book.

The importance of what is known as export practice has always been greatly under-rated, because it is held that the mechanics of getting goods to customers in other countries are capable of being handled by junior and untrained staff. The words 'export clerk', with all that they imply, are often used to describe a person whose function is every bit as valuable as the most senior export executive, whose efforts are frequently nullified by the inability of the company to handle the business he has obtained. This has led to the constant criticism thrown at British exporters regarding late deliveries and poor documentation of export orders. Such criticism, and I speak from many years of being on the receiving end of British exports, are nearly always justified, and are responsible, moreover, for more lost export business than anyone will ever admit.

The new Foundation Course in Export of the British Overseas Trade Board has been designed to overcome to some degree this inability on the part of so many exporters to handle an export transaction efficiently. It is intended that this basic course in export practice should be followed by further study for the Institutes of Export, Marketing, Freight Forwarders and Shipping Executives' final diplomas.

Export practice has been placed before marketing in this book, because no amount of marketing expertise can succeed in the face of poor export practice. But the factors in this part of the book also have a marketing use, because they can be used to obtain business as well as handle it. Parts 2 and 3, therefore, may be said to make up a complete marketing operation, and no one in export can afford not to have a basic knowledge of both sides. The seven chapters in Part 2 are as follows:

Chapter 3: Export Prices, Quotations and Orders. These have to be prepared and handled, but the final price to the customer will also depend on transport, insurance and payment factors, as well as on such marketing factors as production, competition, distribution and promotion. The final price will probably not be settled until a marketing plan has been prepared. But a start has to be made in what may be called the export circle, since what so often happens in practice is that the first step in export is the receipt of an enquiry from overseas.

Chapter 4: The Export Office. The organisation needed to handle export is considered in this chapter, including the people required, their qualifications and the work they will have to do. Export Licensing and Customs Procedures are included here because in the main they precede the dispatch of the goods.

Chapter 5: Export Transportation. This chapter includes both the various methods of transport and the documents used in each. It deals with the total distribution concept. The word 'distribution' has come to be used in two senses, one indicating the physical aspects of export, and the other the channels through which exports pass to their final customers. The latter will be dealt with in Chapter 13, so to avoid confusion this chapter has been called Export Transportation.

Chapter 6: Cargo Insurance. It is customary for all export cargoes to be insured. This chapter shows how this may be done, and the documents required.

Chapter 7: The Finance of Exports. Three aspects are covered. First, how you may obtain payment for your exports. Second, how you can ensure that you are always paid. Third, how you may finance your exports. This use of money will be dealt with again in the final chapter of the book, since the finance of exports is an integral part of any marketing plan.

Chapter 8: Export Practice Procedures. Because so much of the work of handling an export transaction inevitably interlocks and overlaps, this chapter examines the shipping, insurance, finance and documentation required as a whole.

Chapter 9: The Legal Aspects of Export. These are dealt with together in this chapter, since all the elements in export have legal implications.

3

EXPORT PRICES, QUOTATIONS AND ORDERS

Before you can deal with an enquiry from overseas you must fix the price at which you will sell your goods or services, and you must also decide on what terms you will deliver them. You will need to send a quotation to the enquirer; while if an order materialises you must know how to accept it. Hence this chapter has been divided into the following sections:

1. Export prices
2. Export terms of delivery
3. Export quotations
4. Export orders

Export Prices

To be able to fix an export price for your goods or services you must take into account four main factors:

1. Fixed Costs

These are the costs incurred in running your factory and offices, which do not vary with the volume of goods produced. This is an oversimplification, of course; they will vary, but in well-defined steps, such as when you have to build a new factory to take care of increased production requirements. Some share of your fixed costs must be allocated to the export side of your business, and included when you fix an export price.

2. Variable Costs

Basically these are the costs which do vary with the volume of the goods being produced, such as raw materials and labour costs. This is also an oversimplification, because labour, for example, is not a variable cost if you do not lay it off when it is not required. Also included must be the costs of using the company's money in export, and distribution and promotion costs, when these are related to volume.

3. The Profit Element

This is the difference between the total cost of the goods and the revenue obtained from their sale, and is in effect the **gross profit** you make. It may be calculated:

(*a*) By adding a percentage to total costs, known as **cost plus.**
(*b*) By fixing a **gross margin** below which you will not sell.
(*c*) On some **non-related cost basis,** such as charging what the business in total will bear.

4. What the Overseas Customer will Pay

Customers in overseas markets will pay different prices for the same goods, owing to the various economic factors which vary between one country and another, such as:

(*a*) The **demand** for the goods in the country.
(*b*) The **value** of the goods to the customer.
(*c*) The available **options.**
(*d*) The **ability to pay for the goods.**

This subject will be considered in more detail in Chapter 12, because it follows on from a study of the local environment.

Price always basically depends on supply and demand, and as you will appreciate these are not the same for your product in every country of the world. So that when you attempt to formulate a price policy for export you must consider:

1. *Whether to have one export price for all export markets, or a different price for each.* If you plump for the former, you risk losing some business if the price is too high, or some profit if the price is too low. Yet if you calculate a different price for each market, you may find the costs involved are too great to justify the results. One solution is to charge different prices for the major markets, but to adopt a standard one for the smaller ones. When one-off quotations are required for tenders and special contracts, the price the buyer will pay is more difficult to assess, because the options open to him are generally unknown to you. Even so, you should try to obtain some idea of the price the contract will bear before finally fixing your own selling price.

2. *How long a price is to remain valid.* Clearly some time limit must be imposed, especially in days of continually rising costs. If you decide to quote 'Prices ruling at the date of despatch' remember this may cause your customer some problems, because if he has to obtain permission to import the goods, and buy foreign currency with which to pay for them, he must know the amount for which he has to apply. Normally a time limit is placed on any quoted price, according to estimates of costs.

3. *Whether to quote gross or nett prices.* This depends to some degree on the custom of your trade, but most overseas buyers seem to prefer gross prices, less discounts. If you adopt this method you have an opportunity of varying the discounts, and thus altering your price in different markets.

4. *Whether to quote in sterling or the local currency.* Quoting in sterling presents a customer with no difficulty, provided he can obtain the sterling to pay for your goods and provided he is not worried that the rate of exchange may go against him. If you quote in his currency, however, your difficulty is that you may not receive the correct amount when you are paid if the rate of exchange has gone against you. In these days of floating exchange rates both of you may be nervous of losing. But as you will see in Chapter 7, you can insure against making a loss on the exchange rate, and thus you should always quote in the customer's currency if he so requests.

In certain parts of the world you will be obliged to sell at not less than your domestic price, in order to prevent 'dumping', which creates unfair competition for locally made goods. You are unlikely, however, to be prevented from obtaining a higher price for your exports than you would get on the domestic market. The key to good export pricing lies in:

(*a*) Having an accurate costing system, which will tell you exactly what costs are involved in any export transaction.

(*b*) Making a realistic appraisal of what an importer will pay for your goods.

(*c*) Obtaining an accurate estimate of the strength of the demand for your goods.

The weakness in export pricing is that a salesman or a sales agent will usually opt for the lowest price to ensure getting the business. A competent export marketing man, however, is not frightened of price because he knows he will get the business, provided his product is right and its price is realistic under local market conditions.

Should you be unable to obtain an adequate contribution to your company's profit from a particular export market, it is usually better to ignore that market, unless there is some special reason for trying to develop it, such as its long-term prospects. You cannot hope to be truly competitive in every world market, so concentrate on those markets where the price you wish to charge is most acceptable.

Marginal Pricing

Companies which have an excess production capacity sometimes resort to what is known as selling at **marginal prices**, which in effect means selling at prices lower than they would normally charge. This is done by ignoring the fixed costs, on the basis that they have already been accounted for in the original production costs. So by only taking into account the additional variable costs in producing more goods, the price may be lowered, even after allowing for some contribution to the company's profit. It still adds to profit, and can help to minimise loss. But since it is not based on true costs, the picture is a false one.

On the other hand, marginal price selling has its merits provided:

(*a*) That the additional variable costs do not exceed the additional revenue obtained.

(*b*) That there is no chance of selling the goods elsewhere at a higher price.

(*c*) That there is no addition to your fixed costs.

(*d*) That there is nothing better that you could be doing with the money.

It represents, therefore, what you might call opportunist business. It is essentially short-term, and companies which use it tend not to be too serious about export, because they usually pull out as soon as they find buyers on the domestic market willing to pay the full price. You cannot hope to prosper in export unless you charge prices based on true costs, which provide adequate contributions to company profits.

Export Terms of Delivery

Having fixed the basic export prices of your products—and remember that there are many other factors to be considered before you can finalise these prices—you must next consider on what terms you will deliver them to your customers overseas. These terms will also affect the prices you quote.

International terms of delivery have been in use for many years. Although their precise definition varies from country to country, the International Chamber of Commerce has codified them under the name **Incoterms.** When you add this word to a quotation you are telling your customers the exact definition you propose to apply in each case.

Terms of delivery lay down precisely and legally three conditions:

1. What charges and expenses will be incurred by both the exporter and the importer.
2. When and where delivery of the goods takes place.
3. When and where the title to the goods passes from the exporter to the importer.

The most commonly used terms of delivery are:

Ex Works The importer is responsible for all charges from the time that he collects the goods from the exporter's works. At this point the title to the goods passes from the exporter to the importer.

F.O.R. This means 'Free On Rail'. The importer is responsible for all charges as soon as the exporter has delivered the goods to the railhead. Here delivery takes place, and the title to the goods passes from the exporter to the importer.

F.A.S. This means 'Free Alongside Ship'. The importer is responsible for all charges once the exporter has placed the goods on the quay alongside the ship. If the goods are sent out to the ship by lighter, the exporter must pay the lighterage charges. He does not, however, have to pay for loading the goods on to the ship from the lighter, nor does he pay for loading the goods from the quay on to the ship. Delivery takes place on the quay or lighter, when the title to the goods changes hands.

F.O.B. This means 'Free on Board'. It is often qualified by the addition of 'British port', in which case the exporter must deliver to any British port; or of a named port, such as 'F.O.B. Southampton'. The exporter is responsible for all charges incurred in getting the goods 'over the ship's rail', which is where delivery takes place and the title to the goods changes hands. The precise definition of 'over the ship's rail' has been argued about for many years, but it is always taken as the dividing line between the responsibilities of the exporter and importer, so it is normal practice for the exporter to pay port and loading charges.

C. & F.
C.I.F. These mean 'Cost and Freight' and 'Cost, Insurance and Freight'. It is customary to add the port of destination, such as 'C & F. Durban', or 'C.I.F. Singapore', thus indicating precisely to which port the exporter will deliver. All charges, with or without insurance (which is the only difference between the two terms), are paid by the exporter up to arrival in the port of destination.

Here delivery of the goods takes place, and the title to them changes hands.

Franco This word means 'Free', and with the addition of the word 'Domicile' the term is taken to mean that delivery will be made to the importer's warehouse, free of all charges to him. Delivery takes place at this point, and here the title to the goods changes hands.

You will appreciate now how important it is to agree with your customer in advance the meaning you attach to any of these terms.

Modern methods of delivery, using more than one method of transport, are tending to obscure the meanings of some of these terms. For example, shipping by container to Australia, you may find you are quoted a rate which includes the handling charges at both ends, which would not be a strictly F.O.B. contract at all. If you ship on a Groupage basis (see Chapter 5), an F.O.B. contract can easily be turned into a C.I.F. one. Hence, while some adjustment to terms of delivery is likely in the future, this must not be allowed to obscure their real meaning, or their legal implications.

The Effects of Terms of Delivery on Price

According to which terms of delivery you use, so the **price** you quote will need to be adjusted. The simplest way to understand this is to study an example. The one quoted below concerns a shipment of cloth from Britain to Milan by sea. The basic price the exporter wished to receive was \$2.00 a metre. The enquiry was for 3,000 metres. Hence the exporter began by wishing to receive at his works a total of \$6,000.00. The costs at all stages of delivery to Milan were as follows:

Price of the cloth, unpacked, at works	\$6,000.00
Packing costs	300.00
Transport to docks by rail	450.00
Port dues and loading charges	60.00
Freight by sea to Genoa	875.00
Landing charges at Genoa	90.00
Duty payable on 3,000 metres of cloth	1,200.00
Transport from Genoa to Milan	150.00
Insurance, all risks, to Milan	100.00
Total	9,225.00

1. If you quoted 'Ex Works' your price would be \$6,000.00 because you would have no additional costs to add. But in this case you would have to specify 'Packing extra at cost', since export packing is seldom included in the cost. If it is, then your price would be \$6,300.00.

2. If you quoted F.O.R. you would probably not add anything further, unless you were some distance from the railhead.

3. If you quoted F.A.S. you would have to add the cost of taking the goods by rail to the port, so in this case your price would be \$6,750.00.

4. If you quoted F.O.B. you would have to add the port charges, which would include any documentation. Thus your price would now be \$6,810.00

5. With a C.I.F. quotation you have to include the freight to the nearest port, in this case Genoa, and the insurance. While this has been shown as \$100.00 this was right through to Milan, so you might need to add only \$80.00, when your C.I.F. price would be \$7,765.00.

6. Selling on a Franco Domicile basis you would have to add all landing charges at Genoa, the duty payable on the cloth, the full insurance and the freight from Genoa to Milan. Thus your final price, delivered to your customer's warehouse in Milan, would be $9,225.00.

So which terms of delivery should you choose? From the customer's point of view he has least to do when he buys from you on a Franco Domicile basis. He has most to do when he buys Ex Works. Customers often prefer to buy on F.O.B. terms for three reasons:

1. They have other goods being sent to them and wish your goods to be shipped at the same time, possibly saving freight charges.
2. They can use the ships and other services of their own country, thereby saving foreign currency.
3. Their import licences may be granted on an F.O.B. basis.

So clearly you must in the first instance respect your customer's wishes. But from your point of view, you have least to do when you ship Ex Works, and most to do when you use Franco Domicile. You may opt for F.O.B. because while this enables you to control delivery to the ship, you are not involved with calculations of freight or insurance. In extremely competitive situations a small miscalculation on these charges may make all the difference between a profit and a loss.

In the more developed European markets customers are starting to demand quotations on a Franco Domicile basis, and it is in your national interest to comply, because as with C.I.F. this is saving Britain currency by using British transport services. The main thing to avoid is to use F.O.B. or any other term merely because it has always been that way with the company. Times and conditions in the transport field change, and you must adapt to them.

Export Quotations

A quotation may be considered as an **invitation to make an offer.** If this is done the exporter may accept or reject the order, or offer, from the importer. Quotations are usually made in one of three ways:

1. Price Lists

Many companies issue export price lists, quoting their product or products in terms of price and terms of delivery. This is accompanied by a letter, which is the offer, since the price list is strictly an invitation to treat. If frequent price changes are likely, price lists have to be revised, so their duration must be clearly stated. For goods in regular supply they are useful, but where variations in price occur between different markets, then different versions of a price list have to be produced. Price lists are most useful where a wide range of products is on offer, but they tend to restrict the exporter to a rigid pricing policy which, as you have seen, is often a means of losing possible profit.

2. Pro Forma Invoices

For special quotations, or where an importer has to apply for an import licence or permission to buy foreign currency, it is usual for him to ask you to send him a pro forma invoice. This you make out like a normal invoice, showing a description of the goods, their price, terms of delivery and any other details requested, such as the freight and insurance charges.

3. Tenders

In most cases tenders have to be made out on special forms which have to be bought from the authority seeking the tender. The details are usually complicated, and you must be precise in all your replies.

When you make an export quotation, make sure the specifications fit the goods exactly, or the importer may have problems clearing them through the local Customs authorities. There is the classic story of the pro forma invoice which specified electrical goods as being of 50 cycles, and the Customs refusing to release them until they could find 50 bicycles. You must also state packing details precisely. It is no use quoting 'Packed in 24 cases' if you intend to pack them in 12 cases.

It is normal practice to issue **conditional quotations**, these being subject to certain conditions, embodied in what are known as the **Conditions of Sale.** Most companies have formal Conditions of Sale, but for export you should ensure that the following are included:

1. How long the offer is to last, either in precise terms, or subject to certain conditions. This prevents you quoting a price and finding that you can no longer supply the goods at that price.
2. Which terms of delivery you use.
3. Which methods of payment you require.
4. The procedure you adopt regarding insurance.
5. A Reservation of Property clause is normally included, explained in Chapter 9.
6. You should include a statement to the effect that weights and measurements are supplied for transport purposes and do not form part of the contract.
7. When you specify a delivery date, you should qualify it to the effect that it is given in good faith, but that it may have to be amended due to circumstances beyond your control, such as strikes, etc.
8. It is normal to insist that the customer is responsible for obtaining any necessary import licences.
9. You may also wish to include a clause regarding the replacement of damaged or defective goods.
10. As will be explained in Chapter 9, there should be a 'Choice of Laws' clause explaining under which law the contract will be accepted.

Export Orders

If a quotation is an invitation to make an offer, once that offer is accepted it becomes an **order**, or **contract**.

Before you accept an order, and in English law this may be done at present merely by acknowledging it, you must check its **Conditions of Purchase.** Most importers include such conditions on their order. If they are acceptable to you, you may proceed. If not, then you must have them altered before you accept the order. This may seem a tedious process, but if you do not carry out the conditions attached to an order, you are in breach of your contract.

If you receive an order from an agent of any kind acting for an importer, such as a Confirming House (see Chapter 13), you must make sure you know the **principal** with whom you are dealing, in order to establish with whom you are entering into a contract; who will be responsible for shipping the goods; and who will pay for them. You must also make sure that any agent has the authority to act for his principal.

Disputes on export orders usually arise because some mistake or misunderstanding has arisen at the time the quotation was made or the order accepted. So ensure that you and your customer always understand perfectly what is involved before you go ahead. Remember you are dealing with people of other nationalities, who may neither speak the same language nor interpret statements as you do.

Revision

Cover the page with a sheet of paper and uncover one question at a time.

Answers	*Questions*
	1. What is the main difference between Fixed and Variable costs?
1. Variable costs vary with volume, whereas Fixed costs do not.	2. What is meant by 'cost plus'?
2. Adding a percentage of profit to a manufacturing cost.	3. When is Marginal Selling often used in export?
3. When a company is unable to sell all its production on the home market.	4. What are Incoterms?
4. Terms of delivery as defined by the International Chamber of Commerce.	5. What does C.I.F. stand for?
5. Cost, Insurance and Freight.	6. What is a Quotation?
6. An invitation to make an offer.	7. When is a pro forma invoice used?
7. To make a quotation.	8. What is a Conditional Quotation?
8. One where Conditions of Sale are imposed.	9. When an order is acknowledged what does this signify in English law?
9. That it is accepted.	10. Is an agent responsible for payment of an order?
10. Not unless specifically stated.	

Exercises

1. Under what conditions may Marginal Selling be beneficial to an exporting company?
2. What are the main advantages and disadvantages to a customer of buying on F.O.B. terms?
3. What are the essential elements in Conditions of Sale for export?
4. Do you think a standard export price is to a company's advantage?
5. How would you decide which terms of delivery to adopt?
6. What considerations would you bear in mind when arriving at an export price?
7. What are the different ways in which you can send a quotation to an overseas customer?
8. What would you do if the Conditions of Purchase differed from your Conditions of Sale?

4
THE EXPORT OFFICE

As soon as a company starts to obtain export business, some form of export office will be required, along with a system under which it should operate and certain people able to deal with the work. And before any goods can be dispatched, some dealings may be required with the Customs authorities. Hence this chapter has been divided into the following sections:

1. The structure of an export office.
2. The personnel and their work in an export office.
3. The handling of export enquiries, quotations, orders and records.
4. Customs procedures.

The Structure of an Export Office

The three basic functions of an industrial company are **production, sales** and **finance**. To these may be added numerous additional functions such as administration, research and development, statistics and records, promotion, personnel, training and purchasing. Underlying this functional view of an organisation you must appreciate that basically a company consists of people, so however you may organise an export office, you must always consider it in terms of human beings.

There are as many ways of structuring an export office as there are of skinning a cat. In no two companies will you find precisely the same kind of set-up. But the problem may be solved in four basic ways.

1. Export as Part of the Commercial Operation

Since the prime object of export is to obtain additional business for a company from overseas, you can treat export as an integral part of a company's overall commercial operation. Hence you may divide a commercial department into domestic and overseas divisions, under the control of the commercial director.

In this case the remaining export functions such as transportation, insurance, finance and so on can be handled by the company's specialists concerned, and there is as a result no export department as such in the company. This type of set-up is most suitable for a smaller company, and has much to commend it on the basis that a customer is a customer, wherever he happens to be.

2. A Horizontally Based Department

This is the most usual solution, a special department being set up to look after all exports, under an export director or manager. It may be based on a product basis or a geographical one, depending on the nature of the business and its involvement in export.

As it develops there will be a number of senior export executives in charge of sales, research, dispatch, statistics, promotion and personnel, who in turn will have specialist managers and staffs below them.

This is most suitable for medium to large companies handling a good deal of export business, but its weakness is that it tends to keep domestic and export business in two watertight compartments, and this may today be a somewhat old-fashioned outlook.

3. A Vertically Based Department

This also separates domestic and export business, but instead of subdividing on a product or geographical basis, it is vertical in structure to the extent that it consists of specialists in each area. This means every export transaction is handled at some stage by a specialist, all insurance is dealt with by insurance experts, and the same with documentation, etc.

It has much to commend it in that there is an expertise often denied to horizontal organisations, but it often lacks an overall direction, and hence a sense of purpose.

4. A Multi-National Structure

This structure applies only to large companies operating all over the world. There are three main options:

(*a*) *A product-based organisation.* This is usually the case when the organisation is product-oriented, an example being the Sperry Rand Company, which has divisions selling products as diverse as typewriters, shavers, computers and combine harvesters. Each division operates as a self-contained entity, both at home and overseas.

(*b*) *An area-based organisation.* Where a large company has its products in the same field, it may organise itself on a geographical basis. The world is divided into a number of fairly autonomous areas, such as Europe, the America's, etc. This is sound because as conditions vary you are making the best use of local people, who know local conditions better than anyone else.

(*c*) *An export-based organisation.* This describes the structure of a major company which has decided that all its overseas operations shall be handled by one export operation. British Leyland have opted for this type of structure, all the exports of their car, truck and specialist divisions being looked after by one international division. It is a well-defined structure but has two main weaknesses. One is that it tends to increase export prices, because the international division will usually have to buy from the production divisions and re-sell at a profit to finance themselves; the other is that the production divisions do not take export seriously because they cannot see the results of their efforts.

There is, as you will appreciate, no ideal solution to the structure of an export office, but when one is set up you should take into account the following factors.

The Size of the Company

With a small company an export manager and a secretary are all that is needed initially. But as the export business grows, a decision must be taken as to which type of organisation will be most suitable, otherwise the export operation will become unwieldy and unorganised with no one sure what he should be doing.

The Nature of the Company

Selling a highly sophisticated range of industrial equipment, with the necessity for providing efficient after-sales service, will call for a different type of export organisation than that needed to export a fast-moving consumer product like confectionery.

The Overseas Market Involved

The wider the geographical spread of markets, the more complicated the structure will tend to become. It is simpler to organise business in a few West European markets than to trade with places as far apart as Hong Kong, Zambia and Peru.

The Degree of Involvement in Export

If you export from a domestic factory you will not need the same kind of structure as if you establish local manufacturing or sales operations in many parts of the world. Looking after agents or distributors will call for a different structure from that required to look after local companies.

The Experience of the Company in Export

The more experienced the staff the more sophisticated can be the structure. A company starting in export with comparatively inexperienced staff should initially aim to keep its export organisation as simple as possible.

The Use of Outside Services

A great deal will depend on how far the company tends to make use of outside services, such as shipping and forwarding agents, etc. This point will be considered in detail in Chapter 5 as regards the transport function, but it extends rather further in such areas as research, promotion and even selling. This is generally a matter of basic company policy, and it applies to export as much as to the domestic side of the business. Almost every function can be subcontracted, including the selling, which will be covered in Chapters 13 and 14, and the promotion which is dealt with in Chapter 15.

There is an additional problem for companies concerned with the EEC, where there would seem to be three basic options on the organisational side:

1. To treat all Community markets as part of the company's domestic market, on the grounds that the Community is rapidly becoming one market, forming a complete self-contained trading area, a point looked at in more detail in Chapter 10.
2. To treat all parts of the EEC, apart from the domestic market, as export, on the grounds that the sections of the Community will remain virtually export markets for many years to come.
3. To treat the EEC as one market, but having two divisions: (*a*) the domestic market; and (*b*) the non-domestic areas.

A great deal of uncertainty is prevalent in British industry on this problem, and few companies seem as yet to have made up their minds which is the best solution. But as the world becomes smaller, and the Community is one example of how this is happening, the distinctions between domestic and export business are bound to disappear, and any structure should be created with this ultimate goal in mind.

The Personnel in an Export Office

It would be unwise to try to differentiate between those who work on the practice and marketing sides of export, because they both form part of any export office. The only possible exception is those whose work it is to travel overseas on selling missions, who are out of the office for lengthy periods at a time. Such people will be considered in Chapter 14.

The functions of export office staff as regards the practice of export are as follows.

Customer Liaison

Staff are needed to handle customer liaison in respect of enquiries, quotations and orders. They need to advise customers of the progress of their orders, and ensure that delays do not occur. They are the essential back-up to export salesmen, with whom they must work closely.

Transport

The actual transport of goods to overseas markets must be arranged, either directly with the carriers concerned, or through shipping and forwarding agents.

Insurance

Since it is customary for all cargoes to be insured, staff are needed to ensure this is always done, either on behalf of the company or the customer, or by the customer, so that the goods are never left uninsured.

Finance

This is always a problem area since the work touches closely on that of the accounts department of the company. Nevertheless, in an export office there must be people to ensure that some system of credit control is operated; to decide and operate methods of payment; to deal with the bank whenever necessary with regard to payment; and to handle credit insurance by the Export Guarantee Scheme operated by the government or some other means.

Documents

While each section is normally responsible for its own documents, their sheer number means that some form of control has to be exercised so that all the documents for any transaction are brought together and dealt with as required. This means having someone in charge of documentation.

Records, Statistics and Information

In an export office there must be staff able to keep the necessary shipping and sales records and such statistics as are required. In addition, information must be recorded about methods of transport, rates, procedures, and while this may be kept by the individuals concerned, it must be available to anyone in the export office.

It is normal for certain export functions to be carried out by the appropriate departments in the company, but staff will be needed in the export office to liaise with these other departments. The main areas where this is necessary are as follows.

Production

There are two main aspects concerned with the production of goods for export with which the export office staff are concerned. One is the completion, packing and dispatch of goods, in accordance with instructions which the export office will have to issue. The second, which often precedes the other, is the planning and production of goods for export, and the modifications which may be required to existing products for export markets.

In the case of merchants, the buying in of the goods will need to be done either by a separate buying department, or by the export office staff.

Research and Development

The export staff will need to be consulted on various aspects of research and development, so that new products will be considered in the light of both their domestic and export suitability.

Legal Considerations

Normally all legal matters in a company are under the control of the company secretary or a special legal department. Since so many aspects of export have legal implications for the company, the export office staff must work closely with the company's legal personnel.

On the marketing side there are four areas where the export office staff will be concerned, and depending on the size and involvement of the company in export this work will either be handled by the department concerned or by experts in each area working entirely on the export side of the business. These are as follows.

Information and Research

All markets have to be studied, and the information obtained about them will need to be recorded. Where specific research has to be carried out, staff will be needed either to handle this or have it done locally.

Distribution

Where various channels of distribution are used, it is normal for this work to be handled by the export office staff, and not by anyone on the domestic side. The exception concerns subsidiary companies overseas, which may come under the direct control of the Board, and where the contact between such companies and the export office is confined to practical day-to-day transactions.

Promotion

This covers all forms of promotion, from the production of price lists to the carrying out of advertising campaigns in overseas markets, which is sometimes referred to as marketing services. It may be handled by the company's advertising or publicity department, or it may be looked after by specialists in the export office.

Just as there are no two export structures precisely the same, so the functions of the export side are a matter for individual companies to decide. The important thing is to be clear from the outset how the various tasks of the export side of the business are to be handled, who is to handle them, and to build accordingly. But clearly anyone who works on the export side must have certain additional qualifications, of which the most important are dealt with next.

A sense of diplomacy. People working at any level in export must be willing and able to work with people of any nationality, colour, race or religion. They must be able to act with impartiality, tolerance and understanding. To be able to behave in a truly diplomatic way is an essential part of the make-up of a good exporter.

An aptitude for languages. It is true that much of the world's business is conducted in English. But everyone does not speak or write it fluently. All export staff should be encouraged to learn at least one language in addition to English, and if it is not their mother tongue it should be learned as a first requirement in export. French, German and Spanish are the next three most important, but languages like Chinese and Russian may become more important as time goes by. Ideally all correspondence should be answered in the language in which it was first written, and a well-equipped export office should have people fluent in several languages.

A well-developed sense of responsibility. Customers work different hours, different days of the week, and are unaware of your holidays, days off and so on. Hence export staff must be able to act without constantly referring to some form of higher authority. Most export staff would agree that clock-watching is impossible if shipments are to arrive on time anywhere in the world.

An interest in the world. All export staff must have a comprehensive knowledge of geography, and know ports, cities and countries in the world by heart. In Brazzaville I was sent a news magazine with monotonous regularity addressed to me at Brazzaville, Zaïre. Sometimes it reached me, more often it did not. All that kind of thing does is to show your customer you are not greatly interested in export. In addition, export staff must be keenly aware of world events, because if, for example, war or riots break out, the insurance of their cargoes will be affected, or the arrival of the goods delayed.

A liking for export. You may say that a liking for the job is essential in any walk of life. It is more true of export, however, because it produces challenges in complicated procedures, last-minute requests, and involved local regulations which have to be dealt with quickly and accurately, and which will never be handled properly unless the staff genuinely enjoy the work. If staff are not interested in export they should stay out of it, and this applies at any level in the company, especially to senior management.

The training of export staff will be an essential part of any company's training programme, and there are several ways in which this may be accomplished:

Professional Qualifications

In Britain there are three kinds of professional export qualifications which may be gained.

1. *The Certificate in Export Office Practice*. This is primarily for junior staff. It covers four subjects, namely commercial geography, export documentation, and commerce, with options covering law, a language, or other commercial subjects. It may be taken at several colleges of further education in the United Kingdom, and a Certificate is awarded to successful candidates. It is under the control of the Institute of Export.

2. *The Foundation Course in Overseas Trade*. This was started in 1975 by the British Overseas Trade Board, and consists of four subjects, namely international trade and payments, cargo insurance, transportation and documentation, and elements of export law. It is designed to be taken over a year's part time study, and a Certificate is awarded to successful candidates. It is already available at several polytechnics and colleges of further education. Gaining the Certificate will exempt students from Part I of the Institute of Export's examinations; from three subjects in the Institute of Freight Forwarders' examinations; from the entry examination of the Society of Shipping Executives; and from four subjects in the Institute of Marketing's IM Certificate in Marketing Studies.

3. *The Institute of Export's Final Examination*. Students who take Part II of the Institute's examinations, which covers four subjects—namely management accounting, international trade law, and marketing—will earn the right to become full members of the Institute of Export, and be able to put M.I.Ex. (Grad.) after their names.

Courses and Seminars

Diploma courses. There are several diploma courses run by colleges of further education in various parts of the country, which include a language as an integral part of the course.

Management courses. Many of these include international trade, and are available at numerous polytechnics, colleges of higher education, schools of business and institutes. There are management centres in the USA, France, Belgium and Switzerland which offer similar internationally based courses.

Seminars. Both public and private bodies offer seminars of interest to people working in export, those run by the Institutes of Export and Marketing being particularly useful. The Centre for Economic and Political Studies in London is one of several colleges which cater for overseas students wishing to be trained in export.

Other Training

There are several areas where additional training will be of benefit to exporters.

Languages. All staff should be encouraged to learn at least one other language, and this may be done at colleges of further education and at a number of private language schools.

Travel overseas. Wherever possible export staff should be encouraged to visit other countries, even if only on holiday.

In-house training. When a company becomes involved with export it should consider running company training sessions in export, for which there are many consultants and experts available to help with the work.

Reading. All export staff should be encouraged to read widely about other countries and people; and in addition to books, they might also read publications like the *Financial Times* and *The Economist*.

Working overseas. At some stage in any exporter's career it is helpful if he or she can spend some time living and working in another country, both to learn about that country, and to study export from the receiving end.

The Handling of Export Enquiries, Quotations, Orders and Records

There are certain basic principles regarding the handling of export enquiries, quotations and orders which should be applied in any export office.

Enquiries

All enquiries should be dealt with immediately, and answered by the same method by which they are sent, *e.g.* by airmail, telex, etc. If they cannot be dealt with at once, they should be acknowledged to the effect that details are following. They should be followed up if no reaction is received, and a careful record kept of them and any subsequent action.

Quotations

All quotations, except tenders, should be sent as quickly as possible, but with tenders there is usually a date by which they have to be received. Make sure all the relevant details are included in quotations, even if these have not been specified by the enquirer. Quotations must be followed up, and a record kept of what orders were received from them.

Orders

Orders must be acknowledged by return, unless there is a query regarding the terms of purchase. Any points in an order which are unclear, or have been omitted, must be queried at the time. Delivery dates must be agreed, and customers informed at all stages if there seem likely to be any delays. A progress chart should be kept to ensure the smooth delivery of the order and to enable the correct documents to be supplied at the appropriate time.

Companies will wish to instal their own systems of records, but the following may provide a base for any such system.

Customer flow charts. These show each order, the date received, when it was sent for execution, and when dispatched. If you add the approximate date of arrival you may check with your customer that his order has arrived, thus showing that you are concerned that your deliveries shall not be late.

Customer dispatch cards. These show the details of the dispatch of an order overseas, including the method of packing used; the documents required and sent; the method of transport; the insurance and how it was arranged; how the customer paid for the goods; and when the transaction was completed. If all stages are dated, the state of an order can immediately be checked, so if there looks like being any delay the customer may be advised accordingly.

Customer sales cards. The simplest form of sales cards consists of a top card containing all the details of the customer you need to know, such as the marks he uses, the port to which shipment should be made, his wishes about insurance and the method of payment agreed, as well as any special instructions he has given. Successive cards, one for each year, show the details of each order, with cumulative totals, so that all your dealings with him are clearly recorded.

Export sales records. The kind of records you keep will depend on the business you do, but essentially there are three things you will need:

1. Sales by product, by year, by quantity and value to all customers.
2. Sales by product, by year, by quantity and value to individual markets.
3. Sales to all overseas markets of each product by quantity and value.

In addition to these totals, forecasts for each year will have to be made and compared with actual results. These figures can be shown on charts, either in block or graphical form.

Export earnings. In addition to sales records, you should keep records of earnings, i.e. the revenue you obtain compared with the costs incurred, and the amount you contribute to the company's profits. If you sell at standard export prices this will be a simple task, but if you quote according to what the market will bear, you will need a system for showing the earnings and costings on each order.

If you have a central statistical department, you will need to arrange to provide the figures for each export transaction, and also agree how these are to be tabulated. An efficient export manager has the figures always available, and keeps a constant check on how the export side of the business is going.

Customs Procedures

In almost every country of the world exports are subject to some form of control through the Customs Authorities, and there is the equivalent of H.M. Customs and Excise in virtually every overseas market. The Customs are concerned with both imports and exports, and as an exporter you are concerned with the Customs both when your goods leave the country and when they enter your customer's country. For United Kingdom exporters the two main areas with which the Customs are concerned are Export Licensing and Customs Entries.

Export Licensing

There are four ways in which goods for export are subject to export licensing procedures:

1. Certain goods may not be exported at all, and these will be shown on the **Prohibited List.** This list is drawn up by the Export Licensing Branch of the Department of Trade, and includes certain war materials, drugs and antiques among others.
2. Some goods may only be exported under licence. The Export Licensing Branch of the Department of Trade draws up the list showing which goods require an **export licence.** This is set out in groups of products, and includes certain chemicals, atomic energy materials and military equipment. If your goods are on this list, you must obtain **Form A** (see Fig. 1, Appendix 1), and having filled it in, send it in duplicate to the Export Licensing Branch, who will return the copy to you, if approved, which you must then send forward with the goods to enable the Customs to allow them to leave the country.
3. Some countries are on a prohibited list so far as exports are concerned, a current example being Rhodesia.
4. Exports to some countries, while not prohibited, are in certain cases **restricted**. At present exports to China, Chile and Vietnam are in this category.

Apart from the above, exports from the United Kingdom are not subject to any form of licence, although in many countries there is a system of **Open General Licences** for exports, requiring the exporter to specify the details of the goods according to this OGL.

In the United Kingdom there is one other control on exports—namely that placed on **foreign currency,** which will be dealt with in detail in Chapter 7. But at this stage you should note that you may not export goods without being paid for them, to prevent you from being paid in another country to avoid bringing the money back to the United Kingdom. Nor may you receive less than the declared value of the goods for Customs purposes, and avoid the full earnings being paid to the country. The Customs authorities are concerned with both conditions.

Customs Entries

The Customs have the responsibility for seeing that all exports are recorded, and they also of course record all imports. It is on these figures that national statistics of exports and imports are based, which in turn produce the balance of payments figures. In some countries the Customs also have the responsibility for seeing that taxes on exports are paid.

All classifications of goods for Customs purposes have been codified by the publication and acceptance of the **Brussels Nomenclature**, or BTN. This has been agreed by most countries in the world, and the classifications consist of two four-figure numbers which enable the goods to be identified at any time. Your office should have a copy of this book, in Britain called *H.M. Customs & Excise Tariff and Overseas Trade Classification*; and you should quote the required tariff number on your invoices as well as on Customs forms.

Under the Customs and Excise Act of 1952 and the Finance Act of 1971 all goods exported must be either **pre-entered** for Customs, or **declared** under a number given to the exporter of the goods, it being agreed that a detailed entry will be made to the Customs within 14 days of shipment. Hence you must apply to the Customs for what is called a **CAN** (or Customs Assigned Number), which you do on **Form C.274.** This enables you to send goods forward for export without entering them for Customs purposes, provided you quote this number on the shipping documents. The Customs authorities will allow the goods to leave the country so long as the number is shown.

Except in certain cases, which will be dealt with below, you have then to declare the details of the goods for Customs purposes, and this is done on the C.273 forms, of which there are several. **C.273(1)** (see Fig. 2, Appendix 1) is used for exports of a single product; **C.273(4)** is used where there are up to four different products being exported, each having different BTN numbers; and if there are in the same shipment more than four different kinds of goods then C.273(1) is used, but a **Schedule** is attached to it on a special form on which all the goods can be included in their various categories. For shipments by air there is a **C.273(Air)** form. The forms are prepared in duplicate, the copy being returned to the exporter by the Customs in due course. The exceptions to this post-entry for Customs are certain goods which have to be pre-entered with Customs on form **C.63A** (Fig. 3, Appendix 1) before they can be exported. These goods are as follows:

(*a*) All goods on which a **drawback of duty** is claimed—that is to say, where import duty has been paid on the goods which are being re-exported, the import duty may be reclaimed. But you must apply to the Customs before exporting them and produce evidence that you have paid the import duty, and that you are now shipping them out of the country.

(*b*) All goods shipped from a **bonded warehouse.** Goods held in a bonded warehouse are those on which no duty is paid when they are imported, or those on which no Excise duty has been paid, such as whisky or tobacco. The Customs will only release the goods if they are being exported, or the import duty or Excise duty is paid.

(*c*) All goods shipped to a **restricted territory,** or goods for which an export licence is required.

In most cases, therefore, goods shipped from the United Kingdom do not have to be pre-entered with Customs, although this is not the case in many other countries, where pre-entry is more common.

EEC Customs Regulations

In principle all Customs duties between the member states of the Community are being abolished, and in the case of Britain this applies in full from July 1977. All goods entering the Community at any point will pay the **Common Customs Tariff,** or **CCT.** All goods moving from one member state to another pay nothing. Hence the harmonisation of Customs procedures within the Community has had to be arranged.

The first result of this harmonisation has been the adoption of CA numbers and the procedure described above for both post and pre-entries. There are, however, three areas where Customs procedures assume importance.

1. *The origin of the goods*

The Community has adopted a rather different attitude towards the origin of goods qualifying for an absence of Customs duties, and has defined this as

goods in free circulation. This means basically that the goods are wholly produced in the Community, of materials on which duty has been paid and on which no drawback has been claimed, or are imported goods on which the CCT has been paid. To enable these goods to move freely a Community Transit system has been introduced, based on the 'T' forms. There are three of these, **T1** being used only for goods not in free circulation; **T2** and **T2L** only used by the six original member states of the Community; and **T3** and **T3L** (Figs. 4 and 5, Appendix 1) being used by Britain and the other two new members during the transitionary period—that is, until July 1977, when all duties will have been abolished. These T forms are combined movement certificates and evidence of the Community status of the goods. It is likely that after July 1977, Britain will use the T2 and T2L forms. The forms have to be ratified by Customs before the goods leave the country, and go with the goods.

When goods leave any country of the Community en route to a non-Community state, passing through another Community country, bank guarantees may have to be given that should the goods fail to reach their destination, and remain in a Community country, then any Customs duty will be paid in full. There are several forms for these guarantees, notably **C.1145** and **C.1144**; but note that this only applies where shipments are sent by road.

2. *Where goods are sent to an associated Community country*

When goods are sent from a member state of the Community to one of the countries associated with the Community, a different procedure has to be followed. These countries are the remaining EFTA countries—namely Austria, Norway, Sweden, Switzerland, Portugal, Finland and Iceland, and certain Mediterranean countries, notably Israel, Turkey, Greece, Tunisia, Egypt and Cyprus. For these countries the forms **EUR 1** and **EUR 2** have been introduced, establishing the Community nature of the goods, and allowing some preferential rates of duty to be paid. These forms (see Figs. 6 and 7, Appendix 1) act in much the same way as the T forms. But at present there are still some special forms for each country being used instead of EUR 1 and 2, which are used for all EFTA countries and Israel. These are **ATR1** for Turkey; **AG1** for Greece; **ACY** for Cyprus; **AET1** for Egypt and **ATN** for Tunisia. One point to remember about EUR 1 and 2 is that you normally declare on them 'Article 25(1) Satisfied', this referring to the goods being of such a nature that they are in 'free circulation'.

3. *VAT*

At present all goods exported from the United Kingdom are zero-rated for VAT and nothing has to be added by an exporter in this respect. However, it is possible that, when in 1977 goods may circulate freely within the Community and countries associated with it, some form of VAT may be introduced covering British exports to the remainder of the Community. But remember that when dispatching any goods to the Community or countries associated with it, you must include an invoice with the goods, irrespective of the method of payment adopted.

One of the essential tasks of the export office is to establish good relations with the local Customs officers and to ensure that all the necessary entries, etc., are made as described above. The Customs will make occasional checks to see this has been done.

Revision

Cover the page with a sheet of paper and uncover one question at a time.

Answers	*Questions*
	1. What are the three primary functions of an industrial company?
1. Production, sales and finance.	2. In whose hands are legal matters usually left in a company?
2. The company secretary.	3. What is the worst fault of many exporters?
3. Late deliveries.	4. What is a customer flow chart?
4. A chart showing the progress of an export order.	5. What is the Brussels Nomenclature?
5. An internationally accepted classification of goods for Customs purposes.	6. What is the CCT?
6. The Common Customs Tariff, levied on all goods entering the EEC.	7. What is a CA number?
7. A Customs Assigned Number to enable goods to be post-entered for Customs.	8. When is EUR 1 used?
8. For shipments to countries which are associated with the EEC.	9. When is C.273(4) used?
9. When a shipment consists of up to four different types of goods.	10. How are export goods rated for VAT from Britain?
10. Zero-rated.	

Exercises

1. Which are the most important factors affecting a company's export structure?
2. How would you integrate your handling of the EEC markets into your company's structure?
3. What sort of training would you give your export staff?
4. What special qualifications and aptitudes would you look for in your export staff?

5. What documents have to be used for Customs entries?
6. What records would you expect to find in a well-organised export office?
7. How are Customs procedures with countries associated with the EEC affected?
8. Why is customer liaison in export so important?

5

EXPORT TRANSPORTATION

No export transaction can take place unless goods are transported from one country to another, except of course for invisible exports. In order to accomplish the physical exchange of goods, a good deal of paperwork is required, involving the use of internationally accepted documents. These will be dealt with in this chapter while the methods of transport are examined. But because these documents are also needed for other aspects of an export transaction, they will be examined again as a whole in Chapter 8.

Packing is the word most commonly used to describe the protection of goods in transit. **Packaging** is generally used to describe the protection and promotion of consumer goods, and is dealt with in Chapter 12. Methods of packing vary according to the type of transport used, as well as the kind of goods you are exporting. Since packing costs vary, not only is the cost of transportation affected, but so is any decision as to which methods of transport should be used.

The **cost of transport** has increased rapidly, and so has the cost of preparing the necessary documents. On the other hand, transport operators now offer various kinds of through-transport facilities, such as groupage, the grouping of a number of export consignments to a named destination but not necessarily to a single importer. It is used to take advantage of the most favourable freight rates, and provides regular despatches to frequently used destinations. The growth in the use of containers has resulted in lower loading costs, and sometimes cheaper packing costs. All these costs may be grouped together under the term **Total Distribution Cost**, or TDC, and analyses can be made to show differences in total cost between one method of transport and another.

The additional complications of procedures affecting transport between members of the EEC will be included where appropriate. The question of whether a company should attempt to handle all this work itself or sub-contract it to outside specialists, is another export transportation problem to be considered.

Hence this chapter has been divided into four main sections:

1. Methods of transport and their documents
2. Packing
3. The total distribution cost
4. Handling the transport

Methods of Transport and their Documents

There are four main methods of transport, two lesser used ones, and certain problems connected with local transport facilities, and these form the basis of this section.

Carriage of Goods by Sea

The main **advantage** of shipping goods by sea is that it is, in terms of pure freight costs, cheap. Moreover, ships can carry heavy and bulky cargoes which other forms of transport cannot handle. A **disadvantage** is that ships are slow, so that sea transport is unsuitable when time is important. Since few importers or exporters are close to ports a good deal of transhipment may be required, increasing the risks of damage or loss. Even so, the bulk of international trade is still transported by sea.

While there are many kinds of cargo ships, two are now of particular importance, the first being the **container ships**, which are taking the place in many instances of more conventional break-bulk ships. The second are the **roll-on/roll-off** (RO/RO) ferries, designed to carry both rail and road transport, which are of increasing importance on short sea routes.

Pre-Shipping Requirements

When shipping by sea you must first decide which ship will be used. Details of all sailings are found in *Lloyds Loading List* or the *Handy Shipping Guide.* Since most shipping lines, or their agents, employ brokers to obtain business for them, you will probably be sent **Sailing Cards**, giving details of the sailings, where and when loading will take place, and where to apply for space (see Fig. 8, Appendix 1).

Shipping lines are organised into **Conferences**, such as the North Atlantic Conference. By using ships of the same Conference Line you may obtain reductions in the standard freight rates, and rebates for using that particular line exclusively. Details of any rebates will be found in *Croner's World Directory of Freight Conferences*, which shows whether you can obtain contract rates, nett rates or rates subject to rebate.

You book space in a ship by means of a **Cargo Registration Form**, most shipping lines and container services having special forms (see Fig. 9, Appendix 1). These are made out in duplicate, half being returned to you in the form of a calling-forward for shipment notice. This form will call for complete details of the shipment, and on it you indicate any shipping documents required, such as the Bill of Lading, how many originals and copies, and how they are to be made out.

When you send goods to the docks or container bases, you will need to send with them, in addition to the invoices, a **Shipping Note**. In Britain there is a **Standard Shipping Note**, known as an SSN, and it is used for all shipments to inland and dock container points, groupage reception places, as well as to the conventional docks. This Note comes in a six-part carbonated set, obtainable from named suppliers, and no other note may be used (Fig. 10, Appendix 1). The first copy is kept at the port; the second, third and fourth copies are used by the shipping company; the fifth is returned to the haulier as a receipt for the goods; and the sixth is for the exporter's files.

In addition to the SSN, where hazardous cargoes are involved, a **Stowage Order** must accompany the goods, made out on a special form supplied by the shipping line concerned (Fig. 11, Appendix 1). It indicates the nature of the cargo, its flash point, and any special instructions as to stowage which may be necessary, and is also used for goods needing special stowage.

Notice that on all these documents your CA number (or CAN), as described in the previous chapter, will be required to be shown, or that of the shipping and forwarding agent if he is arranging the shipment for you.

Freight Rates

The rates for freight by sea are based on **weight, measurement or ad valorem,** whichever is the greatest. The latter is used only for highly valuable consignments, so that normally freight is payable on weight or measurement, the latter being the more common. In the past a rate was based on a measurement of 40 cubic feet, which was equated to a weight of one ton. Now rates are calculated on a metric basis, one cubic metre equalling one thousand kilograms or one tonne. Normally measurements are in centimetres, and if you multiply these together, you divide by 1,000,000 to obtain the cubic metres. If the measurements are in feet and inches you should use a ready reckoner to convert; but you may like to remember that to convert you multipy the inches of the three dimensions to give so many cubic inches. You then divide by 1,728 to give cubic feet, and if you divide this sum by 35·32 you get cubic metres.

You will be quoted rates which will vary by destination and by commodity; i.e. glassware will be different from artist's materials, just as Mauritius will have a different rate from that for Morocco. Most rates are at present quoted in US dollars, rather than in sterling. Hence you will find that a **CABAF** factor will be involved. This means two things: first, the CA stands for currency adjustment—that is, converting dollars to sterling; second, the BAF stands for bunker adjustment factor, which is an allowance for the refuelling of the ship, due to the increased price of oil.

There are special rates for hazardous cargoes, and there is always a minimum freight rate payable on small consignments irrespective of their size or weight. You can see, therefore, why grouping of small orders can be advantageous for the importer, since he would have to pay minimum rates on all the shipments unless they were combined.

Freight rates are usually paid in advance to destination, but goods may be sent **Freight Forward**, when the freight will be collected by the shipping line before the goods are handed over.

Back Freight is what the shipping company will charge you should they have to bring the goods back to this country, because the importer will not, or cannot, pay for them, or refuses to take delivery of them.

The Bill of Lading

This is the most important shipping document, and is made out either by the shipping line or by the exporter or his agent, and then signed by the line (see Fig. 12, Appendix 1). It is basically three things:

1. *A receipt for the goods*. The shipping line acknowledges receipt of the goods, and according to what is being done with them three different kinds of Bill may be issued. The first is a **Received for Shipment Bill**, issued when the goods have been received, but not loaded on to any particular ship. If, however, the goods have been loaded and shipped, then a **Shipped on Board Bill** will be issued, showing the name of the ship and its destination, together with that of the goods. But should the goods have been received in a damaged condition or are not according to the specifications—for example, some are missing—

then a **Dirty** or **Claused Bill of Lading** will be issued. This will also be done for hazardous cargoes, which may have to be carried on deck. Notice that the Bill will also be marked either Freight Paid or Freight Forward.

2. *A contract of carriage*. The shipping line agrees to take the goods to the destination indicated, or as near to it as the ship may safely proceed. But a ship might have to lie off the harbour because it was unsafe to enter, in which case the owner of the goods would have to pay to have them taken from the ship into the port. The legal implications will be discussed in Chapter 9.

3. *A document of title*. This means that whoever has the Bill may, on presenting it to the shipping line, obtain the goods. Bills are issued in sets of originals, and the first of these to be presented will enable the goods to be handed over. Copies of the Bill are also made out, but these have no value in themselves.

Much will depend on how you make out the Bill. In the first place you indicate the name of the **consignor**, by either your own name or your agent's name. In either case his or your CAN must now be shown on the Bill, or it will not be accepted by the shipping line. Second, you may show the name of your customer, the **consignee**. In this case you are allowing him, when he receives the Bill, to present it and obtain the goods. Or you may make it out to 'Order', in which case when you have endorsed it, it becomes a negotiable instrument. If you then sent it to a bank, they could pass it on to the importer provided he had paid or promised to pay for the goods. This use of a Bill of Lading to ensure payment will be dealt with in Chapter 7. You can of course make out a Bill to any third party if you wish, but do not make it out to a bank, because banks normally prefer not to become involved with the legal implications of a Bill. Third, you indicate who is to be notified when the goods arrive. Here you normally put your **customer's name**, or that of his agent. But this has no legal significance; it is only for the customer's convenience and enables the shipping line to have the goods delivered from the ship.

There are three other kinds of Bills of Lading. A **Stale Bill** is one which arrives after the goods, and should this happen, if the goods have to be stored the importer must pay the cost, while the shipping line has a lien on the goods if such charges are not paid. A **Through Bill** is one which covers shipment to a final destination beyond the port indicated, and this may include other methods of transport, often being used with container shipments. A **Groupage Bill** is not a Bill of Lading in the true legal sense, because the issuer is not the shipping line but the organiser of the service. Hence he receives the original Bill and in turn issues Groupage Bills to each shipper, which in effect are Certificates of Shipment.

If you charter a ship instead of taking space along with other shippers, in place of a Bill of Lading a **Charterparty** will be issued. This covers three basic types of agreement:

1. A specific voyage from one port to another.
2. A specific length of time for which a ship is chartered.
3. Taking over a ship for a contract period, during which time the ship virtually belongs to the charterer.

Normally a ship is chartered for a specific voyage, and in order to arrive at the charter rate it is often agreed in advance what cargo shall be carried and how long the loading and unloading will take. But the Charterparty refers to the ship, not its contents, and as the charterer you would not need Bills of Lading.

Carriage of Goods by Air

Shipments of goods by air continue to grow at a faster rate than other methods of transport, freight being carried on passenger aircraft as well as on special freight planes. Flights now go to almost every major city in the world, and a supplement to *Lloyds Loading List*, called *Cargo by Air*, gives details of the services available.

As you will appreciate there are certain types of goods which are most suitable for shipment by air, including:

(*a*) Goods of high value but small bulk, e.g. diamonds.
(*b*) Perishable goods, e.g. fruit.
(*c*) Seasonable goods, e.g. New Year presents.
(*d*) Short-life products, e.g. pop records or fashion goods.
(*e*) Emergency supplies, e.g. medicines or spare parts.

The two major **advantages** of shipping by air are, first, the speed of transport and, second, that both exporters and importers tend to be closer to cities served by airports than seaports. For example, the airport at Brazzaville is only a few kilometres from the city, whereas the port of Pointe Noire is several hundred kilometres from the capital, and only linked to it by a single-track railway.

The major **disadvantage** of shipping by air is its cost in terms of actual freight rates, but as you will see later these may be offset by other reduced costs such as packing, etc. It is unsuitable, of course, for large and bulky goods over, say, 30 tonnes in weight.

While it is unnecessary to book space on an aircraft, it is usual for an exporter to issue instructions to the airline, or an airfreight forwarder, in much the same way as to a shipping line, and a form similar to a Cargo Registration form for sea is used (see Fig. 13, Appendix 1). No Shipping Note is required at the airport, although the same Customs procedures have to be followed, as have others covering the origin of the goods, etc.

Air Freight Rates

All rates are controlled by **IATA**, the International Air Transport Association, to which some 98 per cent of the world's airlines belong, which means that there is virtually no competition in rates between the various airlines. All freight is charged at so much a kilogram, but for bulky goods with little weight, one kilogram is equal to 7,000 cubic centimetres.

There are six different classifications for air freight rates, these being:

1. Specific commodity rates.
2. Classification rates applying to live animals, newspapers, valuable cargoes, and human remains.
3. General cargo rates, divided into minimum, normal and quantity rates.
4. Unit Load Device (ULD) rates for containers and pallets.

5. Economy pack rates covering dense cargoes of 2,500 cubic centimetres or more on pallets.
6. Special rates for internal services.

The Air Waybill

The basis of all contracts between you as the exporter and the airline is covered in one essential document, the **Air Waybill** (see Fig. 14, Appendix 1). This is (*a*) a receipt for the goods, and (*b*) a contract of carriage. Unlike a Bill of Lading it is not a document of title. Nor is it a negotiable instrument.

Three originals are issued: one for the carrier, one for the importer, and one for the exporter. The person named in the Air Waybill can obtain delivery of the goods, and the Bill is made out as regards its marks to 'Addressed', this being the name and address of the consignee. You must always inform him of its number at once, so that he may take delivery of the goods. Hence you cannot prevent him having them without payment, as you can with a Bill of Lading, but you may consign them to him COD, when the airline will collect payment before handing over the goods.

The essence of shipments by air is speed, and complicated payment procedures are to be avoided if you are to take advantage of shipping by air.

Carriage of Goods by Road

The development of modern road systems and the growing availability of large, well-equipped trucks have resulted in a large increase in road transport, not only in Europe, but in all parts of the world where roads link countries. As an exporter you may use your own trucks or those of an outside contractor.

The main **advantages** of road transport are:

(*a*) Door-to-door delivery from exporter to importer.
(*b*) Elimination of transhipment problems.
(*c*) Availability of specialised trucks for liquids, etc.
(*d*) Less danger from loss or damage.

The main **disadvantages** are:

(*a*) Length of transit time, particularly in Europe where there are now strict regulations affecting the length of time a driver may drive.
(*b*) Limitations on the weight of the goods, basically 30 tonnes.
(*c*) Limitation to short-haul traffic.

In the past, the movement of vehicles across national frontiers has been made possible by the **TIR** system (*Transport International Routiers*), although this has now been abolished within the EEC. The TIR system allows a truck to be sealed on departure and not opened until arrival at its final destination, such trucks being distinguished by the familiar blue and white TIR signs front and rear.

The document used for international road transport is the **CMR** Consignment Note, which acts as a receipt for the goods and a contract of carriage, but is not a document of title. But in addition to all the usual details required about the consignment, there is a space for the carrier to make a note of the condition in which he has received the goods. This CMR is based on the international convention in road haulage, the *Convention de Merchandises per*

Routes, but in the EEC the new combined Certificates of Origin and Movement Certificates, the T forms, will now be used, as explained in Chapter 4.

It is worth noting that in the EEC there is a **Common Transport Policy**, aimed at harmonising as far as possible all the regulations affecting road transport within the Community, including the vehicles that may be used, the conditions under which they may be operated, and some form of uniform system for charging. At present this varies considerably between operators, although it is based on weight or measurement, whichever is the greater, as with sea freight. One cubic metre is taken to equal one tonne by the road hauliers/freight forwarders for shipments to Europe.

Carriage of Goods by Rail

There are three main types of railway traffic into Europe:

1. Freight Liners, where freight is consolidated at container bases or inland clearance depots, and is then integrated with short sea container shipping services.
2. Block train-load systems, involving privately owned wagons for the movement of cars, oil, and other commodities.
3. Train ferry wagons, operated in services organised on a groupage basis, with individual wagons being used to make up a train-load. This is the more usual method, and is covered by the CIM Consignment note (*Convention International Merchandises*), which allows the carriage of goods by rail under one document. This is a receipt for the goods and a contract of carriage, but not a document of title.

The **advantages** of rail traffic are that it is faster than road, especially over distances of more than about 300 kilometres. It is fairly economical, especially under the complete train concept, and rates are based on weight or measurement as for road. The **disadvantages** are delays at terminals and the problem of pilferage, which has come to acquire an air of respectability from railways.

Two modern developments are the specialist operators of rail container services like Intercontainer, who buy freight in bulk and offer the exporter advantageous rates; and TEEM, or the Trans-European Express Goods Trains system, which sets out to provide a fast rail service all over Europe.

Other Methods of Transport

There are three other methods of transport that are of note.

1. *Coastal shipping services*. Exporters situated near smaller sea ports may find it advantageous to send their goods to the larger ports by coastal vessels. While this is a comparatively slow method, it is useful for bulk shipments of raw materials, machinery and heavy plant. The documents can usually be incorporated into the main shipping documents.

2. *Inland waterways*. In the European transport scene the value of canals has been recognised by the EEC and other European countries. In the north of Europe links already exist between Antwerp and Warsaw, and extend down to Stuttgart and Basle. There is an extensive system of canals in France, and another in Yugoslavia. It would not be difficult to link these systems and provide services between the North Sea, the Baltic, the Mediterranean and the

Black Seas. This may be a slow way of transporting goods, but for imperishable and bulky goods it has its uses.

3. *Parcel Post*. If you can export in small consignments you should not overlook the parcel post system which operates all over the world. It is usually fast, and extremely reliable. Its main limitation is weight, since a maximum of 10 kilograms is allowed for any one parcel, except to India and the Philippines. It operates by sea and air, and there is a minimum of formalities. The most important one is a **Customs Declaration**, usually in the form of a small green label, fixed to the outside of the parcel. British Rail have introduced a rail parcel post, and now guarantee delivery anywhere in Europe within a day or so.

Local Transport

One of the faults of exporters is that they often overlook local transport facilities, whereas you should always take into account what happens to your exports when they arrive in their country of destination.

In the example quoted earlier, it is clearly better to ship to Brazzaville whenever possible by air rather than by sea, because of the delays in forwarding goods from the coast up to the capital. Similar conditions exist in neighbouring Zaïre, where the sea port of Matadi is some distance from the capital, Kinshasa.

Your customers should be encouraged to advise you of local transport conditions, which you should study, because they will in many cases indicate which is the best main method of transport to the country. Moreover, the method of packing the goods may have to be amended if, for example, taking them to their final destination involves the use of more unorthodox methods of transport, e.g. by mule, donkey or on people's heads. Importers do not all live close to sea or air ports, railheads, or even truck depots, so that you must understand and make allowances for local internal transport conditions.

Packing

The object of packing is to protect from damage or loss goods in transit from the factory or warehouse until they arrive in the hands of customers overseas. Such risks occur at five main points:

(*a*) When the goods are being loaded.
(*b*) When they are being handled at the docks, airports, railheads, etc.
(*c*) During the voyage itself, by sea, road, rail or air.
(*d*) When they are being unloaded.
(*e*) When they are being transported to their final destination.

Hence you must examine the type of protection your goods need when they are exported to another country, which determines the method of packing required. You must identify the goods, the customer and their destination, which means the goods have to be marked.

Criteria for Export Packing

There are several criteria by which you may judge which form of packing is most suitable:

(*a*) *The method of transport used*. Damage may occur, for example, more readily in a ship than in a plane if the goods are likely to be corroded by sea air. Pilferage is more common from railway wagons than from road containers.

(*b*) *The nature of the goods*. Pottery, for example, is more fragile than wooden toys. Sugar will not break, but absorbs moisture. Steel rods need little protection from breakage, whereas glass containers require protection against being dropped.

(*c*) *The conditions to be encountered*. These may be climatic conditions, especially extreme heat, or cold, and damp. They may be the local unloading conditions, especially in places where modern equipment, such as forklift trucks, is non-existent or out of action. They may also be the actual conditions under which the final transport is conducted.

(*d*) *The regulations to be observed*. Depending on the nature of the goods and the country to which they are being sent, there are many regulations imposed on the materials used for packing. The Netherlands, for example, forbids the use of straw packing. South Africa and New Zealand both insist on declarations that any timber used is free from certain diseases. Your customers will advise of such regulations, which are indicated in *Croner's Directory*. The shipping and airline companies also provide lists of packing regulations.

To appreciate packing criteria and be able to pack goods in the most effective way, you should occasionally visit docks and airports to see for yourself what happens to your goods as they are loaded and unloaded, as well as stowed. When overseas you should do the same, and also ask your customers to advise you of the conditions in which your goods arrived. Always ask them if they have any suggestions as to how your packing could be improved. And before you adopt any new method, test it thoroughly. One way is to dispatch a sample to various destinations, and have it returned to you, so that you may examine any damage that may have taken place. There are several export packing specialists, and you may feel their services should be used, especially when new and complicated methods have to be adopted.

Methods of Packing for Export

There is a tremendous variety of methods of packing. Some goods—such as pipes or lavatory pans—are sent overseas with little or no packing because the risk of damage to them is slight. Some need no more than some form of protective coating, whereas others need cushioning from the risks of being dropped.

For small-sized products, wooden or fibreboard cases are still extensively used, often steel or nylon bound. The use of sacks, steel drums and plastic or glass containers is also widely practised. Furniture may be sent in knocked-down form, while vehicles and apparatus are often sent in a Completely Knocked Down (CKD) form, but generally packed in cases.

A major development is the Unit Load, which now takes two main forms:

(*a*) *Palletised Cargo*. Here the goods are anchored to a pallet or base, made of wood or metal. There are innumerable kinds of pallets, ranging from stillages (base plates), to skeleton pallets (for lightweight goods) and box pallets (where one side can be dropped). The use of pallets has made the

A stillage

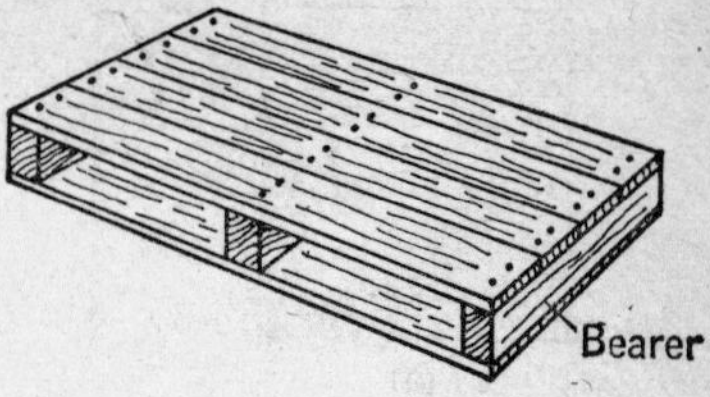

A two-way pallet

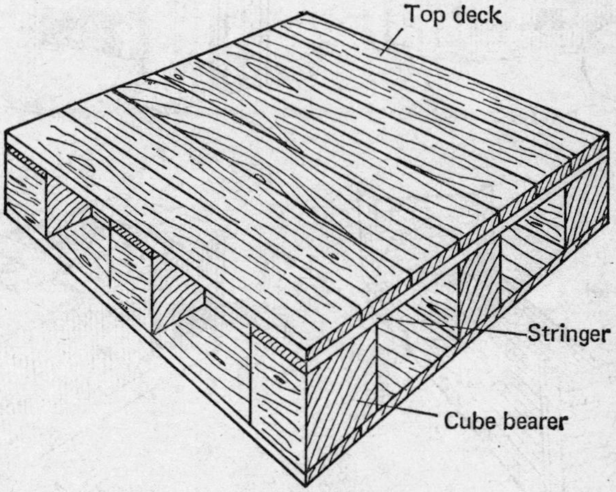

A four-way pallet

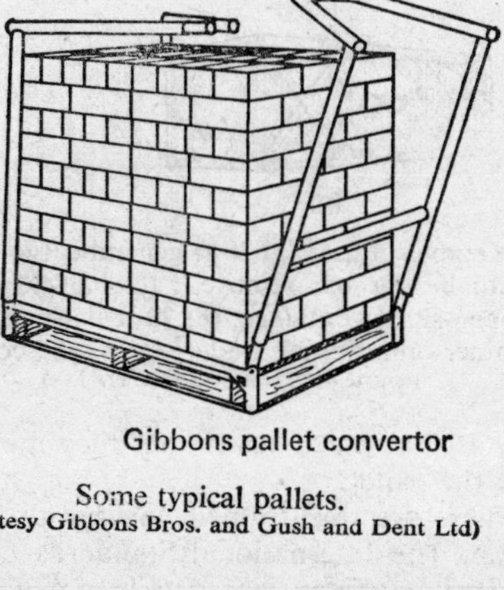

Gibbons pallet convertor

Some typical pallets.
(courtesy Gibbons Bros. and Gush and Dent Ltd)

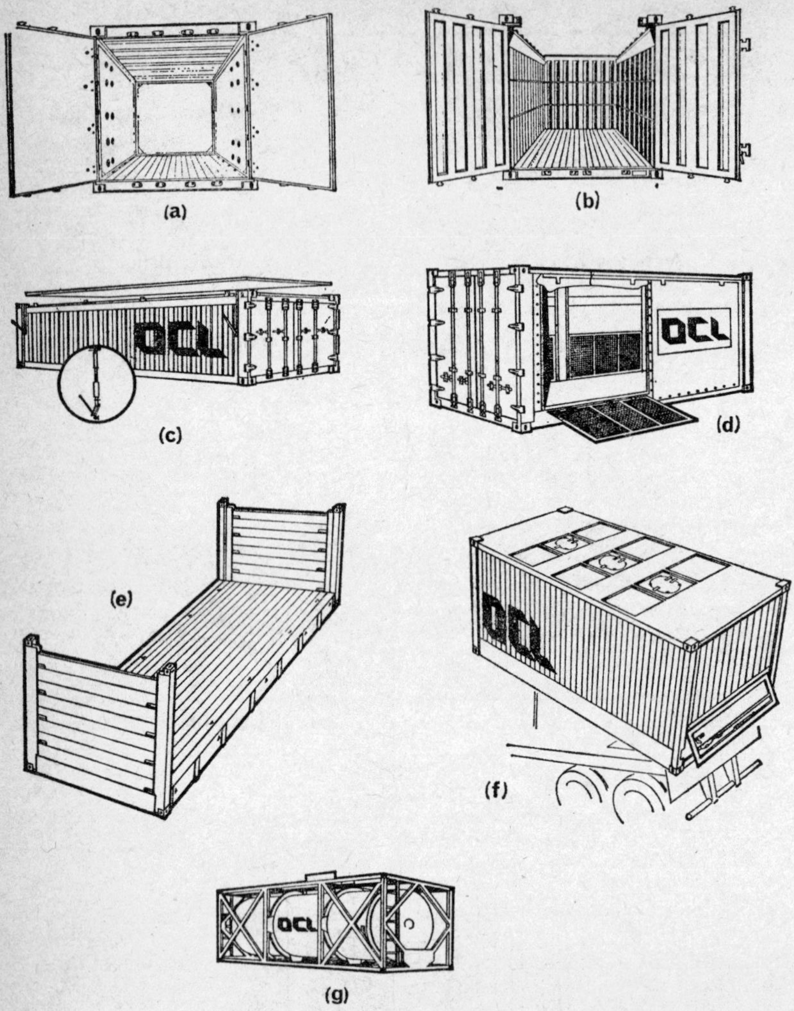

Types of container in common use: (a) 20 ft general cargo container; (b) 20 ft top-loading container with header bar removed; (c) half-height container with solid removable top; (d) open-sided container; (e) 20 ft flat-rack container; (f) dry-bulk container on a tipping trailer; (g) a tank container.
(courtesy Overseas Containers Ltd)

handling of the goods that much easier, but they may still need protection before being put on the pallet.

(*b*) *Containers*. These are steel-framed boxes with panels of steel, wood, plastic or aluminium. The International Standards Organisation (the ISO) has laid down standard container sizes, details of which are published by the British Standards Institution. There are a great many kinds of containers, from end-loading general cargo containers, to open-sided ones, often used for hazardous cargoes, and tank containers for bulk liquids.

The advantages of using containers are fairly obvious, because they can be easily loaded, afford protection to the goods inside, and reduce the risk of pilferage. But they do not relieve you of the responsibility for packing your goods, because it has been found that insufficiently packed goods within a container can suffer serious damage. Moreover, containers are inclined to sweat in humid conditions, and damage the goods inside.

You can buy containers for your own use. You can hire them, or use them on a groupage basis, which means your goods are included with others in the carrier's containers. You will have already noted the growth in the number of container ships, as well as the growing use of containers on aircraft, railways and for road transport.

Cost of Packing

You will recall from Chapter 3 that when considering the effect of terms of delivery on the costs of your exports, packing was shown in the example as 'Additional at Cost'. This is one way of allowing for what may be a considerable additional cost to the exporter, since packing, to be fully effective, must be done without prime regard for cost. Many companies prefer to add this to the cost of the goods, but in order to keep the price as low as possible add only the actual packing cost itself.

The alternative is to allow in the basic export price for the packing cost, and to quote a price inclusive of packing. This method is often used by exporters of goods which have a standard form of packing, like cartons or cases.

Whichever method you adopt you must, however, know what the packing costs are, since these must often be shown separately on an invoice. And remember that packing materials are, in some countries, valuable in themselves, so your customer may be able to sell or re-use the materials.

Marking of Export Shipments

All exports have to be marked in some way or another in order to identify the goods, the customer to whom they are being sent, and their destination.

(*a*) *Shipping marks*. Most customers overseas have their own marks, which they will ask you to use. These usually consist of the initials of the importer, often enclosed in a distinctive shape such as a square or a diamond. Underneath this the port of destination is normally given, as well as the port through which the shipment is being made. It is also quite usual for the customer's order number to be included in a mark. At the bottom of the mark is the number of consignments being sent. This is expressed as the total number, plus the actual number of that package. For example, 'Nos 2/6 UP' would indicate there were six items, of which this was the second.

The weights and measurements are added—that is the gross weight, the nett weight and the tare (packing only)—together with the cube, each figure being shown separately (e.g. 24 cm × 28 cm × 30 cm).

(*b*) *Instructions*. Since exports go to countries where your language may not be spoken, it is usually a waste of time putting any special instructions such as 'Do not drop' on the consignment, necessary though they may be. To overcome this problem use the various internationally accepted signs, such

Some typical shipping marks and instructions.

as a wine glass, to indicate which way up a case should be stood. A broken wine glass indicates that the goods are fragile. Poisonous or dangerous cargo is sometimes marked with a skull and crossbones. You will find that airlines will issue special stickers for hazardous cargo and for certain special cargoes. An umbrella mark means the cargo must be kept dry.

(*c*) *Regulations*. Certain countries have local regulations about the marking of goods, these being found in *Croner's Directory* as you might expect. For Germany, for example, you must show the country of origin on all cases and cartons containing foodstuffs, although the actual contents need not be shown, since this would be an invitation to pilfer. These regulations are also shown in Croner's.

Whatever you put on your goods in the way of marks they must agree exactly with what is put on the documents accompanying them, or your customer will have problems when he tries to obtain the goods. Hence you must ensure the closest cooperation between those marking the consignments and those preparing the documents.

Total Distribution Cost (TDC)

The high proportion of transport costs to the final cost of the goods to the customer—which may be as great as 40 per cent—has led to studies being made of the comparative costs of different methods of transport, everything being taken into account. The factors to be considered are as follows:

(*a*) *The wishes of the customer*. This takes precedence over everything else, although you have a duty to suggest an alternative method if you think it would be in his interests.

(*b*) *The method of supply locally*. This concerns the respective merits of supplying from stocks held in a warehouse locally, as opposed to supplying direct to each customer from the exporter's factory or warehouse.

(*c*) *The nature of the goods*. Clearly some goods, as you have seen, are more suited to certain methods of transport; for example, heavy and bulky machinery is better sent by sea than by air, while most perishable fruit is better sent by air.

(*d*) *The packing required*. Different types of packing will be required, according to both the nature of the goods and the method of transport, because the risks incurred vary.

(*e*) *Insurance*. This may alter according to the length of transit time, and the risks involved.

Bearing the above in mind you might then start to compare transport costs as follows (a case of machinery sent from London to Marseilles).

	Sea	*Road*	*Air*
Packing costs	200	105	125
Documentation	40	36	64
Freight	50	180	130
Insurance	60	59	58
Totals	350	380	367

This shows that it was cheapest in this instance to send the goods by sea, but they took ten days to arrive. By air they arrived the next day and cost less than by road, which took three days. A good deal therefore depended on the speed of delivery required.

When you carry out TDC analyses you will find that certain factors emerge, as they have done from the example above.

Packing

Generally air transport requires less packing than sea, although in this case road transport needed least of all, because the goods were loaded at the exporter's factory and not touched until they reached their final destination. If container transport is used, packing costs will tend to be much the same whichever method of transport is used.

Documentation

Documentation costs do not vary a great deal, although in this case the increased air cost was due to special Customs clearance at the airport.

Freight

As you would have expected, the actual freight costs were cheapest by sea, and most expensive by air. This is normal, but when comparing air and road, the longer the distance the more air gains over road, which also applies to air and rail transport.

Insurance

For short distances, as in the above example, insurance costs do not vary all that much, but for long distances air is likely to gain at the expense of sea, owing to the shorter time for which the goods are held covered.

Delivery times

This is a critical factor, and in the above example the greater air costs were more than compensated for by the shorter delivery time, even road having the edge over sea in this case. But where delivery is made from a warehouse locally, you will find that the cost of getting the goods to the warehouse will depend to some degree on the volume of goods involved. This is because warehousing costs are both fixed and variable. Up to a certain volume you will probably find it cheaper to dispatch by air, but above that level sea transport would cost less. This is because the additional volume increases the variable costs, but not the fixed ones. Hence any comparative transport costs depend to some degree on the volume of the goods concerned.

To be a successful exporter you must continually examine your transport costs, and be prepared to use different methods as and when these show cost and customer advantages. In the past many exporters have used traditional methods without examining the other options open to them. There are now too many such options for this to be a sound policy. The major developments in this field are the combined transport facilities offered by freight forwarders, which cover shipping by any means from what is in effect door-to-door, either as single consignments or as part of a groupage operation. This is especially the case with container loads carried on container ships and aircraft, where delivery to the container base, and collection from it in the country of destination, are the only things the exporter and importer have to arrange.

Handling the Transport Operation

As an exporter you can either handle the whole transport function yourself, or you may subcontract a major part of the work to outside specialists, such as shipping and forwarding agents.

The work these agents will do for you is as follows:

1. Advising on the availability of the different methods of transport to any given destination, and which would be the most effective from the point of view of you and your customer.
2. Providing details of the costs involved, and in some cases being able to obtain preferential rates for you.
3. Handling the booking of shipping space, and even arranging, should you wish, to have the goods collected and taken to the docks or airport.
4. Preparing the shipping documents, paying the freight charges, and attending to Customs entries, as well as handling any other documents required, such as Certificates of Origin, Movement Certificates, etc.
5. Handling the insurance of the cargoes.
6. Having the goods cleared in countries where they have agents.
7. Enabling you to pay charges monthly, instead of whenever shipments are made.

Hence you will not need your own staff to handle this work, and you have access to considerable expertise and experience which you may not possess yourself.

On the other hand, you have to pay for the agents' services. Charges vary as a rule from 3 to 5 per cent of the total freight charges, plus the costs involved in preparing the documents, etc. You also to some degree lose control of your shipments, so that if anything goes wrong, while your customer will blame you, you can only blame the agent, which may not be highly satisfactory. Hence what you are paying for is service, and where your business is important to the agent you are likely to get good service; where it is of minor importance to him, the standard of the service may slip.

So that you must weigh up, according to the size of your export business, the cost of doing the work yourself, as opposed to paying to have it done outside, along with the standard of service you can supply to your export customers as compared with the service provided by an agent. In practice most medium and smaller companies prefer to use an agent, only the largest exporters reckoning they can do the work better, and more cheaply, themselves.

Revision

Cover the page with a sheet of paper and uncover one question at a time.

Answers	*Questions*
	1. What is an SSN and how many copies are used?
1. The new Standard Shipping Note: six copies are used.	2. How is sea freight charged?

Answers	*Questions*
2. By weight, measurement or ad valorem.	3. What does an Air Waybill provide?
3. (*a*) A receipt for the goods. (*b*) A contract of carriage.	4. What is a dirty bill of lading?
4. One issued where the cargo does not conform to the specifications.	5. Where do you find details of ships' sailings?
5. In *Lloyds Loading list*; the *Handy Shipping Guide*; and from sailing cards.	6. What does a broken wine glass signify?
6. That goods are fragile.	7. What is the maximum permitted weight for parcel post?
7. 10 kilograms, but less to India and the Philippines.	8. What is a TDC analysis?
8. An examination of the total transport costs.	9. How much do shipping and forwarding agents normally charge?
9. Between 3 and 5 per cent of the freight charges.	10. What does 1 cubic metre equal in weight?
10. 1,000 kilogram or one tonne.	

Exercises

1. Explain the significance of a Bill of Lading.
2. How would you set about carrying out a TDC analysis?
3. Assess the advantages and disadvantages of using shipping and forwarding agents, as opposed to doing the work yourself.
4. Which types of goods are most suitable for shipment by air?
5. Why should you, as an exporter, study local transport conditions in other countries?
6. What is meant by a unit load, and what significance does it have for an export transaction?
7. How would you mark 15 cases of glass bottles being sent by sea to Hassan Bros. of Nairobi?

6

CARGO INSURANCE

Various forms of insurance have been in existence for hundreds of years, just as many of the terms used today are the same as they were many years ago. The first paragraph of the Marine Insurance Act of 1906, under which all marine insurance is still regulated, states that 'A contract of insurance is a contract whereby the insurer undertakes to indemnify the assured, in manner and to the extent thereby agreed, against marine losses, that is to say, the losses incidental to marine adventure.' So that when you insure a shipment of your goods going to another country, you are still presumed to be sharing in an 'adventure'.

As an exporter you should be familiar with five areas of cargo insurance:

1. The liability for, and principles of, insurance
2. The types of insurance and policies
3. Insurance procedures
4. Warranties and additional risks
5. Insurance claims

While export insurance has often in the past been referred to as marine insurance, this really means transport insurance, since it covers the risks involved in the movement of goods by rail, road and air, as well as by sea. Hence the use of the term Cargo Insurance to describe the insurance which you, as an exporter, will have to handle. You will, of course, also be concerned with Credit Insurance, but this will be dealt with in the next chapter, since it is concerned with the finance of exports.

The Liability for, and Principles of, Insurance

In principle, insurance compensates the owner of the goods, or anyone with an interest in them, for any loss or damage incurred as a result of their being involved in some risk against which insurance cover has been taken out. Hence in all normal export transactions it is usual for goods to be insured against loss or damage during their passage from the exporter to the customer overseas. The **liability for insurance** rests with the owner of the goods. As you saw in Chapter 3, the Terms of Delivery define who is the owner at any given point in their delivery, so that you are able to decide at what point you are responsible for insuring them, and when the customer must take over. For example, in an F.O.B. shipment, the title to the goods passes to your customer when the goods pass over the ship's rail, so that it is your responsibility to insure them up to that point, and your customer's responsibility from then on.

In practice, the exporter normally takes the responsibility for seeing that goods are insured at all stages of their delivery. For example, although in a C.I.F. contract the exporter is only responsible until the arrival of the goods at the port, he would generally make sure they were insured right through to their final destination. Yet, legally, there is no obligation for goods to be insured at all, whether in transit or not. In Britain the only two compulsory insurances are those for motor vehicles and national health. But bearing in mind the risks involved when goods are sent to other countries, compared with the cost of insurance, it is unusual for export shipments not to be covered to some degree by insurance of some kind. Moreover, methods of finance today require in most cases that goods must be insured when they are exported, as part of the contract.

There are three fundamental principles of Cargo Insurance, as follows.

1. Utmost Good Faith

The Marine Insurance Act of 1906 states that 'a contract of marine insurance is a contract based upon the **utmost good faith** . . .' and it states that if utmost good faith is not observed by either party the contract may be avoided by either party. This means that you must, as an exporter, tell underwriters all the circumstances that are material to the risks involved. The statements you make must be truthful, or be made in good faith that they are true. If any material circumstances are withheld, the policy becomes avoidable. And if the insurance is made by a broker acting on behalf of an exporter, then the broker must also add any material facts, if he knows of any. The intention is to allow an underwriter to decide whether or not to accept the risk, and to fix a premium for the insurance. Yet you may presume the underwriter to know his job, or what are matters of common knowledge. This principle is particularly important when you insure under some form of open cover, because the underwriter is accepting your declaration of the shipments being insured.

2. Insurable Interest

If you insure a cargo you must have some **insurable interest in it**. An interest is said to exist where a property is exposed to risks, and the assured has such a relationship that he will benefit by its safe arrival, or will be prejudiced by its loss or damage, and may incur liability in respect thereof. If he is not 'interested', then he is in effect betting or wagering, and this is expressly forbidden.

Interest may be of several kinds. Ownership of the cargo implies a **full interest** in some or all of the property. But a **defeasible interest** is one which ceases, such as when the ownership changes hands during the voyage. A **contingent interest** is one which attaches during a voyage, such as when a buyer acquires an interest in the goods as they are in transit.

In practice the buyer has an insurable interest at the time of a loss, even though he did not have it when the insurance was taken out, which means he takes over the policy which had originally been issued to the exporter. Moreover, a buyer may transfer his interest to a third party, but no one may claim who does not have an interest in the cargo.

3. Indemnity

An insurance policy is a **contract of indemnity**, which means the assured is indemnified against loss. But since it would clearly be impossible to replace the goods, or the ship or aircraft, the indemnity is almost always expressed in monetary terms. Hence a value, known as the **insurable value**, has been introduced, unless of course no value is stated. In this case a policy is an **unvalued policy**, but the Act lays down how the insurable value has to be calculated. Otherwise policies are known as **value policies**, when the value of the cargo is specifically stated.

But note that you cannot recover more than the loss you have suffered, so that when a claim is paid you will be given the full value of the goods insured if the loss is total, but only a percentage of the total if the loss or damage is partial. Yet if the loss is partial, by the right of subrogation underwriters are entitled to the whole amount of any recovery up to, but not exceeding, the amount of the claim they have paid. Hence underwriters take over the interest of the assured in whatever remains of a damaged cargo.

This points to another effect of any cargo insurance, which is that **you may not make a profit as such out of insurance**, although you may include your profit in the total sum assured. Nor may you recover from underwriters as well as the carriers, because you would then be getting more than the total value of the cargo.

In addition to the above main principles of insurance, there is one of considerable importance, namely **proximate cause**. This is concerned with the problem of establishing the actual cause of loss or damage, because in many cases there may well be more than one cause. Hence it has been established that only the proximate or nearest cause shall be considered, so that remote causes will be eliminated. This has the effect of bringing any underwriter's liability within reasonable limits.

As you will see in Chapter 9, all these principles have been embodied in the **Marine Insurance Act of 1906**. As an exporter, arranging for insurance on your export cargoes, you must adhere to them at all times, otherwise you will run the risk of dispatching goods overseas without adequate insurance cover.

Types of Insurance and Policies

While the principles of insurance apply to all forms of insurance, when you send goods overseas by sea you will be concerned with two things, one being the insurance of the goods and the other the insurance of the ship. When you use what is called a **Lloyds S.G. Policy** (Ship and Goods Policy) you will see that there is a clear distinction between the insurance of the ship and that of the cargo, but you will be concerned with both.

At this point you must, moreover, remember that in marine insurance the word **average** has the specialised meaning of 'loss', whereas in non-marine insurance it relates actual values to the sum assured. The principles of average in marine insurance can be seen from the way a claim is assessed for partial loss or damage, by comparing the actual damaged value at destination with the sound value, thus giving a percentage of depreciation, which is then applied to the agreed insured value.

Insurance of the Ship

While ship insurance is carried out by the owners of the vessel, if you are the owner of the goods or are arranging insurance on behalf of the owners, you are sharing in what is still presumed to be an 'adventure'. Hence if the ship has to be saved from some peril, to ensure its safety, by part of the cargo being jettisoned, both the owner of the cargo lost and the owner of the cargo saved are concerned in either a loss, or the avoidance of a loss.

General Average, which covers this eventuality, may be defined as covering the position if any part of the ship or its cargo is voluntarily sacrificed, or if any expenditure is incurred for the purpose of preserving from peril all the interests involved (i.e. the ship and its cargo). For example, water might have to be used to put out a fire, which might then damage some of the cargo, or some cargo might have to be thrown overboard to save the ship from sinking.

When anything of this kind happens, a General Average is declared, which means that every cargo owner has to contribute towards whatever damage the ship or its cargo has suffered, this being done in proportion to the value of the cargo. This amount in each case will be worked out by the average adjusters. Normally cargo is insured against General Average, but if it is not, then the owner is still liable for General Average.

Insurance of the Cargo

Whereas any General Average falls on all concerned in an 'adventure', **Particular Average**, which is concerned with insurance of the cargo, only falls upon the individual. This insurance is embodied in a standard policy issued by Lloyds or an insurance company, or what, as you have seen, is called the S.G. Policy (Ship and Goods Policy). But this is really only the bare bones of insurance of the ship and its cargoes, covering loss and damage from the perils of the sea, fire, thieves, jettison and barratry (which is any wrongful act by the master or crew of the ship). Hence it has to be modified to bring it up to date, and this is done by means of what are known as **Institute Clauses**, of which there are 14. Of these the most important are:

(*a*) *F.P.A.* This means **Free of Particular Average**, the word Particular applying to the cargo insured, and the particular loss incurred. It covers the goods against total loss by sea perils, including damage or loss attributable to fire or collision, and contributes to General Average. But it does not cover any other damage to the goods, and is used, therefore, for goods which are unlikely to suffer damage in transit, such as steel girders.

(*b*) *W.A. or W.P.A.* This means **With Average, or With Particular Average.** It includes the risks under F.P.A., plus total or partial loss or damage due to sea water or heavy weather. It does not include theft, pilferage, or damage in transit.

(*c*) *All Risks.* In theory, by including this clause you insure against **all risks** of loss or damage; but this is not entirely true, because much will depend on the type of goods being insured. For example, any damage caused by the effects of sea air would be excluded, as would be any wear and tear on the goods. Tainting from another cargo is also excluded. Moreover, this insurance only covers the voyage itself, whereas most exporters wish to cover the goods from the time they leave their premises until they arrive at those of the customer.

(*d*) *The Institute Transit Clause.* This used to be called the **Warehouse to Warehouse Clause**, and has been introduced to cover the goods to their final destination. Hence you are insuring against any loss or damage whether caused on the voyage or not; and when the 'place of storage' is specified, this covers any place not strictly a warehouse. But there is one important limitation, namely that there is a limit of 60 days placed on the cover, which means that any claim has to be made within 60 days after the goods have been discharged from the ship.

(*e*) *The War Clause.* This is usually expressed as **F.C. & S.**, meaning **Free from Capture and Seizure**, and is excluded from a policy unless it has been expressly added. Should, therefore, your cargo be passing through an area where war is raging, or likely to break out, you must add this clause, paying the additional premium which will be charged.

(*f*) *The Strikes Clause.* This is usually expressed as **S.R. & C.C.**, which means **Strikes, Riots and Civil Commotions**. These also are expressly excluded, unless you specify their addition under this clause, paying an additional premium as you would for a War Risk clause.

(*g*) *Additional Risks.* There are other clauses covering additional risks against which you may wish to insure, and a number of trade clauses covering specific commodities such as jute and timber. The more important of these clauses are the **Constructive Total Loss** clause, which will be dealt with under Claims; the **Termination of Adventure** clause, which covers the right of a shipowner to terminate the voyage other than at its declared destination; the **Bailee clause**, which protects the rights of the assured if there is any delay in lodging a claim, or fulfilling any conditions of carriage or bailment; and a **Reasonable Dispatch clause**, covering the lodging of claims within a reasonable time.

When you insure shipments by air, note that the Institute of London Underwriters has introduced a set of **Air Cargo clauses** (All Risks). There are 11 of these, based on the marine clauses, including a **Transit** clause, although the period of cover is only up to 30 days after discharge from the aircraft; a **Termination of Adventure** clause where the time for final delivery is limited to 30 days; and a new **Frustration and Confiscation** clause, which has no equivalent in the marine cover. This makes it clear that losses caused by nationalisation, confiscation or requisition are not covered, and that where the transit is frustrated but no physical damage to the goods has occurred, no claim is payable. You should also note that the **Air Civil Riots** clause excludes loss or damage caused by withholding labour or fuel.

When you insure your goods in transit you have, therefore, a wide range of options, and you must decide against which risks you wish to insure. Clearly the more you insure against the higher the premium, so that you must take into account the nature of the goods, the packing provided for them, the kind of voyage involved and the risks to which you believe they will be exposed. For example, insuring logs of wood will usually only call for an F.P.A. cover, because the risk of damage to them would be minimal. But if you were exporting toys you would probably prefer a Transit cover because the toys could easily be damaged during their voyage to their final destination. Yet if you were exporting crockery, liable to be chipped or damaged, you might feel the additional premium was too high and prefer to insure against loss, but find it cheaper to replace any damaged pieces. When you insure on behalf of your customer, you must agree with him the extent of the insurance cover he wishes, as well as what you feel would be reasonable. Naturally, increased insurance premiums increase the final price of the goods, and insurance should be kept to a minimum consistent with adequate cover.

Insurance Procedures

Types of Policy

You have seen how a basic policy has to be amended by you, as an exporter, according to the risks against which you or your customer wish to insure the cargo, and these will be incorporated in the Policy. You may apply either to **Lloyds** or to an **insurance company** for such a policy, and you will see that you must declare the vessel, its ports of sailing and destination, the marks and numbers of your consignment, and the amount for which the cargo is to be insured. If you insure through an insurance company you may deal direct or through a broker. If you insure with Lloyds you must use an authorised Lloyds broker. The broker will try to get the best terms for you, and the details will be recorded on a **'slip'** (see Fig. 15, Appendix 1), on which underwriters put what are called 'lines' indicating how much of the risk each underwriter has taken. This 'slip' has no legal value in itself, but may be used as evidence of a contract of insurance. Lloyds has an enviable reputation throughout the world, and once a risk has been accepted payment will be made in full, if that risk proves to have been incurred. The actual contract will be embodied in the Policy.

If you are a regular exporter you may not wish to have a separate Policy made out for each shipment, in which case you have three options:

1. *You may take out a Floating Policy.* This is issued for a round sum sufficient to cover the cost of shipments for some months. You must declare all shipments, and the Policy remains in force until it has been exhausted. There is normally no time limit, only a limit of value, and the premium is paid when the Policy is made out, although some final adjustment may be necessary.
2. *An Open Cover.* This is a permanent provisional cover to take care of all shipments within a fixed period, usually 12 months. You must declare each shipment, when policies are issued to cover each.
3. *An Open Policy.* This is similar to Open Cover, but it remains in force until cancelled by either party.

When you make individual declarations the insurance company or broker will issue you with a book of **Insurance Declaration Forms** on which the details of the shipments must be made individually (Fig. 16, Appendix 1). In the case of shipments by sea the name of the vessel must always be shown, so that you cannot group shipments for purposes of insurance; but for rail, road or air shipments you may make them monthly en bloc, although you still have to prepare individual **Certificates of Insurance** (Fig. 17, Appendix 1).

The Value for Insurance

As you have seen, you will need to place a value on your cargo for insurance purposes. It is customary to insure export cargoes for 10 to 15 per cent above their C.I.F. value, the additional amount representing cover against incidental losses and out of pocket expenses.

To work this out, suppose the cost of the goods to be $180.00 and the cost of the freight to be $43.50. In this case the C. & F. cost will be $223.50. For the purposes of this calculation this represents 100 per cent, and you need to insure both this and the insurance costs, at the rate of, say, \$0.75 per cent, plus an additional 10 per cent of the total. Hence the sum to be insured will be

$$\underset{1}{(100\% \text{ of C. \& F.}} + \underset{2}{0{\cdot}0075 \times \frac{110}{100} \text{ of C. \& F.})} \times \underset{3}{\frac{110}{100}}$$

1. This is the raw cost
2. This is the extra percentage stepped up by 10 per cent
3. This is the step up of the whole figure by 10 per cent

If you work the above out you will arrive at

$$(100\% \text{ of C. \& F.} + 0{\cdot}00825\% \text{ of C. \& F.}) \times 1{\cdot}1$$
$$= (1{\cdot}0825 \times \$223.50) \times 1{\cdot}1$$
$$= \$247.88, \text{ or say } \$248.00$$

Is the \$248.00 correct? If you add 10 per cent to your C. & F. cost of \$223.50 you get \$247.89, so you have in fact insured to a total of 10 per cent above the C.I.F. value.

Insurance Premiums

Premiums will vary according to the category in which your product is placed for insurance purposes; the type of risks against which you insure; and the destination to which the goods are being sent. Moreover, your record as an exporter will also be taken into account, i.e. whether your packing is considered to be adequate, your procedure for handling claims is satisfactory, and your general handling of insurance business efficient.

To give you some idea of current rates, if you were shipping machinery from Britain to Europe, you might pay about 0·20 per cent, but if you were shipping that machinery to North America you would probably pay up to four times as much, because of the distance involved and the time taken for the goods to arrive. This would be on an All Risks basis; but if you only took out F.P.A. cover, you would probably pay about half these amounts. But if you were shipping crockery, you might well pay 0·20 per cent for no more than F.P.A. cover to Europe from Britain, and find the rate for North America increased to 1·00 per cent. But then take out a Warehouse to Warehouse cover and the rates to Europe would probably go up three times, and as much in proportion to North America. Remember that War Risks and Civil Riots and Commotions clauses will add to the amounts involved, and you will appreciate why you must take a good deal of care in deciding how the goods are to be insured. You also need to obtain the best rates, which do vary quite considerably, so that the services of an insurance broker are invariably required.

Insurance Documents

As you have seen, a Policy is issued for all kinds of insurance effected, but in practice, for regular exporters, a **Certificate of Insurance** is normally used for individual shipments. While this has little or no legal value in itself, it is now taken to be the equivalent to the Policy, and accepted as such in the documentary procedures for Letters of Credit and so on. You will need to show on the Certificate the open contract under which it is issued, and exporters are issued with books of Certificates which they may fill in themselves and send both to the insurance company and with the remainder of the shipping documents. (A selection of insurance documents is given in Appendix 1, Figs. 15–18.)

Similar procedures are followed for shipments insured on rail, by road or by air. The view is currently held that shipments by air are safer because the goods are handled less than they are by other means of transport, but remember that you must arrange to insure the goods on their way to and from airports, and that there is also a risk of mis-delivery or non-delivery, so no insurance would be asking for trouble. Rates by air tend, however, to be lower than by sea, road or rail. If you use parcel post extensively, you can obtain an Open Policy on a Warehouse to Warehouse basis.

The increasing use of containers has led some exporters to feel that insurance is not so necessary because of the greater protection afforded to the goods by the container. This is not so, because it has been found that while the risks of theft and pilferage have been reduced, the risk of damage is still present. For example, damage often occurs inside the container because of faulty packing. There is, as you have seen, a danger of sweating and also a problem of both overheating and freezing of the contents. Containers are themselves often damaged, and have been thrown overboard in bad weather. Hence underwriters have been careful to consider how far containers are inspected before use; how well the goods are packed before being placed in the container; how well the containers are stowed; and how securely they are sealed. Generally speaking there are no special rates for insuring container cargoes, but you must declare them as such. Moreover, it is likely that rates for containerised cargo will decrease as the use of containers becomes more general.

Warranties and Additional Risks

Acting on the principle of 'utmost good faith' is, as you have seen, an implicit part of all insurance. But certain **Warranties** have been introduced over the years, which make the proposer's duties more onerous.

There are two kinds of Warranties, **Express** and **Implied**. The latter do not appear on the Policy, while the former are written in as required. A Warranty is simply a promise by the assured that something shall, or shall not, be done, or that a certain state of affairs does, or does not, exist. They improve the character of an insurance, and help to obtain a more favourable rate.

Express Warranties may be anything introduced to establish more precisely the nature of the risk, one example being the type of packing to be used for easily breakable goods. There are many Express warranties used on the ship itself, known as Institute Warranties, four of which restrict ships sailing to icebound regions in winter in the north, another restricting sailings to the Antarctic, and one prohibiting the carriage of Indian coal as cargo during the summer owing to its highly combustible nature. These Warranties apply, of course, to ships not on regular sailings.

Implied Warranties are harder to understand because they do not actually appear on the Policy, but two of these are important. One is that a ship is deemed to be seaworthy, and this is taken to mean at the beginning of a voyage or at the beginning of each stage of a voyage. Seaworthiness also includes cargo-worthiness. The other is that the adventure insured must be lawful and carried out in a lawful manner. Hence any insurance taken out to protect the proceeds of a robbery, or the carrying of prohibited drugs, would be held to be invalid. There is now a Dangerous Drugs clause which states that no claim will be paid unless the shipment has been authorised by the governments of the importing and exporting countries.

Since you can always insure against additional risks if you so wish, you may like to consider four on which insurance is often effected in export.

1. Exhibition Risks

Exporters who take part in exhibitions overseas will wish to insure their property in transit to and from the site and while it is being used. In addition, some form of third party insurance will be required. Another risk against which it is possible to insure is the loss which might be incurred if the exhibit fails to arrive on time. Basic cover on an All Risks basis can be obtained, plus an additional premium for third party risks.

2. Erection Risks

The intention is to insure against loss or damage to plant or equipment after completion of the voyage, and while it is being erected, installed or assembled. The value on which any premium will be assessed will be the valuation of the plant when it is finally installed, and the period will be from when the equipment is dispatched until it is finally ready for use. Naturally the premium will depend to some extent on what local labour is being used, and if repairs can be made to the equipment if it is damaged en route, or when being erected. But remember that wear and tear will not be covered, nor will defective workmanship, or any contractor's liability, unless additional premiums are paid.

3. Consequential Loss

The intention of this clause is to protect an exporter against any consequential loss arising from damage to goods in transit, which results in a loss at the other end. For example, a machine cannot be used because it is damaged, thereby causing loss in the factory. This loss may also be incurred by your customer, and he can be insured against consequential loss. Two points have to be established. One is the period of the indemnity, and the second the measure of the indemnity. In addition, the way any claim would be met must be established—for example, on the basis of so many weeks' loss of profit, based on the annual profit received.

4. Seller's Interest and Contingency Insurance

This form of insurance is purely for the exporter's benefit, and may not be passed on to the customer, as is normal with other forms of cargo insurance. The risks usually arise under F.O.B., or any other forms of contract, when the contract does not call for immediate payment for the goods on shipment, but at some later date. Title to the goods normally passes to a buyer when he pays for them, but in the export trade the documents of title are frequently handed over before payment is made, such as when payment is agreed some months after the arrival of the goods. Hence the risks are that the customer will not in the long run pay for the goods. He may not accept the documents of title because they do not comply with the contract terms. He may even reject the goods because they are not in accordance with the contract. Of course you could, as an exporter, regain possession of the goods, but you would have no insurance protection for any loss or damage to them. Moreover, in the case of an F.O.B. contract the responsibility for insurance rests with the customer once the goods have passed over the ship's rail.

But you may guard against these risks by taking out a Seller's Interest insurance, which is for the benefit of the seller, and covers, not only all the usual risks, but also insures the goods, if the buyer refuses to take them, against loss or damage.

Insurance Claims

If you have shipped goods by sea, your first task is to replace the goods if they have been lost or damaged by reason of some form of General Average being declared. If they were insured against General Average, your contribution will be recovered from the underwriters or insurance company, and the amount will be decided by the Average Adjusters. If you did not insure the goods, then your contribution will need to be guaranteed by payment of a deposit to the underwriters, or a guarantee for the amount you might be later called upon to pay.

Salvage, which is an award to a third party who gives service to those in peril from maritime causes, may be claimed and awarded, and will be considered at the same time as the General Average is being handled by the Average Adjusters. This will be covered by the General Average insurance. Note that both General Average and salvage give those concerned a lien on the goods.

If you or your customer have to make a claim for any loss or damage to an export cargo, this will be done in the insurer's country, unless in the Policy it has been specified that claims are payable abroad. Since it is often easier for your customer to make the claim and have it settled locally, it is normal practice for Policies and Certificates of Insurance to be endorsed 'Claims payable abroad', particularly if the insurance is being taken out by you on behalf of your customer.

Settlement will be for the insured value of the cargo, and may be for Total or Partial Loss. In the first case the amount payable will be the total insured value, but in the event of a partial loss the claim will be in proportion to the damage incurred. There is also Total Constructive Loss, which means that the cargo is so damaged that to repair it would cost more than its original value—that is to say, it could not be preserved from total loss without an expenditure which would result in the goods having a higher value after it had been incurred.

When you make an insurance claim the following documents must be produced:

1. The Policy or Certificate of Insurance.
2. The invoice issued by the exporter to the customer.
3. An original Bill of Lading, Air Waybill or Consignment Note.
4. A Survey Report, indicating the loss or damage incurred.

5. A copy of any claim made against a carrier of the cargo, if this has been made.

The first thing to be done in the event of a claim is to obtain a **Survey Report**, which may be done by asking any of the Lloyds agents—of whom there are many, located in almost every major city of the world—or the insurance company's local agent, to examine the goods if they have been damaged, or certify if some have been lost.

If the carrier responsible can be identified, a **claim** should at once be made, and efforts made to obtain compensation. There are, as you will see in Chapter 9, limitations on the liability of carriers, agreed by international convention. Any such claims which succeed will result in the insurer obtaining some of the money back which he has paid out to the assured.

Claims must be made promptly, and hence you should always impress on your customers that they must inspect the goods when they arrive to make sure there has been no loss or damage. In some contracts of carriage there is a clause stating that claims must be made within a stated period, while you will remember that it is implicitly implied that all claims will be made with reasonable dispatch. As an exporter you must always give your customer as much help as possible in making an insurance claim.

Most claims go through quickly and easily, provided that the correct procedure is followed and that there is no delay in making the claim.

You will appreciate that cargo insurance is a highly complicated and technical subject, and you are recommended to read further about it if you wish to learn the subject thoroughly.

Revision

Cover the page with a sheet of paper and uncover one question at a time.

Answers	*Questions*
	1. Who is responsible for the insurance of an export cargo?
1. The owner of the cargo.	2. What is Insurable Interest?
2. Any person likely to suffer a loss has an Insurable Interest.	3. What does 'Average' mean when applied to marine insurance?
3. Loss.	4. What is F.C. & S. and what does it mean?
4. The Institute War Risk Clause, meaning Free of Capture and Seizure.	5. What is a Floating Policy?
5. An Open Cover issued for a certain amount.	6. What are 'lines' on a 'slip'?

Answers	*Questions*
	7. What is an 'Express Warranty'?
6. The extent of the risk taken up by each underwriter.	
7. An additional duty, a breach of which makes it harder to recover a loss.	8. What is Consequential Loss?
8. An additional loss suffered by the assured.	9. What is Total Constructive Loss?
9. Damage to goods which would cost more to repair than the original value of the goods.	10. By what amount is it usual to insure an export cargo?
10. From 10 to 15 per cent above C.I.F. value.	

Exercises

1. Calculate the insurance at 10 per cent above C.I.F. value on a C.I.F. contract, where the premium is $1.15 per cent, the cost of the goods $320.00, and the total freight $45.00.
2. On what main factors do underwriters usually base their premiums?
3. Explain the procedure for insuring an export cargo.
4. What documents will be needed to make an insurance claim?
5. What are the main principles on which cargo insurance is based?
6. What is General Average, and what happens when one is declared?

7

THE FINANCE OF EXPORTS

There is little point in exporting goods or services unless you are paid for them. While you inevitably run some risks of non-payment in your domestic market, when you export you face certain additional risks.

1. You will often be dealing with people you may never meet or get to know, let alone trust.
2. While you need to be paid in your own currency, your customer will pay in his, which has then to be converted to yours, but some action may have been taken to prevent this being done as a result of which you do not get paid at all.
3. If you have quoted your customer in his currency, the rate of exchange between your currency and his may have changed adversely before you are paid, resulting in a lower amount being received than you had originally intended.
4. If your customer fails to pay you after you have sent him the goods, you either have to have them returned to you or sold to someone else in that country.
5. Giving credit costs money and can increase your risk of not being paid.

All this may explain why some companies are hesitant about exporting. But if you handle the financial side correctly, there is no reason why your exports should not show a profit, and bad debts be virtually non-existent. In order to handle the financial side of export effectively, there are five main areas with which you should be familiar:

1. *Invoices*. In addition to being the bill for the goods, the invoice has certain additional functions in export.
2. *Methods of payment*. There are several ways by which your customers overseas may pay you for the goods or services.
3. *Foreign Exchange*. However your customer pays you, to some extent you will be concerned with foreign exchange.
4. *ECGD*. The Export Credit Guarantee Department of the Department of Trade is the government body in Britain which insures exporters against risks of non-payment that are commercially difficult to insure. It also provides exporters with a means of obtaining finance, because ECGD backing makes the transaction more secure to the lenders.
5. *The financing of export business*. When you export you are using the company's money, for which you are accountable, and on which you are expected to show a profit.

These are the main headings in this chapter, but in addition there are two things which affect the finance of exports, apart from fixing terms of delivery (which was dealt with in Chapter 3) and the final export price, which cannot be done until all the factors in the export transaction have been considered.

Credit Control

Having agreed to supply an importer, you must as far as possible make sure he is reliable and able, as well as willing, to pay for the goods. This will mean your obtaining a status report on him, either from your bank or from any of the professional organisations which handle this type of enquiry. ECGD will also do this for you, while other suppliers to the importer will also generally tell you something about his record of payment.

You must have, in addition, a system in the company which shows the status of an exporter's account, and the first step after an export order is received is for it to be checked for credit. No order should be passed for execution until this has been done. This is normally handled by the accounts department of the company, but it is part of an export manager's responsibility to ensure this is always done.

The Services of the Banks

In all export transactions the services of a **bank** will be required, and a close relationship must be established with your bank for this purpose. You should note that the major banks have not only been responsible in many instances for opening up export markets, but they also provide the means whereby export trade can take place.

The banks provide many services to exporters, and to take one example, the Midland Bank has a special Panel for Overseas Trade Development, as well as an Overseas Trade Promotion Department and specialist branches dealing with foreign trade. It acts as a merchant banker in export trade, and has a factoring service. Barclays, National Westminster and Lloyds banks offer similar services. Moreover, these banks have branches or associates in most other countries.

This is one area where export differs to some extent from domestic business because export staff will probably have far more dealings with their bank than their opposite numbers on the home side.

In addition, the **merchant banks**, as you will see, arrange credit for major projects overseas, so little international trade could take place without the services of the banks, not only from the point of view of the customer, but also from the exporter's side.

Invoices

In addition to being a 'bill' for the goods, and used whenever a sale is made, an **invoice** is a detailed list of goods supplied, against which an importer may check what he has received from you. It is evidence of a contract, although not actually part of a contract. It forms an essential part of the shipping documents, and will be required in the event of an insurance claim. Additionally, an invoice is often used as a **Certificate of Origin**, and hence as a means of assessing duty by the customer's Customs authorities.

There are four main kinds of invoices used in export:

1. Pro Forma Invoices

These are used for making quotations, and are similar in all respects to ordinary commercial invoices, showing the prospective importer the cost of the goods and how much it will cost him to get them to his country. Importers use pro forma invoices when they have to apply for import licences or permission to spend foreign currency, so that you must ensure that the details on them agree in every respect with the final invoices sent with the shipment, or you will cause your customer needless problems when the goods arrive. These invoices are made out as a rule on the exporter's own invoice forms, and clearly marked 'Pro Forma'.

2. Commercial Invoices

In addition to a detailed description of the goods supplied, commercial invoices in the export trade show how these goods were dispatched, the weights and measurements of the shipment, and both the F.O.B. and C.I.F. charges, however the quotation was originally made. In addition, the B.T.N. number is often included, while any import licence obtained by the customer should also be shown. Details of packing charges will be required, and of course the marks of the consignment.

3. Certified Invoices

These are similar to commercial invoices, but require certification by the company or an outside body, and in most cases these then act also as Certificates of Origin. For this reason, in addition to the selling price of the goods, the Current Domestic Value, or C.D.V., will have to be indicated, in order that the local Customs authorities may be satisfied that no dumping is taking place and that the goods are not being declared at less than their normal value for customs purposes.

There are several kinds of special invoice forms which have to be used by British exporters for various parts of the world. Details of these will be found in Croner's. For example, British goods being exported to Canada have to be declared on Form 725, but on 724E if they are going to Australia, or 728A for New Zealand (see Fig. 19, Appendix 1). These forms are to allow for Commonwealth Preference rates of duty.

The special forms may be certified by the exporter in certain cases. When shipments are made to associated and other parts of the EEC, for example, the exporter declares that the goods are of Community origin, using the words 'European Communities, United Kingdom'.

Some countries require certification of invoices by a Chamber of Commerce or a special Chamber of Commerce invoice (see Fig. 20, Appendix 1). A list of authorised Chambers is published twice a year in the Department of Trade's publication *Trade and Industry*.

4. Consular Invoices

In some cases—notably certain Central and South American countries—there are special consular invoices, which have to be prepared on forms issued by the consulates concerned and which then have to be certified by them. In most cases these also act as Certificates of Origin, although in some a separate Certificate of Origin has to be prepared. Details will be found in Croner's.

You should always get your customer to tell you what type of invoices he will require, and in particular how many copies, because he is the one who has to deal with the local authorities and it is your task to make sure he is equipped in every way to do so. Invoices are key export documents, and must be completely accurate in every respect.

Methods of Payment

The method of payment you adopt for each customer must depend on many factors, such as how well you know him, how much business you are doing with him, the amounts in question, the competitiveness of the market and the Customs of the trade in which you are engaged.

Should you decide to grant credit, you must also decide for how long and on what terms. How a customer is asked to pay is a marketing tool, so that your terms of payment must be determined as carefully as your terms of delivery. Payment terms may have to be settled in accordance with local regulations in some cases.

There are three vital legal conditions affecting payment for exports for British exporters. The first is that **you must be paid in full within six months** for the goods, unless you have special permission to be paid a lesser amount, such as when selling to a subsidiary company overseas. The second is that **you must be paid from an external account** held by your customer. The third is that **the currency he uses must be convertible into sterling**, which naturally follows from his having the use of an external account. And as you have already seen, you are not allowed to hold foreign currency, unless you have special permission to do so, but must surrender it to a bank or authorised dealer. To break these conditions you must obtain permission from the Bank of England, on form SPE (see Fig. 21, Appendix 1), and complete in most cases a CDE. An ECGD policy is required for payments over six months.

Bearing in mind the above, you should consider the seven different methods of payment as follows.

1. Cash in Advance

This can be arranged quite simply by your customer transferring the funds to you, either by a draft or a bank transfer, provided the conditions as set out above are fulfilled. It is usual for the money to be paid before a contract is made.

You would use this method if you did not know your customer at all, and felt it safer to obtain the money before sending the goods. You would also consider it if you had reason to doubt your customer's ability or willingness to pay you. It is highly satisfactory from your point of view, but the least attractive method from your customer's side, because he is paying without any guarantee that he will receive the goods. If you use this method you will have to send the customer all the shipping documents to enable him to take delivery of the shipment when it arrives.

A variation of this method is to take a deposit in advance, and then use one of the other methods to collect the balance. But make sure the deposit is large enough to ensure that the customer will finally pay for the goods, because it is an old dodge to send a small deposit, and when the goods arrive, fail to pay the balance.

2. Documentary Letters of Credit

A Letter of Credit is simply a means of opening a credit in favour of someone, under which payment will be made provided that certain conditions are fulfilled. The 'Documentary' part indicates that delivery of the goods will be effected by means of documents of title.

The procedure is that a customer opens a Credit in your favour for the total sum in question, covering the cost of the goods, freight, insurance and so on. He does this through his bank, which in turn instructs its correspondent bank in your country to pass on the Credit to you, so that there are four parties to a Letter of Credit, which is a form of contract between all of them. On the Credit the customer will impose certain conditions, and payment will not be made until the exporter has fulfilled them all. This in practice means that the amount is not exceeded; that shipment is made by a certain date; that all the documents required are provided by the exporter; that the goods are as specified; and any other conditions the importer may wish to impose. These may include such stipulations that partial shipments are not allowed; that transhipment is prohibited; that certain shipping lines or methods may not be used; and indeed any other conditions the importer wishes. But the point is that provided you fulfil them all, you are certain to receive the money; and your customer is certain to get the goods he has ordered. But of course it means he is paying for them before he gets them, because normally payment is made on shipment. (Figs. 22 and 23 in Appendix 1 give some of the documents involved.)

The use of Documentary Letters of Credit has been codified by the International Chamber of Commerce in its 'Uniform Customs and Practice for Documentary Credits' of 1962, revised in 1974 and brought into effect in 1975. You will find a clause to this effect printed on a Letter of Credit, showing that the bank agrees this interpretation (as you will remember is done with Terms of Delivery under ICC codification).

There are three main types of Documentary Credits:

(*a*) *Revocable Credits.* These may be revoked at any time by the opener, so that you have no real protection against your customer changing his mind and refusing to pay by this method for the goods he has ordered.

(*b*) *Irrevocable Credits.* These may not be revoked, except with the consent of all parties. Hence you are better protected, but of course the free exchange of currency between your customer's country and yours may be stopped; in this case your customer's bank, though willing to pay, may be unable to do so.

(*c*) *Confirmed Credits.* Unless specifically stated, a Credit is unconfirmed. This means that the customer's bank has opened it through a bank in your country, but your bank will not confirm it because the funds have still to be passed from the customer's bank to yours, and this might not be possible. A Confirmed Credit, on the other hand, is one confirmed by your bank because the Credit has already been transferred to them. Thus whatever happens between your country and that of your customer, your bank will pay, provided of course you fulfil all the conditions of the Credit. Hence it is normal practice for exporters to insist on having Confirmed and Irrevocable Credits.

The procedure for payment is normally that you draw a **Bill of Exchange** on the bank confirming the Credit in your country, payable at sight, and quoting the Credit under which you are to be paid. With this Bill you will also need to present all the documents specified in the Credit, and show that you have carried out all the conditions laid down by your customer. Hence the importance of your checking at the outset that you can comply with the conditions, and having them changed if absolutely necessary. It costs money to open a Credit, and more money to have it extended or altered. But better to do this at the time you receive it than at the last moment. Better still, agree all the conditions with your customer before he opens the Credit.

You may come across four other types of Credit:

(*a*) *Term Credits.* These enable an importer to open a Credit in your favour but stipulate payment, not at the time of shipment, but at a later date; in other words he is getting some credit from you. In this case the bank in your country will issue you with what is called a 'fine' bill, which you may discount if you need the money at once, or keep if you have allowed for the cost of the Credit in your price.

(*b*) *Transferable Credits.* These are used when the exporter is not the supplier, part of the Credit being used to pay the supplier and the remainder the actual exporter. You, as an exporter, present your invoice along with the documents, and you will be paid your share, the supplier already having been paid from the Credit.

(*c*) *Back-to-Back Credits.* These are Credits established by an exporter on the strength of those received from customers, to enable him to pay his suppliers.

(*d*) *Revolving Credits.* These are Credits which are automatically renewed as soon as they have been used. They are useful for regular shipments, but today they are not extensively used, because Credits can be so easily renewed by cable or telex.

3. Bills of Exchange

A customer overseas may not wish to pay you in advance because he has no guarantee you will send him the goods for which he has paid; he may not wish to lock up his money in a Documentary Letter of Credit, or pay when the goods are shipped, because it will be some time before he receives them. While you may be anxious to ensure that he does pay, you may feel that it would be more reasonable if he paid when the goods had actually arrived, or even at some specified time after they arrived. In this case you may request him to pay by drawing a **Bill of Exchange** on him, which will grant you some protection against his not paying, provided it is linked with a document of title to the goods such as a Bill of Lading. Moreover, a Bill of Exchange is a legal document, which allows you to take legal action in the event of your customer promising to pay but then defaulting.

As you will see in Chapter 9, a Bill of Exchange is quite simply an order in writing, requesting someone to pay a specified sum of money at some certain date (see Fig. 24, Appendix 1). Hence you obtain payment by drawing a Bill of Exchange on your customer overseas. This is a legal contract, three parties being involved:

(*a*) The person drawing the Bill, or the **drawer**; you as the exporter would probably be the drawer.

(*b*) The person on whom the Bill is drawn, the **drawee**; you as the exporter would normally draw a Bill on your customer, who becomes the drawee.

(*c*) The person to whom payment is made, the **payee**; this will usually be you, as the supplier of the goods.

A Bill of Exchange is made out in a standard way, and you should observe the following when preparing one:

(*a*) By the heading marked Exchange you put the **sum** in figures.
(*b*) You put the **place** where it is drawn in addition to the **date**.
(*c*) You then indicate the **tenor** of the Bill. This means when it is to be paid. Here you may put 'at Sight', meaning the Bill becomes payable as soon as it is presented to the payee; or you may put at a certain number of days 'after Sight'. This is usually expressed in multiples of 30 days, e.g. 30, 60, 180 and so on.
(*d*) Because Bills are issued in sets, like Bills of Lading, you must state whether it is the **first, second or third**, and then add 'the others being unpaid'; this ensures that the first original to be presented is paid, but the rest are then void.
(*e*) **'To the Order of'** means the payee, and in this case you put 'Ourselves', because the customer is to pay you the amount indicated.
(*f*) The **amount** is then repeated in writing.
(*g*) Below this it is customary to indicate **how the Bill is to be paid**. If, for example, it is to be paid in sterling, then you would add 'Payable at the current rates of exchange for sight drafts on London', meaning that the drawee puts up enough money in his country to cover the total in sterling on the day of payment. If certain charges or interest have to be paid by the drawee, these will be indicated at this point, as would any agreement to pay by telegraphic transfer.
(*h*) **Value** means for what payment is being made; this is often marked 'Received', meaning goods have been sent, or simply 'Goods'.
(*i*) You then indicate the name and address of the person on whom you are drawing the Bill—that is, the **customer or drawee.**
(*j*) You add your **own name and address,** indicating to whom payment is to be made, and **sign** it.

Having drawn a Bill of Exchange on your customer, you send it to the bank on a **Bills for Collection** form (Fig. 25, Appendix 1), asking them to present it to your customer, but after signing it yourself on the back or endorsing it in blank. At the same time you instruct the bank how to proceed should the customer refuse to pay or accept the Bill.

At this point the implications of this method of payment begin to become clear:

(*a*) If you ask your customer to pay at Sight, then you may instruct the bank to hand over the relative documents to enable the customer to obtain delivery of the goods, or to withhold them if the customer does not pay. This is known as D/P, or **Documents against Payment**; more loosely it is also called **Cash against Documents.**
(*b*) If you specify payment at so many days' time, the documents of delivery will be handed over, but the customer will write 'Accepted' on the **Bill,** showing that he agrees to pay on the due date. You have thus allowed him credit, but you have his legal promise to pay for the goods. This is known as D/A, or **Documents against Acceptance**. This will only apply for shipments by sea, using the Bill of Lading as a document of title, since Air Waybills, consignment notes and so on are not documents of title. Hence you cannot

prevent a customer obtaining the goods, but you do have a legal document covering payment, on which to take action should the customer default. And if this should happen, the bank must be instructed on the Bills for Collection form what they should do with the goods, e.g. return them to you, sell them in the open market, etc.

Note that strictly speaking a Bill is a Draft until it is accepted, and that once it has been accepted, it may be negotiated and discounted in the money market. Thus you have, with Bills payable at so many days, a means of obtaining immediate payment from the bank or money market. You may allow for the cost of this in the amount charged to the customer.

When a customer defaults on a Bill of Exchange, the bank 'Protests' the Bill, which means they advise people that he is in default and his credit will then be restricted. Hence the use of Bills of Exchange is a method of payment with much to commend it in export trade.

4. Open Account

If you know your customers overseas well, and have no reason to doubt that they will pay for the goods, you may deal with them as you would with customers in the domestic market, and allow them to pay on **open account**. This means that delivery is not tied to payment, but that your normal terms of payment, as laid down in your Conditions of Sale, will apply; for example, payment is to be made 30 days from receipt of the invoice. You may also use a Bill of Exchange for this purpose, as the French do, thus specifying exactly when payment is expected and preventing customers from taking unauthorised credit.

5. Consignment Stock Payments

As will be explained more fully in Chapter 13, you may supply a customer or distributor overseas with stocks of your product for payment after he has re-sold them. The goods remain your property, and you must agree with him exactly when, and at what price, he is to pay for them.

6. Royalties

These will be dealt with more fully in Chapters 12 and 13, but when goods are manufactured and sold overseas by a company licensed by you for this purpose, you will receive payment in the form of royalties, based on the sales made and the cost of supplying the know-how.

7. Barter

When an importer is unable to obtain sufficient foreign exchange to pay for the goods, he may offer to pay in kind. In this case it is usual for a 'factor' to arrange the deal and sell the goods for you. He will then arrange to pay you in money for the goods you have supplied.

Most companies use more than one method of payment, according to the customers with whom they deal and the financial policy they adopt as regards payment for their exports. Even in the same transaction more than one method may be used. For example, on a long-term contract, some money may be paid by the customer in advance; further sums may be paid by means of Documentary Letters of Credit; with Bills of Exchange drawn for the remaining amounts. Variations on the use of several methods of payment are quite common in long-term contracts. It should now be clear that deciding how a customer shall pay for your exports is a marketing decision, since you may use the various methods for obtaining the business and outbidding the competition. This applies particularly to the granting of credit, which will be considered later in this chapter.

Foreign Exchange

However you quote your customer, in his currency or in your own, and however he pays you, you will to some degree be involved with other currencies and foreign exchange.

Under normal circumstances you are not allowed at present to hold any foreign currencies in Britain, but must convert them at once into sterling through an authorised foreign exchange dealer or bank. You may buy a specified amount of foreign currency to go on holiday or on a business trip. You may, however, be granted special permission by the Bank of England to hold foreign currency if, for example, you have subsidiary companies overseas, but you must apply for this facility on form SPE.

The Bank of England at present divides currencies into two kinds. First there is sterling, used in what are called the **Scheduled Territories**. These consist of the United Kingdom and Channel Islands, the Republic of Ireland, and Gibraltar, and within these countries sterling circulates freely. The rest of the world is now classified as the **External Account** area, and payment for British exports may only be made from an external account in any part of that area, this then being converted into sterling.

There are some two hundred foreign currencies in the world today, the rates of most being published in the financial press. You must get to know those with which you are normally dealing, and while many will be familiar to you, how many of you would know that the *kyar* is used in Burma and the *balboa* in Panama? You must know the names, and what they are worth in terms of your own currency. You must also know which, if any, are not convertible into your own currency, as for example the Rhodesian dollar which is not convertible at present into sterling.

If you quote your customer in sterling or your own currency, he will need to sell his currency and buy sufficient of yours to meet the amount he owes you. In this case the exchange rate will not affect the amount you receive, but it will affect the cost to the customer of your goods. At present, as sterling is being devalued in terms of other currencies, British goods are tending to be cheaper to overseas customers than previously, but it is also arguable that their prices might be increased according to what the market will bear, another reason why a knowledge of foreign currencies is so important in export. In addition, should you do anything in an overseas market which involves spending money, such as visiting it or carrying out promotion, you will need to know what this would cost in terms of sterling.

Selling Forward

If you quote your customer in his own currency because he requested this—and many customers do insist today on being quoted in their own currency—

you have the problem of deciding what **rate of exchange** to use for the quotation. This is because, with continually changing rates of exchange, by the time you are paid for the goods you may receive less in sterling than you had originally expected. Of course, you may obtain more, as has been happening with sterling being devalued, but you may reply that you are in the export business and not on the foreign exchange market.

Whenever you quote in your customer's currency, you can protect yourself against loss by selling the foreign currency **'forward'**. To do this you ask your bank, at the time you are making the quotation, for the rate they will charge to buy the foreign exchange from you at the time the customer will be paying. This is the rate you then use for your quotation, and as soon as you receive the order you make a contract with the bank to buy that amount of foreign currency at a stated time in the future, at the rate they have quoted. Thus you are assured that you will receive the correct amount of sterling, whatever has happened to the rate of exchange in the meantime.

You may make such a contract with your bank provided:

(*a*) You have a firm contractual order, because you are not allowed as a company, or an individual, to gamble or deal on the foreign exchange market.

(*b*) That the amount in which you deal does not exceed the amount of the contract.

(*c*) That you are selling the currency in which you will be paid.

(*d*) That the date on which you conclude the contract with the bank is not later than six months after shipment of the goods (but you may specify two dates between which you will be paid from overseas).

(*e*) That there is a forward market in the currency you wish to sell. While this is the case with most of the major currencies, you would have some difficulty in selling some of the Latin American currencies forward.

If you look at foreign exchange listings you will find two rates are quoted:

(*a*) *Spot Rates.* These are the rates ruling for immediate dealings.

(*b*) *Forward Rates.* These are the rates you will be quoted for purchase or delivery at some time in the future. If the rate for delivery is higher than the spot rate it is what is called 'at a premium'; if lower then it is 'at a discount'.

Thus you may quote in another currency with the knowledge that whatever happens between the quotation and payment, you will receive the amount you require in your own currency.

ECGD

You will have noted that one of the problems with export is the possibility that you will not be paid for the goods you send your customers overseas, either because they are unwilling to pay or are prevented from paying by circumstances outside their control. If you sell on the basis of Cash in Advance, you will not have this problem. Moreover, if you are paid by means of a Documentary Confirmed Irrevocable Letter of Credit you will also avoid this problem. But if you are paid on Open Account or by means of a Bill of Exchange, it is possible that your customer may not be able to pay you for some reason outside his control.

Since customers overseas increasingly are not prepared to pay in advance, or when the goods are shipped, by means of a Documentary Letter of Credit, but wish to pay either when the goods have arrived or at some time after that date, you have to be prepared for such payment terms, but you will naturally wish to minimise any risk of not being paid. The facilities of the **Export Credit Guarantee Department** (ECGD) can be used for this purpose, which means in effect you are insuring against the risks of non-payment, these risks being uninsurable on the open market.

ECGD is a government organisation, which takes over the risks of non-payment for exporters, these being primarily:

(*a*) The buyer cannot pay because he has become insolvent.
(*b*) The buyer fails to take up the goods.
(*c*) The buyer is willing to pay but unable to transfer the currency to you because of some action by his, or even your government, which prevents him doing this. Such action may have been caused by war, internal disturbances, or international action.
(*d*) There may be additional charges because the shipments were diverted by factors beyond the control of the carriers.
(*e*) Any political action which prevents the contract being performed, such as the cancellation of an export licence, permission to import and so on.

ECGD issues several kinds of cover to exporters, and you should in your own interests discuss your problems with them to see what help and protection they can give you. This will basically be in the following ways.

1. A Comprehensive Short-Term Policy

This policy covers exports sold on credit terms of up to six months, and is for the exporter doing business on a regular basis. Normally ECGD wish to insure all of an exporter's business, and will not allow cover only for bad risks, for obvious reasons: in practice they require a reasonable proportion of good and bad risks. Most policies are taken out on a yearly basis, a premium being paid at the beginning of each year, depending on the size of the exports involved, the premium being a minimum of £50 and non-refundable. But in addition you also pay a premium every month on the value of the exports you have actually dispatched. At present this type of cover costs about 27p per £100, and is a cost you should include when fixing your export prices.

Up to £250 an initial single contract with a new buyer may be shipped without any prior permission from ECGD. Orders between £250 and £5,000 may be supplied provided you have a recent report from a bank or credit information agency without reference to the ECGD. However, above £5,000 you have to apply in each case, using a special 'Credit Limit Application' form (see Fig. 26, Appendix 1), although this amount may be increased to £20,000 subject to previously good trading with the customer, without any special application. The risks you cover, the amount you will be paid, and when you will be paid are as follows:

(*a*) Insolvency of the buyer: you receive 90 per cent of the loss as soon as proof of insolvency has been established.
(*b*) Failure of the buyer to pay: you receive 90 per cent of the loss, payable six months after the due date of payment.

(*c*) Failure of the buyer to take up the goods: you get 90 per cent after the first 20 per cent of the loss, a month after they have been re-sold.

(*d*) Any failure to pay as a result of some political action: here you receive 95 per cent of the loss, four months after the events which caused the failure to pay, and this is of course one of your main reasons for using ECGD facilities.

Notice that these guarantees cover the goods from the date of dispatch, but you can extend the cover to include it from the date of the contract—which is known as the pre-credit risk—against which you will receive 90 per cent of the loss, for an additional premium.

2. Specific Medium-Term Policies

These have been introduced to cover contracts for capital goods or projects up to terms of five years and you need to negotiate them with ECGD in each case. The amount of the cover will depend on the nature of the contract. However, ECGD has now introduced new regulations whereby the exporter's report on the customer is accepted up to £15,000 and even above.

3. Special Policies

These are mainly for large capital projects and for various other forms of cover on activities in export. They include, for example, consultancy services for major contracts, as well as the contracts themselves; payment received for the sale of licences to manufacture and sell; selling foreign goods or selling from stocks held overseas; and a costs escalation policy designed to protect exporters against the worst effects of increasing costs due to inflation (although at the time of writing the latter is not a really effective means of insuring against the results of inflationary costs, and it only applies to contracts worth over £2 million and of more than two years' duration).

If the cover you require does not fall into any of these categories you should discuss the problem with the Department, because any reasonable proposition will be carefully considered.

Considerations for using ECGD Facilities

Whether or not you should make use of government facilities for covering insurance for the payment of exports depends on a number of factors:

(*a*) If you are assured of being paid because you have received the money in advance, or have a confirmed irrevocable Letter of Credit, you may well decide no other insurance against not being paid is necessary.

(*b*) If you use any of the other methods of payment, you have to decide whether there is a serious risk of your customer not paying you, either because of some inability of his part to do so, or because he is prevented from so doing because of political action outside his control. This will depend to some degree on the countries involved, and clearly those exporters who had no ECGD cover would have been caught on outstanding amounts due to them in the case of Cyprus and Rhodesia, to mention two fairly recent examples of government and political action affecting payment for exports from the United Kingdom. You might at this point reflect how you would rate the possibilities of problems arising in the case of countries like Portugal, the Lebanon or Spain.

(*c*) You may feel that, as in the case of selling in a foreign currency without wishing to gamble on the foreign exchange market, you should not gamble on the future political climates of overseas markets, yet make sure that whatever happens you will not suffer any loss because payment for your goods is not forthcoming.

(*d*) On the other hand, you may prefer to keep your price to its lowest by omitting this form of protection, because you will probably include the cost of ECGD cover when working out your total export costs.

(*e*) You may decide it would be cheaper to self-insure against losses of this kind by establishing a sinking fund of your own, out of which any such losses may be paid.

Before coming to any final decision you should also consider if there is any other way of protecting yourself against any losses due to non-payment, and you may also wish to consider the problem of the finance of your export trade with or without ECGD backing.

The Financing of Export Business

You may also protect yourself against non-payment from overseas by using the services of a **credit factoring company**. These companies in effect take over the collection of the amount due to you from customers overseas, so that whatever happens to prevent your customer paying is the factors' worry, because you will be paid by them. You will also be relieved of the problem of establishing the credit-worthiness of customers overseas, and you will be protected against any fluctuations in the rates of foreign exchange. Thus the use of a credit factoring company, such as Credit Factoring In ernational, which is a member of the National Westminster banking group, may relieve you of most of the problems of being paid for your exports. For this, and other services, you will pay a charge of something like 2 or 3 per cent of the total amount of your exports, a figure which you will take into account when preparing your export costs.

The problem of deciding whether to finance your export business yourself or whether to finance it from outside still remains, however, to be settled, but if you do wish to use outside sources you have three main options.

1. ECGD-backed Credit

If you take out ECGD cover for your exports you may obtain, with their help, three kinds of supplier credit:

(*a*) If you have a policy for more than twelve months, and the credit is for less than two years, you can obtain a Bill or Note, which will enable you to borrow 100 per cent of the amount outstanding on an export order at the banks' base rate plus ½ per cent. For this you pay ECGD a premium of ⅛ per cent. Payment will be made, after the goods have been shipped, by the customer by means of a Bill of Exchange.

(*b*) If you sell on Open Account, on proof of shipment you can obtain a loan from the bank on the same terms as above; and if you grant your customer credit of up to 180 days, you will be able to borrow 90 per cent of the value of the shipment.

(*c*) If you deal with medium-term contracts, i.e. up to two years, you can borrow from the bank on even more favourable terms, because with the backing of an ECGD policy the bank is empowered by the government to lend up to 90 per cent of the order's value at 7 per cent for periods up to two years, and for longer-term contracts at 7½ per cent. This you will appreciate is a major concession, and a means of raising money at a lower rate than is possible for domestic business. This then is another factor of which you must take account when deciding whether or not to use ECGD facilities.

2. Bills of Exchange

If you use this method of payment, and you are granting your customer credit, when you receive the accepted Bill you may discount it in the money market, which means you sell it at something less than its face value. Since you will, as you will see later, allow for the cost of granting credit in your export costings, this discounting of Bills of Exchange is a useful way of financing your exports.

3. Factoring Companies

If you use the services of a factoring company you may be paid before payment is received from the customers overseas, for which service the factoring company will charge something like 3½ per cent over the banks' base rate, which makes it in line with normal overdraft facilities. In practice, most exporters make use of this facility on a seasonable basis, and many combine it with other ways of raising money. You should note here that the task of collecting money from customers overseas is also taken off your hands by the factoring company, which will reduce your accounting overheads.

Closely connected with the provision of finance for exports and the supplier credits available as above, are two kinds of buyer credits. These are often arranged in conjunction with ECGD and similar bodies elsewhere in the world. In Britain buyer credits are usually operated along the following lines:

(*a*) On medium and some longer-term contracts a consortium of banks with the backing of ECGD allow a line of credit to an importer overseas. They usually stipulate that the importer will pay the first 20 per cent of the contract, but that 80 per cent of the remainder is available to him as a credit with which to pay his suppliers.

(*b*) On major contracts a consortium of banks backed by ECGD will arrange a credit of around 90 per cent of the value of the contract, but stipulate that they will be responsible for paying the suppliers. In this case they prepare what is called a 'shopping list', and if you happen to be one of the companies on that list you will be paid, not by the importer, but by the banking consortium.

There is one important difference between supplier and buyer credits. With supplier credits you, as the exporter, will be responsible for ensuring that the lender is repaid, which is to say that the bank or finance house has recourse to you in the long run. But with buyer credits you, as the exporter, run no risks, because you will be paid either by the importer or the banks supplying the credit, and they have no recourse to you for ultimate repayment of the loan.

If you decide to finance your own exports, you will need to consider two major problems: the cost of credit and the cost of company money.

The Cost of Credit

To provide credit for an export customer will cost you money, and this you must allow for when you prepare your export costings. You may provide credit in two main ways:

(*a*) You can build the cost of the credit into your export prices, and offer a discount off those prices if the credit is not required by the customer who prefers to pay cash.

To calculate the cost of credit, you first take the base lending rate of the banks and add to it their own lending rates; these might, for example, be 11 per cent and 4 per cent, making the total cost of borrowing money 15 per cent. If you offer a customer 90 days' credit this will be a little under 4 per cent, or 1/25th. Suppose your F.O.B. price is $100 and you wish to offer 90 days' credit, then what price will you charge the customer? Because the 4 per cent is 1/25th, by a well-known mathematical formula you add 1/24th, (of 100 in this case) which is $4.17, which means your price would then be $104.17, for payment at 90 days for $100 of goods. But you could offer your customer a 4 per cent cash discount (4 per cent of $104.17 being $4.17), and you would still receive your $100.

In practice most exporters work out various credit costs in advance, and when negotiating with a customer they use a 'crib' which allows them to see at once what the cost of the credit is on any given amount. In this way they adjust their price, by means of discounts, in line with the customer's requirements, but ensuring in each case that the customer is in fact paying for his credit.

(*b*) You may charge an importer for credit by applying interest rates for the period of the credit. In this case you would, when drawing a Bill of Exchange on the customer for payment at so many days' time, add a clause to the Bill to the effect that 'this draft bears interest at 4 per cent over the base rate, calculated from the date of the acceptance of the Bill until receipt of the proceeds'. You would use the appropriate rate, and you will remember that a draft becomes a bill when it has been accepted.

Credit is, of course, a marketing weapon, and you will use it as a means of persuading your customer to buy from you rather than from your competitors. Preferably you will allow for it in your price, but you may charge for it on a Bill of Exchange. You may also deduct it from export's contribution to a company's profits, but this often leads to its cost being overlooked, unless a really accurate costing system is used.

The Cost of Company Money

You will need to calculate the cost of using the company's money if you finance your own exports, and to take this into consideration when calculating the profit export contributes to the company. Because you are making use of money which might be employed elsewhere, export will need to earn sufficient to pay for the cost of that money. You should also compare the cost of using company money with that of borrowing it from outside sources.

There are several ways of measuring the export performance of a company in this way, perhaps the most common being to take the return earned on the amount of capital employed. You might arrive at something like this:

Total export sales	$980,000
Less total cost of sales	800,000
	180,000
Less Administration and fixed costs	100,000
	80,000
Investment in export department	275,000
Accounts receivable	250,000
Fixed assets	10,000
	535,000

In this case the return on your investment would be

$$\frac{80{,}000 \times 100}{535{,}000} = 15\%$$

Hence you may measure export performance by calculating the total contribution, dividing it by the capital employed, and multiplying the result by 100, which gives the percentage figure. The major problem here is to decide what should, or should not, be included in each part of the formula, which shows how important it is in export to have a complete costing system, a point which must have become apparent when considering how you arrive at any worthwhile export price. You then have to decide whether 15 per cent is a reasonable return, and if it is, then your exports are in good shape.

There are many other kinds of control ratios you can use, such as the ratio of sales to assets; how long collecting money owed to you takes; and the ratio of current assets to current liabilities. But the above is one of the simplest and enables you to fix definite export targets.

If you decide to export for the first time, you may need to consider raising the company's capital by a further issue in order to provide the funds to finance your export business, assuming you decide that financing from outside sources is not for you. This would prevent your possibly having to plough back profits from the domestic side of the business in order to finance your exports, which your shareholders might dislike, since it would undoubtedly mean lower dividends for them, at any rate in the short term.

To Ensure a Viable Export Operation

Much of the controversy surrounding export results from the view that exports are unprofitable, and that the company might be advised to steer clear of export business. No company should embark on any export activities unless it ensures that they will be a viable proposition, and to achieve this you might consider the following:

(*a*) First define the goals of the company's export trade and its position in the company's total business. Unless you do this you will probably always have dissension about the conduct of exporting, and the money needed to do it, with the result that you will probably handle export badly and end up with an unviable operation.

(*b*) Set definite export targets, such as what return on capital is required, and see that all the export personnel keep to these targets.

(*c*) While costs invariably mean different things to different people, include your export costs on the same basis as you calculate your domestic operation's costs, so that both domestic and export costs are comparable.

(*d*) Have a definite pricing policy for exports, which produces the required return on the capital employed and also produces the required contribution to the company's profits. If you do use marginal pricing for specific occasions, be clear what this entails, and do not delude yourself as to the contribution you obtain from it.

(*e*) Have a definite payment policy, and ensure that the total costs of obtaining payment are included in your export costs.

(*f*) Finance your exports either internally or externally, but make sure you finance them in the way most economical to the company.

(*g*) Plot the company's future in export, which will include such considerations as to whether you wish to increase direct exports, or manufacture overseas; whether you should concentrate on selling know-how instead of products; and where the company is to arrive in terms of its overseas operations. These considerations will be dealt with in Chapter 16, but they cannot be decided without a full appreciation of the financing of a company's export operations, whatever these may be.

You will appreciate that export directors and managers will be involved in financial decision-making for virtually every export transaction, so that they should be trained accordingly and encouraged to look on export business mainly in terms of its contribution to company profits. Any other kind of exporting is best left alone.

Revision

Cover the page with a sheet of paper and uncover one question at a time.

Answers	*Questions*
	1. For what is a pro forma invoice often used?
1. To provide a quotation.	2. What does C.D.V. mean?
2. Current Domestic Value.	3. What is a back-to-back credit?
3. A credit established by an exporter on the strength of a customer's credit.	4. What is the tenor of a Bill of Exchange?
4. The period for which it is to run.	5. How can a Bill of Exchange be used to protect a supplier against the risk of non-payment?

Answers	*Questions*
5. By linking it to a Bill of Lading, which is not handed over until the Bill is paid or accepted.	6. When are goods held on consignment usually paid for?
6. After they have been sold.	7. Which are the Scheduled Territories?
7. The United Kingdom and Channel Islands, Eire and Gibraltar.	8. What is the present average cost of ECGD cover?
8. 27p per £100.	9. What is a 'spot' rate for foreign currency?
9. The rate quoted for immediate dealings.	10. What is discounting a Bill of Exchange?
10. Selling it for less than its face value.	

Exercises

1. Discuss the advantages and disadvantages to an importer of being asked to pay for his imports by means of a Documentary Letter of Credit.
2. How would you ensure that you receive the correct amount of sterling from an importer whom you had quoted in his currency?
3. What options, and how can they be exercised, has an exporter who decides to grant credit to his customers overseas?
4. Discuss the kinds of finance which are available to an exporter who has ECGD cover.
5. Under what conditions would you allow a customer overseas to pay on Open Account?
6. Make out a Bill of Exchange, requiring Hassan Bros. of Nairobi to pay you $9852.76 in ninety days' time.
7. What measures would you take to ensure exports were profitable to a company?
8. Discuss the reasoning you would exercise when considering whether or not to use the facilities of ECGD.

8

EXPORT PRACTICE PROCEDURES

The object of all export practice procedures is to help an exporter move the goods from his factory or warehouse to that of the importer at the minimum cost, but with the maximum effectiveness, and to be paid for the goods as promptly as possible. While these procedures may seem complicated, if you understand how the various elements are coordinated you should have no difficulty in welding them into a continuous and efficient operation.

This chapter, therefore, seeks to draw together the various elements of export practice under the following headings:

1. The movement of the goods overseas
2. The documents used for transport
3. The aligned system of documentation
4. Payment for exports
5. A summary of an export transaction

You may then examine the legal aspects of the export process in the next chapter, because you should have begun to be familiar with the areas of export practice likely to be affected by the law. This will conclude Part 2 of this book. Along with procedures, the documents used will also be summarised.

The Movement of Goods Overseas

How this is accomplished will depend on several factors of which the following are important:

(*a*) Where the goods are being sent.
(*b*) The type of goods being dispatched.
(*c*) The wishes of the customer.
(*d*) A comparison of the costs involved between different methods of transport.
(*e*) Some consideration of the marketing policy you adopt, which will be dealt with in Part 3 of this book.

For example, if you have to send a consignment of pharmaceuticals to Oslo from London, you might pack them in a container, have it taken to the airport, and then flown direct to Oslo, where the customer would only have to collect it at the local airport.

If, on the other hand, you have to send a consignment of machinery from Birmingham to Bukoba in Tanzania, this might be a more complicated operation. Assuming you packed the machinery in 20 cases, you would have to have these taken to the docks, whence they would be transported by sea to Dar-es-Salaam. Here they might be loaded on to railway wagons and taken to the inland port of Mwanza on Lake Victoria, and thence shipped by lake steamer to Bukoba. The customer might collect them by truck or even by hand.

The movement of goods being exported will involve you in making four major decisions:

1. You must know by what **date the goods have to be dispatched** in order that they may arrive by their due delivery date. This means you must know a good deal about the time taken by the various methods of transport to most places in the world. For example, you must know how much longer it would take the pharmaceuticals to reach Oslo by sea. Or in the case of the 20 cases of machinery, how would the cost of flying them to as near Bukoba as possible compensate for the quicker delivery, and how much quicker would this actually be? How long does the up-country shipment take, and how often is there a sailing to Dar-es-Salaam?

Exporters often fail to pay sufficient attention to this point, with the result that deliveries are late, often mainly because of factors they did not take into account, such as ports being congested, or shipping space being unable to obtain at short notice. Your customer is only concerned with the goods when they reach him; it is up to you to ensure that they do so when he wants them, and not when you get them there.

2. Bearing in mind the wishes of the customer, you have to decide which **method of transport** is best for each transaction. Would it have been cheaper, and hardly less time-consuming, to have sent the pharmaceuticals to Oslo by sea? Is it sensible to use complicated methods of transhipment when a more direct delivery may be obtained using air freight? After all, the machinery may well have been delayed after it reached Dar-es-Salaam, but that does not help the customer in Bukoba.

So you must decide each case on its merits, which means knowing a great deal, not only about shipping from your own country, but also about transport in your customer's country.

3. You must decide which **method of packing** you will use, according to the method of transport used. Putting the pharmaceuticals in a container to Oslo might call for a different kind of packing than if you had sent them by a conventional cargo vessel. You might need much less protection against damage to the machinery going to Bukoba if it went by air than if it were sent by sea, rail and inland steamer. So you must vary the packing of your goods to suit the method of transport.

4. This also affects the **insurance of the goods**, which might in the case of pharmaceuticals to Oslo not vary a great deal by sea or air; but in the case of the machinery to Bukoba would be very different for shipment by sea, as opposed to air. Hence you cannot automatically insure your goods in the same way for every shipment, but should aim to protect them within reason, and take into account the risks they will run according to how they are being transported.

If you use shipping and forwarding agencies to handle this work for you, make sure you instruct them accordingly. Make sure you know what they are doing, and check to see that it is the best for both you and your customers. By all means use their expertise, but remember that if anything goes wrong your customer will blame you, and if he refuses to buy again from you, it is your loss; so you cannot subrogate all responsibility in transport to someone else.

In order to minimise the problems involved in transporting your goods to your customers overseas you should **plot the movement of the goods** on some form of chart, and the following steps should be included:

1. The preparation of the goods by a specified date.
2. A check that the goods are exactly according to the customer's specifications.
3. Ensure that the packing and marking of the goods is done according to their method of transport and the customer's needs.
4. Ensure that the goods are dispatched to the docks, airport, rail or road receiving depot at the right time.
5. Ensure that the goods have been loaded on to the ship, aircraft, etc., in good order and condition.
6. Ensure that the correct insurance has been taken out.
7. Ensure that the goods arrive in their country of destination.
8. Ensure that they have been unloaded, complete and undamaged, and cleared through Customs without problems.
9. Ensure that they are being sent on to the customer's destination, wherever this happens to be.
10. Ensure that they have arrived safely and on the due date.

Remember that the goods are your moral if not legal responsibility until they reach your customer, and you must follow them through to their final destination. This will enable you to correct problems as they occur, and keep your customer advised at all times as to the progress of his order. In this way you eliminate late deliveries; so having made a promise to an importer, you are always able to keep to it.

Documents used for Transport

One of your main concerns will be with the documents used to move goods from your country to another, and while these have all been mentioned in previous chapters it may be useful to summarise them here. In addition, Appendix 1 illustrates a selection of the documents described. Some will be internal documents and others external ones. It will be helpful to examine the external ones first.

External Documents Required

1. If an export licence is required this must be obtained on **Application Form A** from the Export Licensing Branch of the Department of Trade.
2. You will need to enter the goods for Customs purposes, and in the case of goods requiring an export licence this must be done on **Form 63A**; otherwise you may quote your CA Number and provide the details after shipment.
3. You will need to **book space** by sea or air, etc., and most shipping and air lines have their own forms on which this can be done.
4. If you ship by sea you will have to send the goods to the docks, or Inland Clearance Depot, accompanied by a **Standard Shipping Note**, or SSN.
5. If the goods require special stowage—for example, because they are of

a hazardous nature—they will need to be accompanied by a special **Stowage Order,** issued by the shipping and air lines.

6. To have them transported overseas will require:

(*a*) For shipments by sea, a **Bill of Lading,** issued by the shipping lines;
(*b*) for shipments by air, an **Air Waybill,** issued by the airlines;
(*c*) a **CIM Consignment Note** for shipments by rail;
(*d*) a **CMR Consignment Note** issued by the road hauliers for shipments by road.

7. A set of commercial **invoices,** the forms used depending on the destination of the goods. These may require to be certified by a Chamber of Commerce or a consulate, or even be on special Chamber of Commerce or Consular forms.

8. A **Certificate of Insurance.**

9. For goods consigned to or through the EEC or associated countries, you will require the **T3** or **T3L** forms for EEC shipments (up until July 1, 1977), which form both Movement Certificates and Certificates of Origin; or for goods going to countries in association with the EEC the **EUR 1** and **2** documents, or their equivalents for countries like Cyprus, etc. All these documents are specified for each country in *Croner's Reference Book for Exporters*, and precise details are given as to how the documents must be worded, etc.

10. You will then need to enter the shipments for Customs, which you do on the **C.273** series of forms. To enable you to handle Customs entries you will also require the Brussels Tariff, and in the case of shipments by sea a *Lloyds Loading List*. The Customs Codes which you have to use are contained in the Customs Notice No. 37.

The actual composition of the documents for each shipment will of course vary, but you should note that a full set of documents will usually include invoices of whichever kind are necessary; Bills of Lading; Insurance Certificates; and some form of Certificate of Origin. Thus the movement document, the Customs document, the insurance document and the invoice are the key documents in an export transaction.

Internal Documents Required

These will vary from company to company, but you may identify the areas where some form of document will be necessary to get the goods sent to customers overseas.

1. Forms covering quotations in response to enquiries, which may also be done on pro forma invoices of the company, these forms to include Conditions of Sale.

2. Forms for processing orders received to the factory or warehouse; or to outside suppliers if the goods are being bought in.

3. Specifications as to how the goods are to be packed and marked.

4. Details of weights and measurements of the goods.

5. Any forms used to book the transport requirements and receive calling-up notices issued by the shipping and airlines, etc.

6. Forms to enable the goods to be insured under whichever policy the company uses.

7. Forms of instructions for the goods to be delivered to the docks, airports, etc.
8. Forms to enable the progress of the order to be checked.
9. Forms on which to record the export office's statistics.

You will of course need an efficient filing system, so that you can check at any time how the transport was arranged and which documents were used, etc.

The Aligned System of Documentation

It will have become clear to you that a great deal of the information needed to complete the documentation of an export transaction will need to be used many times, and you could list this information as follows:

1. The exporter, i.e. your name and address.
2. The consignee or importer, and his name and address.
3. The forwarding agent, and his name and address, if one is used.
4. The Customs entries and status of the goods, along with the BTN classification of the goods being exported.
5. The port of loading, dispatch and destination of the goods.
6. The goods, their weights, measurements and value.
7. The vessel or airline being used.
8. The transport documents involved.
9. Details of any insurance effected on the goods.
10. The freight paid.

In order to prevent an exporter having to have these details typed many times, a system of **Aligned documentation** has been created by an organisation, funded by the Department of Trade, known as SITPRO, or the Simplification of International Trade Procedures Board. This body works closely with international bodies like the United Nations Economic Commission for Europe, who are concerned with documentation in international trade.

The credit for the system must go to the Swedes, who were the first to produce a system for use in Sweden, but it is increasingly being used in Britain, and is constantly being revised and updated. In essence, the system is one of alignment, and requires that all the details are placed in a particular place on all the forms. Where certain details are not required the corresponding space is blanked out. But by means of a duplicator the details can be simultaneously reproduced on all the documents necessary for the order. Because the idea is for these forms to be used in many countries, and because all the details are always in the same place, then whichever language the forms are printed in, the details can be understood by comparing the wording in each part of the forms. Hence the basis of the system is the **master document**, on which all the relevant details are shown (see Fig. 27, Appendix 1).

The documents which can at present be reproduced under this system are as follows:

1. An acknowledgement of the order
2. Cargo booking instructions
3. The Standard Shipping Note
4. The Bill of Lading

5. The EUR 1 Certificate
6. A Certificate of Insurance
7. Invoices, including the Commonwealth Combined Invoice and Certificate of Origin

A good deal remains to be done, because all the necessary documents cannot as yet be reproduced on this system, but SITPRO are working to produce a complete set of all documents. The paper size of the forms is the standard A4 ISO size, and many companies have been able to include their internal documents in the system. The main advantages are a saving in costs and greater accuracy, because once the details have been checked as correct, mistakes cannot creep in, as they so often do when they have to be copied many times. If you wish to consider using the system you should get in touch with SITPRO at 8 Barton Avenue, Dunstable, Beds.

Payment for Exports

Since payment for exports is often closely allied to delivery, and requires documents of its own, the following are important:

1. Invoices, representing a bill for the goods
2. Documentary Letters of Credit
3. Bills of Exchange
4. Bills for Collection forms
5. Forward Exchange contracts with a bank
6. Exchange Control form SPE
7. ECGD Credit Limit Application forms

While these have all been considered in previous chapters, you should note:

1. Invoices are perhaps the most important documents the company has to produce; they are usually the first to be produced; and the information on them will be needed over and over again.

2. Documentary Letters of Credit are used to safeguard the interests of the exporter, and are used in the case of shipments by sea as a means of obtaining payment, before any document of title, e.g. the Bill of Lading, leaves the exporter.

3. Bills of Exchange drawn by the exporter on the customer can also be used in conjunction with the Bill of Lading to ensure payment, or a promise to pay, before the Bill of Lading is handed over to enable the importer to take delivery of the goods.

4. Hence you will, in many cases, be concerned to produce a complete set of documents for use by the customer. You must accordingly have a system which allows for all the documents to be gathered up together, and then sent to the customer, either directly or through a bank. Your accounts department may well deal with the bank; your responsibility is to ensure all the correct documents are produced at the right time.

5. Remember that in the case of ECGD cover you must clear some shipments before they are made, in order not to exceed the credit limits of the importer.

6. Remember also that you are in duty bound to declare all your shipments to the Customs, either on a pre-entry or post-entry basis, quoting the final F.O.B. value.

The work of an export office revolves around the procedures to be followed in the export transaction, and while these may vary to some degree, basically they remain the same. But each order must be followed through until the final payment is made and the export statistics of the company are complete. An export manager must be familiar with every stage of the work, at whatever level he or she operates, because however well you may obtain the business from overseas, unless you handle it efficiently you will seldom obtain any repeat orders.

Revision

Cover the page with a sheet of paper and uncover one question at a time.

Answers	*Questions*
	1. What should always be your prime consideration when choosing a particular method of transport?
1. The wishes of the customer.	2. Where is Mwanza?
2. On Lake Victoria.	3. On what do you apply for an export licence?
3. Form A.	4. What document accompanies the goods if they are of a hazardous nature?
4. A Special Stowage Order.	5. What is an EUR 1?
5. A movement certificate for goods sent to EFTA countries from the EEC countries.	6. What document is used for special applications to ECGD?
6. A Credit Limit Application form.	7. On what sized paper is the aligned system of documents based?
7. A4.	8. What is SITPRO?
8. The Simplification of International Trade Procedures Board.	9. Name a document of title.
9. A Bill of Lading.	10. What can an invoice be besides a bill for the goods?
10. A Certificate of Origin.	

Exercises

1. What major decisions do you have to make when moving goods overseas?
2. What will a system of aligned documents do to help an exporter with the paper work, and how does the system work?
3. What kind of internal documents would be required in an export office?
4. What documents would be required to ensure that you are paid for the goods?
5. How would you try to keep track of a customer's order from when it is received, until the customer pays for it?

9

THE LEGAL ASPECTS OF EXPORT

It cannot be too strongly stressed that as an exporter you should never attempt to be your own lawyer. Only once in my export career have I tried, when an imitation of the product I was selling appeared on the market. So I raided the warehouse where the imitation was being made, only to find it empty. As a result I was sued by the owner for defamation of character. My company nearly fired me for this ill-advised attempt to take the law into my own hands.

This is not a book on law, and this chapter is only intended to acquaint you with the main areas where the law affects export transactions, and with the principal Acts which govern them. Should you unhappily become entangled with the law while exporting, you must employ a competent lawyer. But because international trade is based on the law, you should be aware at least of how you might at some time or other be affected.

The five main areas concerned are:

1. The international sale of goods
2. The carriage of goods
3. The insurance of goods
4. Payment for goods
5. The EEC and English law

These are the main sections in this chapter, and each will be examined separately from the point of view of English law and International law as it affects the exporter. If you are a reader from another country you must relate what is written here to the laws of your own country, as these affect international trade, and as your laws are affected by International law.

There are, of course, many other areas where the law may affect your export business. These areas will include Customs regulations; technical standards and specifications; patents; trade marks; consumer protection; and company laws. But these laws will be those applying locally to each of your export markets, and will often be different from country to country. You must make sure, therefore, that you check with your customer what the laws in his country are in such cases, so that you do not break any local laws when exporting.

In addition to obtaining far more tuition in the law than one chapter in this book can provide, you should also have some idea of the sources of law; the administration of justice and judicial precedent; and some knowledge of fundamental legal concepts such as contract, tort, ownership and possession, mortgages, pledges and legal persons. The most important point about the law as it affects export is that in practice you will not come up against it, provided you know the legal implications of what you are doing and take steps to ensure that you do not break English, International or local laws. It is these implications with which this chapter is most concerned.

The International Sale of Goods

In any international contract the negotiation of that contract is one of the most important factors, since if this is done properly legal problems should not arise, provided that both the exporter and his customer carry out and perform the contract strictly in accordance with the terms laid down in it. Hence the importance of offers, quotations, orders and their fulfilment, as covered in Chapter 3 of this book.

In Britain the basis of the law covering the sale of goods is contained in the **Sale of Goods Act of 1893**. This sets out, in six parts and 64 sections, the basis of a contract of sale, although the law of contract is much wider than that of the sale of goods. The six parts of the Sale of Goods Act cover:

1. The **formation** of the contract, including the contract itself, the formalities, the subject matter (i.e. the goods, their price, etc.), the conditions and warranties, and sale by sample.
2. The **effects** of the contract, including the transfer of property from seller to buyer, and the transfer of the title of the goods.
3. The **performance** of the contract, covering such points as the duties of the seller and buyer, the rules governing delivery, the right to examine the goods, their acceptance, and the liability of the buyer if he refuses delivery of the goods.
4. The **rights of the unpaid seller** against the goods, his lien on them, the right of stoppage in transit and re-sale rights.
5. **Actions for breach of contract**, and the remedies of both buyer and seller in this respect.
6. The **rights and duties** under the Act enforceable by action, the interpretation of terms used, and so on.

Since the essence of the sale of goods is the transfer of them from seller to buyer, you can see why the Terms of Delivery, as set out in Chapter 3, are so important, and you can also see why your own Conditions of Sale are important.

But this Sale of Goods Act is an English Act, and since you are dealing with customers who are subject to their own laws in their own countries, you should note that in 1964 two international conventions were held at The Hague, where laws governing the international sale of goods were codified and agreed by some 27 countries. Their proposals were incorporated into English law in the **Uniform Laws of International Sales Act of 1967**, which became fully effective in 1972. These laws consist of two main Schedules:

1. The Uniform Law on the Formation of Contracts for the International Sale of Goods.
2. The Uniform Law on the International Sale of Goods.

The intention was to reconcile English and European laws on offer and acceptance, and hence a contract to be agreed between an exporter and an importer. But there was no attempt to define, for example, terms of delivery used internationally, leaving the parties to be bound by the common usage of such terms, as agreed between them. It does, however, distinguish between fundamental and non-fundamental breach of contract, which is not in the Sale of Goods Act, and which is an important point because the essence of export is the contract you make with your customer overseas and the performance of that contract between him and yourself.

There are certain features of these Acts which you should note.

Agents

There are two areas where you may be affected by laws governing agents and contracts made with them:

(*a*) Where you deal with Confirming Houses (as will be dealt with more fully in Chapter 13) you must decide in advance with them whether they are acting as agents for their principals, or as principals in their own right. In law a person is an agent when he is authorised to act for someone else, whether the principal is named or not. So decide from the outset with whom you are making a contract, a point well covered in the Sale of Goods Act.

(*b*) When you make agreements with intermediaries of some kind (dealt with in Chapter 13), these agreements will be legally binding on you both, and anything the intermediary does, he will do on your behalf. This will be covered by the Contract of Agency, incorporated into the Sale of Goods Act, which in particular makes provision for the protection of agents. Hence when you draw up agreements with intermediaries to act for you, make sure the agreements are legally checked before being signed.

The Goods

As you would expect, there is an implied condition in a contract that the goods shall correspond with the description given, so if in fact an item is not as specified, the contract may be held to be broken. If, therefore, you supply after offering a sample, you should only accept the order on the condition that the customer agrees he is buying according to that sample.

Payment and Delivery

Unless it has been otherwise agreed, delivery of the goods and payment for them are concurrent conditions. The price in an F.O.B. contract is at the seller's place, but in a C.I.F. contract it is at the buyer's place, because under these terms of delivery this is where the documents change hands. Normally, however, payment and delivery are settled by you and your customer on terms mutually agreed between you. For example, if he pays you by means of a Documentary Credit you will be paid in your country, which is where delivery is made; whereas if he pays by means of a remittance against a draft drawn by you on him, you will be paid in his country, which is where delivery of the goods takes place. These, as you will appreciate, are irrespective of whether the goods are sold by you on F.O.B. or C.I.F. terms.

The Transfer of Property

The word 'property' is used legally to mean the title to the goods. While in law payment and delivery are linked, in export the property may pass to your customer before it is either delivered or paid for. As you have seen, there are ways by which you can ensure that the property does not pass until delivery, and payment has been made. But suppose your customer accepts a draft drawn on him at 60 days; while you will then deliver the goods to him, he may not in fact pay you at the end of the 60 days. To overcome this problem your best remedy is to include in your Conditions of Sale, as dealt with in Chapter 3, a Property Reservation Clause. This states that the title to the goods sold shall be reserved to the seller, and will not pass to the buyer until the purchase price is paid in cash.

The Transfer of Possession

This is not the same as the transfer of property, because in this case you actually deliver the goods, whereas previously you were transferring the title to the goods. But if you deliver the goods to a carrier, note that in law you are normally presumed to have delivered them to your customer.

Rejection and Acceptance

The Act lays down quite specifically the rights of a buyer to accept or reject goods, and the remedies of the seller and the buyer for any breach of contract, which is defined as the non-performance of any condition in the contract. In addition to the rejection and acceptance of a contract, there can be a repudiation of the contract. This is basically an intimation by one party that he does not intend to proceed with the contract. But it is rather harder to define frustration of a contract, which is held to occur, and have any validity, only if something so unexpected happens that, if it could have been foreseen, the two parties to the contract would never have made it. What it does not mean is that if something unexpected happens you can shelter behind it, should you not carry out the contract. Since it is not easy, therefore, to say when a contract has been frustrated, a clause may be included in a contract defining both parties' mutual rights if events beyond their control occur, and this is known as a Force Majeure clause. In law such a clause means every event beyond the control of the parties concerned, and it can be worded quite precisely to prevent any future misunderstanding. It is usually insufficient, however, to refer to the 'usual' Force Majeure clause, so it is better to define it carefully, unless in a particular trade it has a definite meaning.

Conflict of Laws

This is an important point in export because there is a clear distinction between private international law, which is any national system prevailing in your own or your customer's country, and public international law, which is the international custom prevailing between the nations of the world. Most contracts are subject to private international law. But if, for example, you sell to a customer in the Netherlands, will your contract be subject to English or Dutch law? And under which law will its performance be judged? If you go to arbitration the arbitrator first has to decide this point, so to save what is a difficult problem you should include in your Conditions of Sale a **'Choice of Laws'** clause. This would normally state that the contract and its performance will be subject to English or Dutch law, as the two parties will agree in advance. You may therefore stipulate English law, and leave it to your customer to alter the contract should he insist on Dutch law being used.

The Length of an Offer

In these days of escalating costs it is normal practice to include in an offer a condition that it is only valid for a stated length of time, and many Conditions of Sale contain a clause to that effect. But you should note that while this is legally enforceable under International law, it is not in English law, although there is a move by the Law Commission to have English law altered to conform to international practice.

As you will see later in this chapter, the law of contract as it affects international business is constantly being changed, and the EEC is much concerned with it, as it affects business within the Community.

The Carriage of Goods

Most methods of transport are governed by laws and regulations which are legally enforceable. Hence when you use any means of transport you are likely to be subject to some legal constraints. Moreover, the documents used to arrange transport of goods from one country to another also contain legally enforceable conditions, which may affect your use of them. But while each nation has its own transport laws and regulations, the conflicts between them have been largely avoided by the Convention system, which is a means of obtaining agreement between countries on matters affecting the carriers and users in transport.

You should therefore be aware of the main legal constraints affecting the four main methods of transport—namely, sea, air, rail and road.

Carriage of Goods by Sea

When you ship goods by sea, the condition under which a shipowner will carry your goods are contained in the **Carriage of Goods by Sea Act** of 1924, and the subsequent Act of the same name of 1971, although the latter has not been implemented at the time of writing. These Acts have been based on the Hague Rules for International Carriage by Sea, as amended by the Brussels Protocol of 1968, which makes the international rules effective in the United Kingdom.

As you saw in Chapter 5, shipment by sea involves the use of a Bill of Lading, which acts as a contract of freight, as a receipt for the goods, and as a document of title. The conditions under which the shipowner will carry your goods from one country to another are set out in the Bill of Lading. On the front it is clearly stated that the Bill is issued subject to the Exceptions and Conditions referred to as set out, in small print, on the back of the Bill.

The first of these is at present called the **Clause Paramount**, which states that the shipowners enter into a contract with you according to the Rules as set out in the Schedule to the Carriage of Goods by Sea Act, with the exception of the clauses referring to the pre-carriage and on-carriage of goods. But the 1971 Act does not require a Clause Paramount to be included in a Bill of Lading.

The remaining clauses cover a great many conditions, including the carriage of hazardous cargoes; the freight charges; the possible transhipment of the goods; and the handling of valuable, perishable and fragile goods. There is a clause relating to General Average, usually subject to the York/Antwerp rules of 1974, and several clauses affecting collisions, in particular the Jason clause applying in both-to-blame cases. You may feel that the shipowners have included so many exceptions that the contract is all on their side. But there are sound legal precedents why these conditions have been so carefully stated, and in practice most shipments reach their destinations safely and in good order, so you should not be unduly put off by such an array of 'small print'.

If you refer to the bottom of the front of a Bill, you will see that there is a reference to the fact that the goods are 'Shipped in apparent good order and condition unless otherwise stated hereon . . .', a legal reference to the points made in Chapter 5, from which you will remember that you normally expect to receive a 'Shipped on board' Bill of Lading showing the goods are on the named vessel, as opposed to a 'Received for Shipment' Bill, which merely acknowledges that the shipowners have had the goods but have not yet loaded them. In both cases the Bill will be clean, unless it has been claused because of some defect or shortage in the goods as stated by the exporter, in which case it becomes a 'dirty' or claused Bill.

The **liability of the shipowners** has been laid down in the Carriage of Goods by Sea Acts, although there was a conflict of opinion over the £100 per package clause in the 1923 Convention, because the English Courts took this to mean sterling, and foreign courts to mean gold value, which would have been considerably more than sterling. To save expensive litigation the British Maritime Law Association agreed to pay up to £200 sterling per package. But as soon as the 1971 Act is implemented both British and foreign courts will have to follow the 1968 Protocol which states that the liability is 30 gold francs per kilo. There has also been some dispute about what constitutes a package in view of the increasing use of containers. It has now been agreed in the 1968 Protocol that if the container has been consolidated, the individual packages count as a package, otherwise the whole container is a package.

Carriage of Goods by Air

The conditions under which goods will be carried by air are contained in the **Carriage by Air Act** of 1961, which replaces for most countries an earlier Act of 1932, although some still technically apply it. The law is based on the Warsaw Rules, which gives them international status, and a number of other Conventions. There are also some Supplementary Provisions in a Carriage by Air Act of 1962.

The **liability of the carrier** is now fixed at 250 gold francs per kilogram, since air freight, as you have seen, is usually based on weight, not measurement. There are, in addition, many internationally accepted regulations, agreed by all the airlines under IATA and set out on the back of the Air Waybill, usually on the originals only, but of rather less complexity than those found on a Bill of Lading. These include rules for the carrying of hazardous cargo, their packing, labelling, and the provision of special certificates for them; and in particular the liability of the carrier.

Reference is also made to the delivery of the goods to the consignee, and you will remember that an Air Waybill, while a contract of carriage and a receipt for them, is not a document of title, so that the goods will be handed over to the person named in the Waybill without his having to produce it, although he will be asked to quote its number. Note that in law a shipper is responsible, when shipping by air, for ensuring that any necessary import licences are available at the airport of destination to enable the goods to enter the country. This is not, however, the case with shipments by sea.

Carriage of Goods by Rail

There is no specific Act covering the carriage of goods by rail, but the **CIM Rules** (International Carriage by Rail) set out the regulations under which goods are carried. The **liability of the carriers** is limited to 100 gold francs per kilogram. The conditions are set out in the Rail Consignment Note, which is both a contract of carriage and a receipt for the goods, but not of course a document of title. If you ship from Britain to European countries, British Rail have a Through Consignment Note of their own, which includes the CIM Rules in its conditions of carriage. Carriage of goods by rail is a good example of how Conventions are used to formulate internationally accepted rules which have the force of law behind them.

Carriage of Goods by Road

In Britain there is a **Carriage of Goods by Road Act** of 1965. This includes the provisions of the CMR Rules, and both are included in the International CMR Consignment note. This, like the Rail note, is both a contract of freight and a receipt for the goods, but not a document of title. It limits the **liability of the carriers** to 25 gold francs per kilo.

There is a possibility that legal rules will be introduced in the not too distant future covering combined transport—that is, where more than one method of transport is used for the same shipment—but so far nothing has been agreed internationally.

The Insurance of Goods

The basis of all cargo insurance affecting export consignments is contained in the **Marine Insurance Act** of 1906, and the later one of 1909. While these were designed to cover insurance of cargoes when shipped by sea, the insurance of cargoes sent by air and other means is based on similar principles.

The 1906 Act is set out in 94 sections, and if you read these in conjunction with the points raised in Chapter 6 you will find the main legal implications of cargo insurance well covered. You might note, however, that most insurance disputes have been settled by arbitration, not litigation, so that there are not so many legal precedents on which to base the laws.

The sections of this Act are set out as follows:

Sections 1–3: These define Marine Insurance, and also the 'Adventure' and the 'Perils' against which insurance may be taken.

Sections 4–15: These define the principles of 'Insurable Interest', or who can benefit from the insurance, and also to whom any insurable interest may be assigned, and how this can be done.

Section 16: This covers the measure of Insurable Interest, and on goods is taken to be the cost of the goods, plus shipping and insurance costs, now normally calculated, as you have seen, as C.I.F. plus 10 or 15 per cent.

Sections 17–21: The Disclosures and Representations that must be made, and the principle of 'Utmost Good Faith'.

Sections 22–31: These cover the Policy itself, show what must be included, and consider the contract embodied in a policy.

Section 32: Double Insurance is defined (that is, when a cargo is insured more than once).

Sections 33–41: Here you will find the various Warranties, both Express and Implied.

Sections 43–49: The definition of the Voyage, and the laws regarding changes to the voyage, deviations from it, and delays.

Sections 50–51: When and how a Policy may be assigned, important when you consider your customer's interest in it.

Sections 52–54: The Premiums to be paid, and the duties of the broker who arranges the insurance.

Sections 55–66: These cover Loss and Abandonment, including Total Constructive Loss. They also deal with General Average and Particular Average losses.

Sections 67–78: These define the measure of Indemnity, both for Total and for Partial Loss.

Sections 79–85: These sections cover the rights of the Insurer on payment; the return of the premium; and problems of Mutual Insurance (when two people mutually agree to insure each other against loss).

Sections 86–94: These include various supplemental articles, such as the interpretation to be given to terms used; the use of the 'slip' as evidence of insurance having been taken out; and a definition of what is meant by the 'reasonable time' within which a claim must be made.

The 1909 Act was passed specifically to cover the prohibition of gambling on the Maritime Perils, because you will remember that it is forbidden to gamble on marine insurance, and the two Acts are usually quoted as 'The Marine Insurance Acts of 1906 and 1909'. You will recall that in Chapter 6 it was stated that no other form of international trade had quite such an early history and interest as marine insurance, and you may like to note that there was passed in 1601 the Elizabethan Act, which describes the objects and functions of marine insurance in picturesque but perfectly clear language, and which allows, so it says, 'all merchants to venture more willingly and freely'. Without it international trade could hardly take place with the security that it does.

Payment for Goods

However your customer overseas pays you, you will be taking on obligations that can be legally enforced. You are, after all, making a contract with your customer, which will be subject to both the Sale of Goods Act of 1893 and the Uniform Laws on International Sales Act of 1967, and your concern is to ensure that you are paid in accordance with the terms of the contract. If you consider the main methods of payment for exports you will find the legal obligations contained in the methods to be as follows:

Cash in Advance

Only the delivery is subject to law, because you will not dispatch the goods until payment has been made. But how you are paid will depend on the provisions of the Exchange Control Act of 1947, and subsequent various amendments to it. These were discussed in Chapter 7.

Documentary Credits

In addition to the ordinary law of contract, it is customary to make the opening of a documentary credit, by the buyer in favour of the exporter, subject to the International Chamber of Commerce's 'Uniform Customs and Practice for Documentary Credits 1974', these taking the place of those issued in 1962. These practices are not laws, or legally effective, in that they have no statutory force, but of course can be enforced on the basis of a contract between the parties. The advantage of these rules, however, is that as they state the methods and procedures for operating such credits, and as the banks endorse their advice of such credits to the effect that these will be subject to these rules, then because they have been internationally accepted most parties will strictly abide by them. So although there is no specific Act covering documentary credits, there are more or less universally accepted international rules, which makes the provisions of the contract much clearer.

Bills of Exchange

Using a Bill of Exchange to obtain payment from a customer overseas is making use of a document which has been defined in the Bill of Exchange Act of 1882. This states that the Bill of Exchange is 'an unconditional order in writing, addressed by one person to another, signed by the person giving it, requiring the person to whom it is addressed to pay on demand, or at a fixed or determinable future, a certain sum of money to or to the order of a specified person, or to bearer'. And you may consider that as an explanation of a Bill of Exchange nothing could be clearer. Its use in international transactions was sanctioned in the Sale of Goods Act of 1893, because it is so often used in conjuction with a Bill of Lading, to effect the transfer of property on consideration, or payment, being made by the buyer to the seller. So that by using a Bill of Lading you are intending that the goods shall be transferred to your customer, but by adding a Bill of Exchange you are also deciding that the title to the goods shall not pass until consideration, in the form of acceptance, has been made.

When a Bill of Exchange is used as a means of payment for export transactions, it is now internationally accepted practice that this shall be under the International Chamber of Commerce's 'Uniform Rules for the Collection of Commercial Paper' of 1968. These rules lay down precisely the procedures to be followed for presenting, accepting, paying and protesting the Bills. Hence when you use this method of payment you are using a well-defined legal method of obtaining payment, more so than by other means.

Open Account

In this case you merely have a contract with your customer to pay after he has received the goods, although you should, in your Conditions of Sale, specify when this is to be. Should you wish to safeguard your payments by customers, you may of course draw a Bill of Exchange on them at specific dates, as is the custom for example in France. In this case you would have an easier way of taking action against them, should they fail to pay or accept the Bills drawn on them.

When you are paid under a barter deal, or by means of royalties under some form of licensing deal, or for stock which you supplied to a customer on consignment, you are only concerned with the contract to determine how payment is to be made.

Should you sell currency forward as a means of being able to quote in your customer's currency, in order to be sure of receiving the correct amount of your own currency you will make a contract with your bank to this effect.

The EEC and English Law

By the European Communities Act of 1972, Community Law has become part of English Law. It is not, however, the intention of the Community to create a uniform law to supersede national systems, but only to harmonise and unify the laws of the member states in so far as it is necessary to establish a Common Market. Lord Denning has, nevertheless, stated that 'We must speak and think of Community Law, of Community rights and obligations, and we must give effect to them'. Hence if you trade with the Community you should be aware of Community laws as they affect your business. There is an increasing number of these Community laws, details of which are contained in the **Community Law Reports**, which also set out the judicial decisions of the Court of Justice.

You should remember that the aim of the Community is to establish a single market, not a set of national ones, so one example of Community legal intentions is that there shall be the same laws everywhere affecting competition. All the laws affecting the functioning of the Community are being harmonised, as are those affecting the establishment and operation of companies in the Community. It is intended that the Court of Justice's decisions shall be binding in all member states, and to this extent the jurisdiction of the courts of member states will be curtailed. If the Commission of the Community decides something is to be done, and the member states agree, then the Council of the Community has wide powers to carry out recommendations.

As a British exporter you should, therefore, be aware of four areas where Community law is likely to affect you.

1. The Law of Contract

European law is, as you may know, based on five codes: the civil, commercial, and criminal, and the civil and criminal procedures. It seems likely that the civil and commercial codes will be combined in both Community and English law. A new law of Contract is being prepared in England, and the intention is to bring this into line with both the European Laws of Contract and the American Uniform Commercial Code. The changes likely in English law will be in such areas as the acceptance of an offer by post; the necessity for the acceptance to be exactly the same as the offer; and the abolition of the old rule of '*Caveat emptor*', or 'let the buyer beware'.

2. The International Sale of Goods

A great deal of progress has already been made since Britain adopted the Uniform Laws on International Sales Act of 1967. But under English law you do not as yet have to make a contract under these Uniform laws, although this is likely to become an accepted practice in the Community.

3. Company Law

English Company law is based on the Companies Acts of 1948 and 1967, but under the European Communities Act of 1972 you must now:

(*a*) State on your letterheadings the number of your company registration and your registered office, and have these publicly announced in the London or Edinburgh Gazettes.

(*b*) Remember that no company can now plead that its directors acted beyond their powers, which is a restriction of the '*ultra vires*' doctrine.

There are many other areas in Company Law where changes are likely. These include the laws affecting public and private companies; the powers and composition of boards of directors; the employees' rights to participate in the management of a company; the two-tier system of supervisory and executive boards of directors; the rights of a European company (*Société Europeènne*) to the status of a national company in all member states; and the appointments to the boards of private and public companies. At the same time English law is likely to affect Community law in such matters as the publications of a company's accounts and the disclosure of its activities, which are two areas where European laws tend to lag behind English law.

4. The Law of Competition

The intention here is for the Community to break down national barriers, especially in two areas:

(*a*) Exclusive marketing agreements with agents or distributors. These are not prohibited, but the rights of a buyer to buy from anywhere in the Community, irrespective of any such agreements, are now fully established.

(*b*) The protection of property in the form of trade marks, patents and copyright, together with the goodwill of the business. No decisions have yet been taken on how property is to be protected, or how various laws on this point are to be harmonised.

You should note that in Great Britain there are now three systems of law: English law, Scottish law, and the federal law of the Community. This is similar to the system in the USA but is entirely new in Britain's case. You must therefore be aware of the various changes that will probably occur in constitutional, administrative, taxation and commercial law as a result of Britain joining the Community.

Should you wish to pursue your studies of the law as it affects exporting, the main areas where you should do this are as follows:

1. *The International Sale of Goods*. You should examine the standardisation of international terms; the sources of international sales law in the United Kingdom; performance, breach and frustration of contracts; and the Uniform Laws on International Sales in particular.
2. *Representatives overseas*. Here the main areas are the agreements made with overseas intermediaries; laws affecting branch and subsidiary companies overseas; and the competition laws of both the United Kingdom and the EEC.
3. *The legal aspects of the finance of exports*. In particular you should examine in detail both Documentary Credits and Bills of Exchange, and laws affecting merchant finance for exports.
4. *The legal aspects of insurance*. Both marine and aviation insurance laws

need to be studied in greater detail; and in addition container rules and regulations, and the Uniform Rules for a Combined Transport Document.

5. *The legal aspects of the carriage of goods.* For transport by sea you should examine the Bills of Lading Act of 1855 and the Carriage of Goods by Sea Acts of 1924 and 1971; for transport by air the Carriage by Air Acts of 1932, 1961, and 1962, and IATA regulations; the rules affecting container traffic; together with the Uniform Rules for a Combined Transport Document.

6. *Arbitration and litigation.* The English Arbitration Acts of 1950 and 1975, the Court of Arbitration of the International Chamber of Commerce, and European arbitration are the important areas to examine. As regards litigation, you should study the enforcement of English judgements abroad, the recognition of foreign judgements in England, and the Foreign Judgements (Reciprocal Enforcement) Act of 1933.

Revision

Cover the page with a sheet of paper and uncover one question at a time.

Answers	*Questions*
	1. On which Act are contracts for the sale of goods based in English law?
1. The Sale of Goods Act of 1893.	2. Where is 'price' defined in an F.O.B. contract?
2. At the seller's place.	3. What does the Clause Paramount in a Bill of Lading state?
3. That the contract is according to the Carriage of Goods Act of 1924.	4. Are you legally bound to insure export cargo?
4. Not unless it is a part of the Contract of Sale.	5. What is the implication when a Bill of Lading is tied to a Bill of Exchange?
5. That the title to the goods shall not pass until acceptance of the Bill of Exchange.	6. Which Act covers the International Contract of Sale?
6. The Uniform Laws on International Sales Act of 1967, effective 1973.	7. On what Acts is English Company Law based?
7. The Companies Acts of 1948 and 1967.	8. What does 'caveat emptor' mean?
8. Let the buyer beware.	9. What kinds of Warranties are there?

Answers	*Questions*
9. Express and Implied.	10. Where can you find details of EEC laws?
10. In the Community Law Reports.	

Exercises

1. Why, how and where would you include a 'Property Reservation' clause in an overseas contract?
2. What are the main differences between a Breach of contract, a Repudiated contract and a Frustrated contract?
3. What are the main areas covered by the Marine Insurance Act of 1906?
4. Discuss the three methods of payment most affected by the law, and say how this is so.
5. Discuss the main implications of Community Law on English business law.
6. What effects is Community Law likely to have on English Company Law?

PART 3

EXPORT MARKETING

While this part of the book concentrates on those aspects of export which are generally referred under the heading of 'marketing', you must not forget that many of the factors in export practice discussed in Part 2 have a marketing function. These two sides of export are, therefore, closely related, and form part of one complete operation.

It must already be apparent that when you export you will be dealing with local environmental factors which are usually different from those in your own country. Local transport conditions, customs procedures and legal requirements are but three which have already been examined. When it comes to selling your exports, these local environmental conditions assume a greater importance because they dictate to a major degree what customers will buy, and what, therefore, you must supply. These factors also indicate the best methods of getting your exports to the customers concerned, both from the transport and distribution points of view. Hence a study of local environmental conditions is essential for both export practice and selling. Such studies involve your obtaining a great deal of information, one area being about local prices. So far you have seen how an export price may be built on basic manufacturing costs, plus such additional costs as are contained in the terms of delivery you quote, the terms of payment you require, the packing that is necessary, the costs of documentation, and the way in which the insurance of goods is arranged. What we have not yet considered is the price the local market will pay, which depends on the local environment. Nor have we yet considered costs in relation to selling, channels of distribution or promotion.

In addition to the price you charge for your exports, you have still to consider the export itself—that is, the product or service you sell. Few products are exported in exactly the same form as they are sold in the domestic market. Most require some modification, either to themselves, or to their packaging if they are packaged products. This represents a further cost factor.

If you wish to appreciate the importance of efficient export practice you should work for a time as an importer, when you will quickly see how necessary efficient export practice is. But the importer is often not the final user. Hence you must study local channels of distribution, because this will serve to identify your final users, and show you how best to reach them.

Enquiries seldom come floating into an export office out of the blue, so to speak. To ensure that they do reach you, you must go out and get them, and this involves personal selling in overseas markets. And to be able to sell successfully, you must promote your exports by means of various forms of publicity, because you can never hope to be in personal contact with everyone who makes, or influences, a buying decision.

If you prefer to export in a haphazard manner, merely fulfilling such orders from overseas as may arrive on your desk, you will almost certainly find export is both unprofitable and unrewarding. Like any other business activity it has to be methodically planned. This will involve preparing an export strategy and export marketing plans, as well as executing them, and finally evaluating the results obtained. These inevitably cover the whole range of export activities, and will need to be based on all three parts in this book. Hence Part 3 has been divided into seven chapters as follows:

Chapter 10: The Local Environment. While you will seldom know as much about any overseas environment as you might wish, these are certain essentials you must learn about the environments in which you operate.

Chapter 11: Information and Research. Since you need to obtain information you must know where to find it, and how to get at it, as well as how to use it.

Chapter 12: Products and Production. Basically you sell the result of using some skill to produce a product or service. But how best to use that skill for export? And how best to adapt that skill to local conditions?

Chapter 13: Channels of Distribution. While you have seen how products may be physically transported to those who need them, you have not yet identified your final users, nor have you considered how they can best be supplied through the various channels of distribution.

Chapter 14: Personal Selling Overseas. While you have examined the kind of export office staff you need in export, you have not yet considered the field staff. You must know what they should do, and how their work can best be handled.

Chapter 15: Promotion. You will need to reinforce all your personal efforts with the use of certain forms of promotion, or your efforts will be directed along such a narrow front that those expected export sales will not materialise.

Chapter 16: Marketing Plans. Only planned export operations have any chance of success in a modern competitive world market place. And only marketing plans based on sound strategy have any chance of success in export.

Now that you have reached this point, you will see that you are back more or less to where you started. But the most important aspect of this section of the book is that marketing is primarily concerned with change, because it is a way of satisfying the needs and wants of people, who are in themselves constantly changing. Success in export is only possible by taking advantage of a constantly changing world. In this section of the book you will be planning for future export business, secure in the knowledge that once you obtain it, you can handle it effectively.

10

THE LOCAL ENVIRONMENT

When you export you need in most cases to adapt your product and the way you sell it to the local environment of the people to whom you are selling. This you can only do successfully if you know a good deal about the environment concerned.

When you market at home you start with a considerable knowledge of the environment, because you were probably born and brought up in it. Certainly you live the major part of your life in it. When you market overseas you have to acquire that local knowledge. Clearly, however, you can never hope to learn as much about other parts of the world as you know about your own area, nor could you in a lifetime hope to do so. It is unnecessary to know everything about each overseas market, but there are four essential factors of which you must know something:

1. The geographical conditions
2. The political conditions
3. The economic conditions
4. The social or cultural conditions

Since there is a tendency for countries to be joined together in groups for purposes of international trade, you should be aware of the characteristics of these groups, and thus be able to do business in the groups as a whole.

The world is made up of some 150 to 200 nations, depending on how you define a nation. It has become customary, therefore, for these nations to be considered as markets. You talk about the Swiss market or the Japanese market. But strictly speaking this is quite inaccurate, because no one sells to the whole market in either Switzerland or Japan. They should more properly be termed **political markets**, because they have been defined by some political action. They will seldom, if ever, correspond to your own export markets, because you will only sell to segments of them. These segments are called **demand markets**, and represent those people with whom you do business, or expect to provide you with business.

You will find that demand markets have certain similar characteristics, and some different ones, but by and large they will probably be more similar than dissimilar. Your major task is to define and get to know in detail your demand markets, which you can do by getting to know their environmental backgrounds under the four headings given above.

Once you begin to define demand markets you start to select export markets, both the new ones to be tackled for the first time, and the current ones to be developed on the strength of existing sales. Your aim should be to find, and develop, demand markets which are as nearly approximate to your domestic market as possible, in order to limit as much as you can the necessity for modifying your product and changing methods of distribution and promotion. Hence this chapter has been divided into the following sections:

1. The characteristics of political markets
2. The conditions in political market areas
3. The classification of demand markets
4. Export market selection

The Characteristics of Political Markets

The four headings mentioned earlier are a convenient way of classifying the information you require to obtain about political markets, some of which will have a bearing on your own exports.

Geographical Conditions

Since every exporter must be something of an expert on world geography you might start by studying an atlas until you can, with some assurance, say where all the political markets are, what they are called, their size, physical conditions, and their climate, as well as how they are placed in relation to each other. You should know, for example, that South-West Africa is now called Namibia. You should be able to place Honduras accurately on the map, as opposed to British Honduras. You should know that it is as far from the east coast of Canada to the west, as it is from Britain to Canada. You should know that Colombia is both a republic in South America and a town in Brazil, and not confuse it with British Columbia, a province of Canada. If you receive enquiries from either Mahé or Port Moresby, you must know the former is in the Seychelles and the latter in New Guinea, which has no connection with Guyana. The size of a country is important from a communications point of view, and particularly in relation to its population. Australia is many times larger than Japan, but has only a tenth of its population; while if you visit Hong Kong you will be amazed to find such a tiny piece of land holding nearly four million people.

The **physical characteristics** are important for several reasons. Mountains still create communications barriers, the Andes cutting off the east of South America from the west. Rivers provide the means of life in many areas; where would South-East Asia be without the Mekong? Deserts are also dividers of people. There is a vast difference between those who live north of the Sahara to those who live to the south.

Physical characteristics affect where people, your customers, live, as well as how they live. There is usually a sound reason why any centre of population exists where it is. The city of Istanbul stands on the edge of the Bosporus, linking Europe with Asia, and at the entrance to the Black Sea. The desert characteristics of the people in Kuwait are quite different from the mountain features of those who live in the Italian Alps.

Climate probably has a greater effect on people than any other physical condition. It dictates in many cases how much people work, because it is harder to sustain long working hours in a tropical climate like that of the Ivory Coast, than it is in the more temperate climate of Belgium. The long winters tend to make the Scandinavians gloomy and introspective. Climate affects what people wear and how they live. It affects products, in relation to their packaging and performance. In Liberia, for instance, it was found necessary to alter the gum used to bind books, because the insects there liked the taste of the gum used in other parts of the world so much that they ate it up, with the result that the books fell apart in the warehouses.

Physical characteristics tend to cut across political boundaries. Hence it is often better to classify your export markets by their physical conditions. For example, you might do this if you sell heating or air-conditioning equipment, and this is one way of pinpointing demand markets. If you sell household equipment you may only need to take into account those parts of the world where climatic conditions make a form of shelter as important as food.

You must become as familiar with the geography of the world as you are about it in your own country, and in particular about the geographical conditions of your own demand markets.

Political Conditions

The controlling role of different political systems has, over the years, greatly interfered with the way people in different nations trade with each other. Basically you can divide the world into those areas where you may only sell to state trading organisations and those where you also trade with private individuals or corporations. State trading is mainly confined to the **Planned Economies**, and to countries such as China, Burma, Sri Lanka, Cuba and Vietnam. The struggle in Angola was about whether to follow countries like Tanzania into the state trading world, or remain a country of free enterprise. In the state trading areas of the world you will seldom be allowed politically to sell consumer products, and you will be encouraged to sell the means of production rather than the results. But this also applies in areas where the local production of products is politically encouraged, such as Mexico and most of the Latin American nations. You could say this tendency is apparent in most of the developing countries of the world, and that only among the richer nations is trade all that free.

Politics affects the amount of trade carried out between countries. The better the terms Britain is on with the People's Republic of China, for example, the greater the chances of trade between them. Because Britain will not have political relations with Rhodesia at present, there is no trade at all. Politics, by creating war or civil riots and commotions, often hampers trade, as in the case of Cyprus when it was invaded by the Turks in 1974. Because politics have such a distinct effect on trade you may, as you saw in Chapter 7, insure against the results of political action affecting payment for your exports.

As an exporter you should, of course, never be politically minded yourself. You should observe, since only by forecasting future political trends can you decide whether trade in any particular political area of the world will be possible for you, and under what conditions. You will hardly need reminding that political forecasting is as hazardous as picking the winner of a horse race, but it is an essential part of any export marketing operation.

Economic Conditions

Nations trade with each other, not only for political reasons, but also for economic ones. What a nation produces dictates to some degree what it will be able both to import and export. Hence a study of any nation's import and

export figures will show you to some extent what you may sell there. Japan, for example, has to import large quantities of raw materials to feed her factories, but Japan needs to import comparatively few consumer products, which she makes herself. Saudi Arabia, on the other hand, exports oil as a raw material, but at present has to import nearly all the manufactured goods she needs. The highly developed nations like the USA and those in Western Europe import raw materials and export manufactures; but they also import manufactures, because as you saw in Part 1, the wealthier nations tend to trade more with each other, because they can all afford to buy as well as sell.

Since the distinction between rich and poor nations is normally expressed in monetary terms, a country's ability to import will be measured in terms of its **currency**. You must know what this will buy in terms of other currencies, and the degree to which it may be converted into your own currency. The strength of the Swiss franc means that Switzerland may buy from virtually any country in the world almost anything she needs; and the same could be said of West Germany, the USA and France, as well as Sweden and Japan. The weakness of the Uruguayan peso, however, prevents the Uruguayans from buying from overseas much more than absolute necessities.

The **economic dynamism** of a nation also reflects its value as a market for imported goods. West Germany, after the war, was left with virtually nothing, but was determined to regain something of her former position in the world. Thanks to hard work and help from her victors, Germany today is one of the world's richest countries, as may be seen from the fact that a German housewife spends a third of her income on luxury goods. Contrast this with the Indian housewife, who has insufficient income to buy the barest necessities of life. You may classify standards of living in many ways, but you should consider those countries with high, middle and low incomes per capita, because this will indicate areas where you are likely to obtain business overseas, although it will not show you any precise demand markets for your exports. It will, however, prevent you from wasting time on parts of the world where you are unlikely to succeed because the economic conditions are an unsurmountable barrier.

Social Conditions

Markets are no more or less than the people in them, so that your most important assessment of any political market must be based on the social and cultural conditions in the world, as they vary between different nations. Moreover, these conditions will start to indicate your demand markets. When you make a study of social conditions overseas you may classify the information under the following headings:

(*a*) *The Population*

Initially you must know the **number of people** with whom you are likely to have to deal in any political market, because this shows the limit of your demand market. You must know where the people live, and how they are broken down by age, sex and physical characteristics. Some population figures are no more than estimates, but the most reliable figures are those issued by the United Nations. The total world population is estimated to be between three and four thousand million, and this is expected to increase to six thousand million by the turn of the century.

(*b*) *The Ability to Buy*

Numbers of people are, however, of little use as a rule unless they are related to an **ability to buy,** which is the first essential requirement of any demand market. Hence you must learn per capita income figures, although these may be misleading, because they do not take into account any means of financing purchases. For example, a poor woman in a poor country may not be able to afford a sewing machine. But she will, if she can borrow the money, even at an exorbitant rate of interest, buy one, because it will give her a means of clothing herself and her family, and of earning money. In some instances people buy more expensive goods because it gives them some sort of status. So to an ability to buy you should add a willingness to buy.

(*c*) *The Social System*

Social systems evolve from history, and studying history will help you to learn the **social customs** of areas important to you, as well as explain the buying motivations of those areas. When you sell to the Turks, for example, you should generally be extra firm, because they themselves, being part of a rigid social order derived from the days of the great Ottoman Empire, are often domineering and uncompromising buyers.

Social systems affect in some cases the values placed on different needs. In many markets in Africa, for example, the male domination in a family will result in a far higher proportion of any disposable income being spent on a man's clothes than on those for the woman. In the USA you might remark that the reverse could be true.

(*d*) *The Family*

To define a family will need different definitions in various parts of the world, families being important because they represent in many areas definite buying groups. Families may stretch from two to two hundred, and be loose or close-knit units. The more advanced the society, the more likely the unit is to be small, but the more often will purchases be made on a unit basis. Variations also occur between the influence of the father or mother on purchases of any kind. In the East, women buy less frequently than the men, whereas in Europe they generally account for a majority of the articles bought. Family relationships also affect ownership, because in many Eastern areas property is on a more communal basis than in the Western world.

(*e*) *The Religious System*

One major effect of different religious systems is the attitude towards marriage and, therefore, towards family life. Wives may be regarded mainly as economic assets; they may have to be purchased. Hence any appeal to a buyer on the grounds of winning a man's love, or a woman's affection, may be an entirely alien approach.

Religion affects when people work and why they work. Friday is a holiday in predominantly Muslim areas; Saturday in mainly Jewish ones; Sunday in Christian ones. It is more important to a non-religious person to earn money than it is to a Hindu, who is more inclined to accept his lot in life, as ordained by a Superior Being.

The influence of religion on life is less strong in more advanced societies than in more primitive ones, but note that in the latter superstition often replaces religion, so that you may find the power of a witch doctor even greater than that of the religious leader. There are some six hundred million Christians in the world, of whom two thirds are Roman Catholic and one third Protestant. There are around 400 million Hindus, and about the same number of Muslims, with nearly as many practising Confucianism, Taoism and Buddhism. You may reflect on the influence of different forms of religion on family planning, in view of the steadily increasing growth of the world's population.

(*f*) *The Tribal System*

Tribal systems exist all over the world. In the more advanced societies the tribes are described as classes, and these are determined by birth, possessions and status, the latter a result in many cases of education. Any tribal system is a powerful buying influence because goods can provide class membership, and are often a symbol of them. In less advanced societies movements between one class and another are often less easy than in the more advanced ones, but in general tribal systems of some kind provide strong motivational buying influences.

(*g*) *The Educational System*

In addition to affecting the tribal differences within societies, the educational system in an area affects buying decisions in two main ways. One is the degree to which people are literate, and able to understand selling messages. The more illiterate a community, the more unpredictable and uncontrollable the buying motivations may be. The second is the importance of the different languages in the world, a factor which affects exporters at every stage of their work. You will need to study languages, because they are the main means of communicating with your potential customers. You should appreciate that there are some three thousand known languages, but happily only about a dozen are of commercial importance. Of these English and French are predominant, along with Spanish, German, Arabic, Russian, Chinese and Portuguese.

A nation's educational system also affects its **management structure,** because where a language has been imposed, so usually has the business pattern. For example, in the former French possessions in Africa, you will find a French system of management, and in former British possessions a British one. In most of the South American countries the management system is similar to that in Spain. But overlaid on these systems, to a greater or lesser degree, is the American management system, adopted especially in modern technical areas such as computers and transport. These systems will affect your ways of doing business, and are essential studies for anyone in export.

The characteristics of political markets are not necessarily confined within political boundaries, and they do not in themselves determine demand markets, but they have enormous influence over the composition of demand markets, and the conditions in them. Hence, only by becoming knowledgeable about these characteristics can you hope to understand how your own demand markets are made up, and what you must do, and not do, to sell to them.

The Conditions in Political Market Areas

Over and above political markets, there are now superimposed certain **trading areas**, consisting of groups of countries acting together for mutual benefit. Because they are composed of political markets, they are called **political market areas**. While they may display many of their individual political characteristics, they inevitably develop characteristics of their own, as did the great empires of the past. The three political market areas of most importance to you at present are as follows.

1. The Planned Economies

This is the name now given to what used to be called the Comecon Countries; it consists of the countries of the Soviet Union (itself a collection of republics), East Germany (known as the Democratic Republic of Germany), Poland, Bulgaria, Rumania, Czechoslovakia, Hungary and Poland. This area has four main trading characteristics:

(*a*) Consumer goods are seldom imported, most imports from the rest of the world consisting of the means of manufacturing consumer goods. With industrial goods the position is similar, although a greater amount of finished industrial goods is imported than of consumer goods.

(*b*) Importing is in the hands of the state, and looked after by state trading organisations, although there is a tendency for individual factories, for example, to be able to specify what they require, rather than always have what the state trading organisations decree.

(*c*) The major demand is for know-how and technical assistance, purchased in the form of the right to manufacture under licence.

(*d*) Some trade is conducted on the basis of barter, owing to a shortage of foreign currency and a reluctance to spend what they have. One interesting recent development, which may serve as a sign of some change in traditional attitudes towards trade, is the introduction of a quality mark on locally made consumer products, indicating the origin of the manufacture, thus giving the consumer some protection against unsatisfactory products.

To develop trade with these Planned Economies you must get to know the state buying organisations, and exercise as much persuasion on them as you can. But you will also need to adapt your methods according to the nationality of those concerned, because there is a considerable difference, for example, in dealing with a Pole as opposed to say a Hungarian or a Russian.

2. The European Economic Community

The EEC consists of nine member states, these being France, West Germany (officially the Federal Republic of Germany), the Netherlands, Belgium, Luxemburg (in this instance counted as a separate state from Belgium), Great Britain, Denmark, Italy and the Republic of Ireland (Eire). The Treaty of Rome, on which the Community has been based, states that it is the intention to create a truly economic community, or common market, and while the political implications have hitherto been kept in the background, the long-term intention is to create a completely integrated community. Associated with the EEC are the remaining countries of Europe, except Spain, with Greece, Turkey, and a number of other Mediterranean countries.

This is a market as large as any in the world, consisting of more than 250 million people, with an extremely high standard of living. The major implication, from a British point of view, is that goods are to be sold freely within the Community—that is, without paying any Customs duties—provided they are of Community origin. This will be achieved by the middle of 1977 in the case of British goods, by which time no customs duties will be payable on any Community goods transferred between one member state and another. Hence it will become one market in this respect for all those within it, and the same duties will be payable on all goods entering the Community, irrespective of the point at which they enter. This one market presents, from the point of the British exporter, two major problems:

(*a*) *Intense competition.* While competition will be intense throughout the Community, it will also be intense in the exporter's domestic market, and under Community rules no protection may be given by means of import restrictions. Thus the opportunities of trading within such a major part of the world's richest markets are matched by the difficulties of resisting the efforts of your competitors from the other states, both from an export and a domestic point of view.

(*b*) *Is the EEC an export market?* You will recall that this question was raised when considering the organisation of an export office in Chapter 3. From a marketing angle, much depends on the extent to which the Community becomes an integrated market for your product, as opposed to nine separate markets.

On the one hand, you may notice the increasing 'Europeanisation' of the Community in such areas as travel, dress, sport and many other leisure pursuits, and your product may need little modification to be sold throughout the Common Market. On the other hand, you may find that the Germans remain German and the French retain all their native characteristics to the extent that you are dealing with separate marketing areas, with idiosyncrasies of their own. You may also feel these will persist within the foreseeable future.

There are, however, signs that the Community will, in many respects, develop at an increasingly fast pace into one market, so that a shirt manufacturer, for example, will need to make and sell what might be termed 'European' shirts, styled and manufactured to European tastes, rather than to British or Italian tastes specifically, because these tastes will become increasingly standardised so far as the Community is concerned. You must make up your own mind which point of view will prevail in your particular case. But you may also consider that in the area of distribution, for example, you should follow the example of Marks and Spencer, who are convinced they can operate in France and Belgium much as they do in Britain; while many other British manufacturers are tying up with local distribution companies in Europe with the intention of creating a Community-wide network of distribution facilities for their products. While in the personal area, you may also reflect that you will have to be prepared to work anywhere in the Community, with the same readiness as you might now be required to work anywhere in Britain.

Since all environments are constantly changing, you should recognise that the EEC is probably changing from a marketing point of view more rapidly and fundamentally than most, and that if it succeeds in anything like the way it is intended, then European characteristics are likely to be far more important than national ones. Hence you may well find that your own demand markets in the Common Market are far more common than you might imagine and, moreover, that this tendency will increase in the future.

3. The Free Trade Areas

In the world today there are several **free trade areas** which, while allowing goods to move freely, are not so advanced in their outlook as the EEC. Their significance is greater to those within these areas than to those seeking to do business with them from outside, although Customs duties will probably have been harmonised in the areas.

The most important of these is probably the **European Free Trade Area** (EFTA), of which Britain was a member until she joined the Community. However, all EFTA members enjoy a close relationship with the EEC, so that for all practical purposes almost the whole of Western Europe can be included as part of the European marketing area. This also extends to some degree to Mediterranean countries, especially Greece and Turkey, although here the Europeanisation process is considerably less marked.

There are many other free trade areas, notably in Central and South America, and the Caribbean. The **Latin American Free Trade Area (LAFTA)** consists of Mexico, along with most of the major countries of South America; while the Central American Republics have formed an organisation called CACM, the **Central American Common Market.** The English-speaking countries in the Caribbean have an organisation known as CARIFTA, or the **Caribbean Free Trade Area.** There are several groupings in Africa organised along similar lines, one example being **UDEAC**, which consists of the Republic of the Congo, Gabon, Cameroon and the Republic of Central Africa. These free trade areas tend to come and go, and some are more effective than others. They make little practical difference to the way in which you conduct business there, but if they develop you will find that area demand markets will become more important, the only one of these so far to have any real significance in this respect being the EEC, apart from the Planned Economies area, where a rather different method of trading is imperative.

The Classification of Demand Markets

Demand markets exist for different products in many parts of the world, but differ from political markets in two main ways:

(*a*) Demand markets are not necessarily confined within political boundaries. A demand market for ship-building equipment, for example, will consist of those people connected with building ships, to a large extent irrespective of the countries in which they are established, their requirements being similar wherever they are located.

(*b*) Demand markets, while often existing within political boundaries, seldom if ever make up the whole of a political market. If you export tractors to France, you are only concerned with the farmers in France, not with all the French people.

An exporter's demand market will vary according to the type of product he exports, the kind of purchasers there are for it, and the way the product is sold. The effect of the local environmental conditions determines the character of each demand market.

The Type of Product

As a rule, demand markets for industrial goods are less subject to local environmental conditions than those for consumer products, because there is a tendency for industrial needs to be more standardised in varying environments. Specifications are increasingly being standardised all over the world, more so in the case of industrial than consumer products. But two important environmental influences which do affect industrial goods are climate and altitude, these affecting the performance of various kinds of machinery, and you might indeed classify demand markets for, say, machinery, by dividing them into those with low, medium and high altitudes; or those with cold, warm and hot climates.

But if you export a consumer product like instant coffee, you will find that the differences between demand markets will be rather more marked, because you will have to cater for differing tastes in the blend of the coffee, as well as varying package requirements. So instead of classifying your demand markets by nationality—e.g. the Swiss or the Australian markets—you could take all the areas where Blend A in Package 1 are accepted as one demand market; then those where Blend B and Package 2 are required as another demand market; and so on, irrespective of their political backgrounds. You should, therefore, work out some forms of classification for your own exports, decide which ones you need, and proceed to determine your demand markets in that way, these being your effective export markets.

The Type of Purchaser

Because environmental differences often play a significant part in determining methods of purchasing, you might need to subdivide your product/packaging demand markets according to the type of consumers you have in various parts of the world. You might, for example, have one classification for your machinery in hot-climate, low-altitude demand markets, but if you apply this to Middle East countries you might have to subdivide by language and perhaps politics. Israel can hardly be included in the Arab states for political reasons. Iran, where they speak Farsi, cannot be included with Egypt, where they speak Arabic.

Exporting consumer products will produce many purchasing differences, because housewives, for example, are often quite different in their approach to a purchase. You might find that housewives in France and Sweden liked basically the same product, although one would need the package in French and the other in Swedish. But the French housewife might well buy for reasons of price and value for money, whereas the Swedish housewife might be more concerned with quality and status. You will find it difficult to promote a consumer product in a demand market unless you take purchasing motives and habits as factors affecting the character of demand markets.

The Way a Product is Bought

For industrial products you might start in this case by dividing your demand markets into those where purchasing is in the hands of state enterprises and those where buying is done by private companies or individuals. You might then group demand markets according to the way contracts are placed. For example, you might group markets like those in Latin America where buying decisions are tedious and slow, as opposed to those in North America where they tend to be much faster. Or you might group markets according to how far inducements, which will be dealt with in more detail in Chapter 14, are necessary, and those where they are seldom asked or accepted.

As regards consumer products, purchasing methods affect several marketing areas. In the case of razor blades, for example, in some demand markets they are sold singly instead of in packets, thus affecting the type of packaging required. Cigarettes may also be sold singly by small boys in the street, instead of in packets in stores.

Hence your aim, when classifying your own demand markets overseas, should be to isolate those customers who:

(*a*) Buy a similar product in all respects.
(*b*) Buy that product for similar basic reasons.
(*c*) Buy in much the same way.

These represent your actual export markets, and they will vary according to the local environment to a greater or lesser extent. But that environment, which so often is the result of political action of some kind, is merely the background to the market, so the classification is not according to the political area but to the demand for your product and the way in which this is expressed.

Export Market Selection

Whether you are exporting for the first time or are seeking to develop your export trade, whether you are exporting an entirely new product, or are trying to develop exports of an existing product, you will be concerned to select the markets in which to do this although, as you have seen, a market is not a political area but a set of customers forming a demand group or market.

To select export demand markets for initial attack or development you should find the answers to the following questions:

1. *Where are there potential customers who need your product?* This will eliminate all areas where business is impossible because your product is not needed. For example, you would not find much demand for heavy clothing in the tropical regions of Africa, except among those who intended to travel to the cooler climates of Europe. You would not find much need for books or magazines among people whose illiteracy was high. But you would note demand markets for heavy clothing in cold climates or where heating was inadequate. You would find a demand for a publication where literacy was high, and people anxious to read.

2. *Where are there potential customers able to buy the product?* This will eliminate areas where people could not afford your product even though they might need it. For example, women in poor parts of the world may need kitchen equipment, but be forced to spend all their available resources on food. This will also eliminate areas where importers do not have sufficient foreign currency to spend on your products, and those areas where the necessary capital to invest in production facilities is lacking. But you would find

demand markets for kitchen equipment in areas where the housewife had a reasonable disposable income, just as you would note demand markets for industrial products where capital was available, and foreign currency not a problem.

3. *Where are potential customers who could be supplied?* Clearly you need to eliminate customers who are not allowed to buy your products. If you export consumer goods, you would find that most of the Planned Economies are forbidden to import them. If you sell consumer goods, such as those loosely classified as hard liquor, you would find most Muslim markets are closed for religious reasons. On the other hand, you can supply industrial products to countries where their import is encouraged because they are not made locally; and you can sell hard liquor to people who are allowed to buy it freely.

4. *Are there any special characteristics about an export product which might be required?* This will indicate what modifications to your product will be required, which will be dealt with in detail in the next chapter. To some degree, however, your selection of possible demand markets will depend on the extent of any modifications and the cost of making them. In some cases this consideration may eliminate certain overseas demand markets.

5. *What competition may be expected, and are there any reasons why certain exports would be preferred?* It is unlikely that you will find a responsive demand market unless your product has some advantage over its competitors in terms of price, delivery, quality, design or innovation. To identify a true demand market you must also be sure you can provide convincing reasons for the purchase of your product, as opposed to a competitive one. You will, of course, never find all these factors in your favour, but you must have some, or you will be unable to break into a demand market.

6. *Are sufficient potential sales possible to make the cost of distributing, selling and promoting the product profitable?* This question will require the preparation of a complete marketing strategy and plan before it can be answered fully, a subject dealt with in Chapter 16 of this book. But it is the crucial, final one which determines whether the possible demand market is worth tackling.

You will appreciate that the number of demand markets which meet all these requirements will be limited, and this serves to emphasise that one of the secrets of success in export is a concentration of effort in a few overseas demand markets. Far too many exporters try to sell everywhere they feel they can obtain some business. The way to real profitability is to limit your efforts to true demand markets, and to tackle these a few at a time.

You may at the outset of this chapter have felt that the amount of local environmental knowledge required was too great ever to be obtained satisfactorily. But you should by now be able to distinguish between the information you must have, and that which is unessential for your purpose. Hence you should make a list of that essential information and disregard the rest. You will inevitably acquire a good deal of general knowledge about any environment, but you must be extremely well informed only about certain aspects, these being those which affect your own trade. This is the only practical way to approach the problem of dealing with the numerous local environmental conditions of the world.

Revision

Cover the page with a sheet of paper and uncover one question at a time.

Answers	*Questions*
	1. What is a political market?
1. A market defined by some political action.	2. What was the former name of Namibia?
2. South-West Africa.	3. What is the population of Hong Kong?
3. About four million.	4. What currency is used in Uruguay?
4. The peso.	5. What is the equivalent of the tribal system in developed countries?
5. The class system.	6. By when should all customs duties between Britain and the EEC be be abolished?
6. The middle of 1977.	7. Which are the world's predominant business languages?
7. English and French.	8. What is LAFTA?
8. The Latin American Free Trade Association.	9. What language is spoken in Iran?
9. Farsi.	10. Who generally dominates a family in Africa?
10. The man of the household.	

Exercises

1. Define the essential differences between political and demand markets.
2. In what ways can different climates affect the exporter?
3. Discuss the implications of the EEC as a market for your goods, and the effect of it on your company.
4. Which are the main characteristics of the Planned Economies, and how do they affect your business relations with them?
5. When you examine local social and cultural conditions, which areas are of major importance to exporters?
6. What marketing uses can you make of export practice, as set out in Part 2 of this book?
7. Make a list of the essential characteristics of any local environment which you would need to know in your particular case.

11

INFORMATION AND RESEARCH

You will appreciate from the previous chapter that there are two main kinds of information about the local overseas environment that you will need to obtain:

1. **Background information.** This is a factor in export marketing you cannot easily control or change. Hence you will need to accept and adapt to the local conditions found in overseas markets.

2. **Specific information** relating to your particular export trade. It is within your power to alter what you export, how you export it and how you sell it. You may alter a trend in a specific export field, and you can start a new one. Hence the environmental conditions in this sphere are to some extent within your control.

The information specified above may be obtained in two basic ways:

(*a*) From published data, which is available to all. This is sometimes referred to as carrying out desk research, because it involves studying existing data from a desk.

(*b*) From specific data obtained by yourself or by someone working for you. This is sometimes referred to as field research, because it involves going out into the field and finding the information.

You will need, therefore, to know the sources of published information because this will indicate where you can obtain it. You will also need to know how to obtain information yourself from overseas. Hence this chapter has been divided into the following sections:

1. Sources of background information
2. Sources of specific information
3. Market research overseas
4. Other forms of overseas research

Sources of Background Information

From the British exporter's point of view, the following sources are some of the most important:

The British Government

For a complete list of government services for exporters you should obtain a copy of their *Export Handbook*, published by the British Overseas Trade Board and issued free of charge. The most important services are:

(*a*) Issuing the *Hints to Businessmen* series of booklets, which contain all the general information about a country that you initially need to know.

(*b*) Running the Computerised Intelligence Service in the form of the

Export Daily Gazette, for which a subscription is payable, and which advises exporters of contracts notified and opportunities open to exporters.

(*c*) Providing names and addresses of buying houses and potential importers established in this country, to whom you may also sell.

(*d*) The provision of two excellent sources of information about overseas conditions in the Statistics and Market Intelligence Library and the Statistics Division of the Department of Trade and Department of Industry.

(*e*) The issuing of a weekly publication called *Trade and Industry*, especially useful since it contains up-to-date details of changes in tariffs, Customs duties and documentation procedures.

(*f*) The work of the Statistical Office of H.M. Customs and Excise, which provides details of Britain's exports and imports for all countries of the world, and issues booklets about the regulations and procedures required from exporters.

(*g*) The work of the Central Office of Information, which exists to publicise British achievements overseas, as well as give out details of British products available for overseas importers.

(*h*) The work of the Export Credit Guarantee Department which, as you saw in Chapter 7, provides information about the commercial standing of importers overseas, as well as a means of insuring against the risks of non-payment for exports from this country.

Names and addresses of all the relevant bodies are included in the *Export Handbook*, which is published annually.

The United Nations

Through its various agencies, of which there are several, the UN publishes a great deal of information gathered in each country of the world, and is generally extremely reliable. For details of what you may obtain, contact the Information Office at 14, Stratford Place, London W.1.

OECD

The Organisation for Economic Cooperation and Development also issues a great deal of information about international trade. Its headquarters are in Paris, but you may find its publications at H.M. Stationery offices in Britain.

The EEC

As you might expect, the Community issues a great deal of information about its activities, regulations and so on. To obtain any of this information you should contact their Information Office at 23, Chesham Street, London, S.W.1.

The Chambers of Commerce

In addition to handling the certification of documents, most Chambers of Commerce take an active part in promoting British exports. A list of British chambers of commerce is in the *Export Handbook* and in *Croner's Directory*; while you can also consult the Association of British Chambers of Commerce at 11, Dean Farrar Street, London, S.W.1.

The CBI

The Confederation of British Industry is anxious to help companies to export, and you will find a good deal of useful information is available from this body, which includes the private and public sectors of industry in its membership. Contact the CBI at 21, Tothill Street, London, S.W.1.

Trade Associations

In whichever trade you operate, you will almost certainly find that it has a trade association and, moreover, that it will probably have a special section devoted to export, such as the British Business Equipment Association does.

Other Official Bodies

There are several of these, most being concerned in some way with providing information for exporters. They are listed in the *Export Handbook*, but you might take note of the Institutes of Export, Marketing, Directors, and Management, as well as the Institute of Practitioners in Advertising. Most have head offices in London, with provincial branches. You might also think in terms of the Export Clubs, of which there are currently about 40 in the country, loosely sponsored by the BOTB.

Embassies of Other Countries

Although their primary purpose is to push the exports of their own countries in Britain, foreign embassies have much useful information about their own countries which they will supply. They should always be contacted if you are visiting their countries for the first time, while they are useful sources of information about local companies seeking business from Britain.

The Banks

All the major banks issue a great deal of useful information about overseas countries and the conditions in them, as well as details of financial dealings with importers.

The Media

There is so much information available to exporters in the media in the United Kingdom that it is necessary to be selective in any studying. But you might note, in particular, papers like *The Times* and the *Financial Times*, which publish excellent surveys from time to time on overseas countries. You might also study *The Economist*, published weekly. More specifically you should read *Export*, the monthly publication of the Institute of Export, and the monthly *Export Times*. *Marketing* is another magazine of interest, and so are the international news magazines like *Time* and *Newsweek*. You will also occasionally learn much about conditions in other countries from television programmes.

Books

Go to your own public library and you will find a mass of books about other countries, which can provide much helpful background material. No exporter who aims to be a real professional ever neglects reading as widely as possible about other countries. For this reason there is, at the end of this book, a bibliography showing the main books about export published in English, with an indication of the areas each covers.

All the above information is available to you in this country, but when you are overseas you will also find many sources of information in the form of existing data, and you should think in terms of the following sources.

Overseas Government Statistics

Every government in the world publishes some statistics, and you should consult the BOTB for the details of where you may contact these sources overseas.

Local British Chambers of Commerce

There are, in most countries, Chambers of Commerce set up to encourage trade between the countries, such as the British Swiss Chamber of Commerce in Zürich and Lausanne. The *Export Handbook* gives a list of these.

UK Embassies and High Commissions

In all British government offices overseas there is a Commercial Section, whose task it is to provide British visitors to that country with all the information they need. The best policy is to advise them, via the Export Services Branch of the BOTB, of your visit and tell them what you wish to know. They will then prepare the information and have it ready for you on your arrival.

Local Banks

As in this country, banks in overseas markets are knowledgeable about local conditions, and you should obtain from them as much information as you can. Your own bank in Britain will have local banks, or branches, with whom it habitually works, and will provide you with the necessary introductions to them.

Local Media

If you read the local media when you are overseas you will learn a great deal about local conditions. Even if you cannot read the local language, you can still learn a great deal by studying the advertisements, which will tell you what is being sold and promoted. You might also watch the local television stations for the same reason, and listen to the local radio programmes.

As you can see, there is a great deal of information available to you both in your country and overseas about local environmental conditions, and a variety of sources of such information. Your main problem is to handle it in such a way that it does not become a burden, which means that in most cases the source is more important than the actual information. But it will mostly be of a general nature, and while you may come across details applying directly to your own particular export business, you will find this is limited. Even so, there are certain sources of specific information you should note.

Sources of Specific Information

Government Services

You may ask the Export Services Branch of the BOTB to carry out a survey applicable to your own type of business. This they will do through the Commercial Sections of the Embassies and High Commissions overseas. They will also, in certain circumstances, help with the cost of having some market research done locally on subjects of special interest to you.

Published Surveys

The most important sources here are the surveys of specific industries published by the Economist Intelligence Unit, which you can buy from them. These probably get closer to defining your demand markets than almost anything else published.

Local Buying Organisations

As you will see in the next chapter, there are many local buying organisations of overseas importers in Britain, and they will tell you whether your product is likely to succeed or not in the countries they represent, and the outlets for which they buy.

Local Commission Agents and Distributors

If you use agents in overseas markets, as described in Chapter 13, you will be able to consult them for their views on market opportunities and details about possible demand markets. But remember that these intermediaries may not necessarily be knowledgeable about research, and because their main function is to sell, may tend to be over-optimistic about prospects, as is the habit with many salesmen.

Thus you may be able to obtain some specific information about your own demand markets, although most of this you will have to obtain by carrying out research yourself in the overseas areas concerned.

Market Research Overseas

A major part of an exporter's need for information is to establish his demand markets overseas, so that market research is the main form of research he is likely to undertake. There are three main ways in which such research may be carried out.

1. By Means of Trade Missions

The BOTB encourages and helps British businessmen to visit overseas markets on official trade missions. These have the advantage that many sources of information are available to exporters which might otherwise be closed to them. On such missions you will meet senior government officials, senior local businessmen, and you will have the opportunity of talking to people, therefore, who will be able to indicate opportunities for you. Such missions are also a means of actually obtaining business, as well as doing some market research, and the cost is generally rather less than attempting to go on your own.

2. Personal Visits

It is important to remember that a personal visit is not research in the strict sense, because it is research by observation, and you may be 100 per cent wrong in your conclusions. For example, if you visit the Netherlands, you might meet several Dutchmen who speak English, and conclude that all

Dutchmen speak English, which is not so. Hence much will depend on whom you meet and how accurate they are in what they tell you, as well as how well you phrase the questions.

The tendency with this form of research is for it to be based on opinion rather than on fact. But even so it is a form of research much practised by exporters, and has the prime advantage that it enables you to see for yourself what local conditions are like, as they apply to your own particular export business.

If you visit trade fairs and exhibitions overseas you will certainly be able to see what competitive products are on the local market, and at what prices. For example, a visit to the Furniture Exhibition in Cologne will give you an accurate picture of the furniture market in Europe. Moreover, a great deal of export business is gained by exporters visiting overseas markets themselves, sizing up the opportunities and then taking advantage of them. After all, export is well suited to those with entrepreneurial abilities, while you may care to reflect that one order is worth a great many research reports.

3. Carrying out Market Research Overseas

To define any demand market there is, however, no substitute for well planned and executed market research. But remember, research will not make the decisions for you. It will only provide the facts on which you may base your decisions.

Worthwhile market research always has specific objectives, and usually needs to be reduced to fairly simple terms, often in the form of hypotheses. For example, to find out by research what price you should sell your product at in Spain, you might define this by saying, 'If I find the price can be between 1000 and 1500 pesetas, then I am in business; but if it is less than this then the Spanish market will not provide me with any worthwhile business.' This clearly indicates the scope of the research, and the objective will, in this case, quite simply be to find out factually if you can sell at prices between those two limits.

If you are not specific about your proposed research you will find:

(*a*) You are likely to waste a good deal of money, because you obtain information not strictly relevant to the problem to be researched.

(*b*) Information is likely to be inaccurate, because the purpose of the research became blurred.

Limitations on Market Research Overseas

There are certain limitations on doing market research in other parts of the world, of which you should be aware. These include:

(*a*) Whereas in Britain and America and some parts of Europe, any systematic approach to business by the use of research is acceptable, in some areas this is not so. In Latin America, for example, people will often say how useful they consider market research to be, but in reality not believe its results, unless these happen to coincide with their own opinions.

(*b*) In many developing countries local business people hesitate to admit there are certain areas they do not understand, one being market research. Hence they have a tendency to make up their minds what to do, irrespective of what facts the research produces.

(*c*) In many parts of the world, mainly the developing areas, questions are either not answered or are answered incorrectly. In some areas this is because of fear of anyone seemingly in authority. In others, because the desire to please influences the answers.

(*d*) In those parts of the world where accurate statistics are hard to find the base of the sample on which the research is built may be inaccurate.

Hence you should approach any research overseas with some caution in all but the most developed countries. Here you may proceed, secure in the knowledge that you can obtain a truly quantitative answer that will provide you with a real assessment of your demand markets.

When you commission market research overseas you need to be aware of certain problems:

(*a*) *Language.* If you have market research carried out in another language, you must ensure that the people doing it fully understand what you are seeking and that they use the correct words in their own language. This means re-writing the questions; while you should always have the re-written version put back into English to make sure nothing vital has been altered. One example of how easy it is to make a mistake with language is the use of the words 'alcoholic drinks'. What drinks are included in such a term varies from country to country; beer in Greece for instance is not considered alcoholic, whereas in Britain it would be included under such a heading.

(*b*) *Scope of the research.* Unless you are careful, there are certain countries where a simple basic research ends by being transformed into a full-scale enquiry, far greater than was originally intended. The French, for example, usually wish to elaborate research proposals and to discover reasons behind questions, which you may have decided were unnecessary. This generally increases the cost, so you must be firm in sticking to the prime purpose of an overseas research, limiting its scope to that purpose, which as you have seen already is best based on testing some hypothesis.

(*c*) *Multi-market research.* You will naturally wish to try to compare research results from different markets overseas, in order to decide which markets would be most receptive to your product. This would be important, for example, in the Common Market countries. But if you do try to carry out multi-market research, remember that it is usually a highly complex operation involving a carefully chosen form of central control; a complete understanding by all concerned of the purpose and scope of the research; an ability to re-write this in terms of local conditions; and a predetermined uniform way of measuring the results. It has been found that this cannot easily be achieved by mail, and that personal visits to each country concerned are necessary.

(*d*) *Local research facilities.* These vary enormously from country to country. In most of the developed countries there are competent, well-organised research agencies, able to carry out market research in the approved manner. You can obtain the names of such organisations from the BOTB or organisations such as the Market Research Society in London and the European Industrial Research Association. But before you commission research from research agencies overseas you should visit them, and brief them on the spot to obtain the best results.

If you use a research agency in Britain you may feel that they should be in charge of any overseas research. Many British research agencies have working arrangements with agencies in other countries, especially in Europe and America, and this is a good way of doing market research in those places.

You may also use the research department of an advertising agency, because most such agencies include research as part of the facilities offered to their clients. Large international agencies can handle multi-market research in many areas, while local advertising agencies usually have research facilities you can use. In smaller and less developed countries you must be wary of bogus claims to be able to carry out research, especially where the use of research techniques is, as you have seen, often unacceptable to the local people.

When you wish to find out details of your demand markets, and when you have to ascertain the composition of these demand markets, you should always use market research whenever possible, because you need to know facts, not merely opinions. And because environmental conditions vary so much in the world, as you have seen, you must get to know the facts as they affect your export business. In this way alone can you prepare any soundly based marketing strategy or plans.

Other Forms of Overseas Research

So far the emphasis has been on overseas market research, because most exporters need to know all they can about their demand markets as a first priority. But there are other forms of research which many exporters will need to use.

Product Research

This covers the design, development and testing of new products, as well as the pricing of these products; in the case of consumer goods, the packaging may also need to be tested. You will wish to research the acceptability of colours, trade names, marks and other means of identification. All the points which will be covered in the next chapter about the export itself may have to be researched before finally being adopted, particularly where modifications to an existing product have to be made in order to establish its credibility or permit its sale.

Distribution Research

In Chapter 13 the various channels of distribution are covered, but you may well need to establish which will be the best for you to use. Only research will give you the facts about channels of distribution in any overseas market. You may also need to carry out research to establish the extent of your distribution before, for example, embarking on an advertising campaign. You may need to check on the activities of a distributor to see if he is giving you the distribution you require from him, or to show him where he needs to concentrate.

Customer Research

In export you are, especially with industrial goods, often selling to customers you do not meet, which is not always the case in the domestic market;

whereas with consumer products in both cases you expect the final customers to be unknown to you. In both, research is invaluable for finding out what the customers think of your product. Market research will give you the answers for consumer goods. But there is no reason why you cannot also carry out research among your customers when selling industrial goods, and more exporters could with profit think along these lines.

Promotion Research

When you are investing money in various forms of promotion, as will be explained in Chapter 15, you may wish to find out how successful this has been, or where the promotion is going wrong. You can use research to provide you with the answers, and this is particularly important when you are attacking a major demand market overseas. You can find out how suitable your promotion themes are, how far the media you use are reaching the customers you want, and what effect your promotion is having on purchasing habits.

In all these areas you will use variations of techniques of research which are fairly common throughout the world. That is to say you may use some or all of the following:

(*a*) Specially conducted surveys among a sample of the population to enable you to project figures on a wider scale. These surveys may be carried out by personal interviewing using questionnaires, or by post.

(*b*) Continuous audits by specialist companies, generally used in the grocery and chemist fields on the retail outlets.

(*c*) New product testing on selected panels of consumers, in either structured or unstructured forms.

(*d*) Motivational studies to discover people's hidden, as opposed to their stated, motives for purchasing.

Every exporter should, therefore, allocate some part of his resources to research overseas. This should be on a continuing basis, and is a cost to be taken into account when preparing a total cost of exports on which to base a selling price. You will appreciate from the previous chapter just how dangerous it is to rely on 'hit and miss' methods in export, because of the innumerable variables in export marketing caused by local environmental conditions. You will understand from this chapter that the means of obtaining the required information about conditions overseas exists in many forms. If you wish to succeed in export you will of necessity have to make use of many of them.

Revision

Cover the page with a sheet of paper and uncover one question at a time.

Answers	*Questions*
	1. What is meant by desk research?
1. Examining information which is already published.	2. Who publishes the *Export Handbook*?

Answers	*Questions*
2. The British Overseas Trade Board.	3. Where can you find statistics on Britain's export and import trade?
3. At the Statistical Office of H.M. Customs and Excise.	4. What is the CBI?
4. The Confederation of British Industry.	5. What is OECD?
5. The Organisation for Economic Cooperation and Development.	6. Who is least fitted to carry out research?
6. The salesman.	7. Which body publicises British goods overseas?
7. The COI or Central Office of Information.	8. What are quantitative results?
8. Results based on statistics.	9. In which publications will you find a summary of each country's conditions?
9. The *Hints to Businessmen* series.	10. Which main British newspapers publish surveys of local conditions overseas?
10. *The Times* and *Financial Times*.	

Exercises

1. Does field research have any value in exporting, and in what way does it differ from desk research?
2. In which main areas will the British government provide information for exporters?
3. Explain how you would set about obtaining specific information about an overseas demand market.
4. If you decide to do some multi-market research in Europe, what sort of problems might you expect to meet?
5. Which ways do you have of carrying out market research in overseas markets?
6. 'There is too much information available about the local environment'. Discuss the implications of this statement for the exporter.

12

PRODUCTS AND PRODUCTION

Having examined the local environmental conditions, you must next consider the product you intend to export to your demand markets, whether you make this yourself, buy it from others, or allow others to make it for you locally. Any product is the result of using a skill. If, for example, you make equipment used in open-cast mining, your real skill lies in knowing how to move earth. Should your demand market for the equipment diminish, you could apply your skill to satisfy other demand markets which require equipment to move earth, such as that used for building highways or clearing building sites. In export you use your skills to produce products which have to satisfy one of two basic requirements:

1. A product which differs radically from that sold on your domestic market, because there would otherwise be no demand for it overseas.
2. A product which may require certain modifications to it so that it will meet local environmental requirements, but which will remain basically the same as your domestic product.

The first requirement is usually a difficult one to meet. For example, if you make electric locomotives, you might need to alter these to diesel-driven ones because of a lack of electricity in the demand markets concerned. While you might use basically similar skills, you would in this case probably suffer in two ways. First, you would not benefit from any economies of scale of production, which you usually obtain when you add export to domestic business. Second, you would lose the advantages of operating on a worldwide scale, because you are selling what is in many ways a different product. It is possible to succeed in export by making a product specially for overseas markets, and not selling it domestically, but most companies prefer to stay away from such operations because of the production problems involved.

The second requirement—making some modifications to a product sold domestically in order to make it match the local demand market requirements—is one which most exporters can face, since it is seldom too difficult to achieve, and in most cases is a worthwhile operation. You might, for example, be able to adapt your locomotive to operate in varying climates or at different altitudes, whereas changing it from electric to diesel power would be too fundamental a change to contemplate profitably.

Where you manufacture for export markets depends on several factors, such as gaining access to markets protected by high tariff barriers; the economics of extending your home plant to accommodate increased production for export; or the necessity of selling know-how to enable others to make your product for you because its import is forbidden for some reason.

In addition to modifying the product itself, you may also need to modify its presentation, and in the case of consumer products this would include alterations to its packaging. Such modifications will of course add to your costs of production, which will in turn affect your export price. Hence this chapter has been divided into the following sections:

1. Product modifications for export
2. Manufacturing overseas
3. Selling know-how overseas
4. Product presentation for export
5. Price as affected by the local environmental conditions

Product Modifications for Export

There are some products which require virtually no modification for sale in overseas markets. One example would be maggots exported for the use of fishermen in Belgium and the Netherlands in the same state as they are bred in Britain. Other examples would be any basically national products, like bowler hats, or Union Jacks, or even livestock in the shape of pedigree bulls.

For most manufactured products, however, some modifications are usually necessary, and these may be as follows:

The Main Purpose of a Product

A bicycle is used in the Netherlands as a means of transport, whereas in the USA it is used more as a means of pleasure. Hence you might need to add a small motor to the bicycle for sale in the Netherlands, which would be less necessary for the American market. Another example might be umbrellas, used both to keep off the wet and the sun in many markets, this necessitating some modification to the material used to cover the frames.

The Secondary Purpose of a Product

A radio, for example, is used universally for receiving news or some form of entertainment. But in certain parts of the world it is also a status symbol. This requires the set to be housed in a cabinet of brighter colours and maybe of more modern design than where its use is purely utilitarian.

The Durability and Quality of a Product

In Europe women demand clothes which last longer than those worn by their opposite numbers in North America, because European women are seldom so concerned with the latest fashion and tend to be more thrifty by nature. High quality is important anywhere that durability is important; it is less important in parts of the world where frequent renewals of the product take place.

The Design of a Product

Design often needs modifying to suit local tastes, and is one of the most common areas where product modifications are required. Some colours are either acceptable, or totally unacceptable, in various parts of the world. White, for example, is the colour of mourning in many Eastern markets, but a generally popular colour in most European markets.

The Operation and Maintenance of a Product

Much will depend in this case on the supply of skilled labour. A printing press of some kind may well need modifying if there is likely to be an absence of people able to maintain it in working order. Moreover, in many parts of the world maintenance is still not considered to be of importance, with the result that machinery is often run into the ground. Where after-sales service is necessary, modifications may be able to reduce the need for it, or even almost abolish it altogether.

The Basic Raw Materials

Clothing in hot and humid climates is preferably made of cotton, not of man-made synthetic fibres, so you may well need to vary the basic raw materials used in the manufacture of your export product.

The Finished State

Consider a product like a laxative. In some parts of the world it may have to be much stronger to have any real effect than in others. You have already seen that an instant coffee may have to be produced in varying blends to suit local tastes. What is considered a hot sauce in Europe would be felt to be almost insipid in many Central American markets.

The Method of Manufacture

In areas where there is a preponderance of mass-produced articles, there is often a demand for hand-made ones. One British exporter, for example, concentrates on selling hand-knitted sweaters, at a high price, to those who want something different from the normal machine-made sweaters.

The Style of the Product

All style is a highly individual taste. The Scandinavians, for example, tend to prefer textured glass, while the Germans prefer pure shapes. But some styles may be exported, British-style furniture, for example, being sold at present in several Middle East countries.

The Specifications of a Product

With the gradual adoption of the metric system and a considerable amount of standardisation of specifications, the need for adapting specifications tends to become less, although there are still areas where this is an important product factor. Voltages, for example, still vary, as do the types of plugs and sockets used for electrical apparatus.

The Size of a Product

There are three areas where the size of a product varies according to local conditions. One is the size itself, a saw for example, varying in size according to the type of wood on which it is used. Second, there is the size of the user, clothing for example varying according to race and type of person. Third, there is the ability to buy, which means that well-off people may buy economy sizes, whereas poorer people have to buy less economically by taking the smallest size of a product.

Local Legal Requirements

Most countries have differing laws affecting what may or may not be sold. For example, in most Scandinavian countries electrical apparatus needs to be protected more strictly against the possibility of fire than in many other countries, the reason being of course that wooden houses present a greater fire hazard than brick ones. The Americans have now introduced more stringent regulations affecting anti-pollution measures which have to be incorporated into vehicles.

None of the above modifications, however, affects your basic demand markets because you are still selling to people with similar needs and wants. All you are doing is to modify your product to suit a number of local requirements. And these, in a rapidly shrinking world market place, are tending to diminish. As examples of extremely standardised world products you might think of traffic lights, which are nearly always the same wherever they are installed, and the more common forms of road signs.

As an exporter you must be aware of the local conditions, and ensure that your product conforms to them whenever this is necessary, or desirable, from the customer's point of view. You cannot, for instance, ignore the fact that the Germans prefer oak furniture, whereas most Britons go for walnut or mahogany. If you are designing a new product for export, you should try to produce it so that as few local modifications as possible are required, a point which becomes increasingly important in the Common Market where, as has already been suggested, there is a tendency for many products to become 'Europeanised'.

You must always be aware of opportunities which you might at first fail to recognise. For example, you would hardly think it possible to export sand to a country like Saudi Arabia. Yet a certain kind of sand, used to test cement, is sent there, because none of the local sand is suitable.

Manufacturing Overseas

As you will see from Chapter 16, in which the strategy of exporting is considered, where you manufacture is a matter of policy, but there are several reasons why you may elect to have your product made elsewhere, and not supply export markets from your domestic base.

(*a*) Some demand markets may prohibit the importation of a product for political or economic reasons. Brazil, for example, now manufactures locally nearly all consumer goods and only allows imports of essential capital goods and raw materials.

(*b*) A local factory may be able to deliver more quickly and economically than the domestic factory, because of the distances involved, transport problems and so on. The congestion of ports, as at present with Lagos in Nigeria, favours those foreign products which are made in Nigeria. The size of the North American market is such that supplies sent from Europe will usually take that much longer than when manufactured locally within the USA.

(*c*) The cost of raw materials and labour may be lower than in the exporter's own country, so that it is cheaper to manufacture overseas.

(*d*) Modifications may be more economical in other factories, because they do not interrupt any domestic production lines.

(*e*) As a matter of financial policy investment in overseas manufacturing plant may be better than extending a factory at home.

Hence the source of supply of your exports has to be decided from the outset, and you should consider this in relation to the long-term aims of the company, the resources available, and the strength of your various demand markets. When you manufacture overseas you will find three main options:

1. You may build a factory in another country to manufacture the product for sale in that country.

2. You may set up a factory overseas to supply a number of countries in that area. This may be important in the EEC, because a factory on the other side of the Channel can greatly help distribution.

3. You may set up a factory in conjunction with a local company, in the form of a joint venture. You might do this in, say, Zaïre, and this is becoming, in developing countries particularly, a common method of operation, since it allows local people a stake in the business.

Which of these options you choose depends on the product, the countries concerned, and your own policy, but you must ask yourself:

(*a*) Will the prospective return on the capital involved represent an adequate contribution to the company's profits?

(*b*) Is there anything better you might do with the money involved?

(*c*) Whether the future of the country where local production facilities are established seems reasonably secure—a question you might, for example, consider if you were setting up a factory in the Republic of the Argentine at present.

(*d*) Whether the demand markets are sufficiently strong and stable to provide an adequate outlet for the goods to be produced in the local factory.

(*e*) How far the policy of the company has developed towards becoming what is in effect a multi-national company, because as soon as local factories are set up overseas you start to embark on a multi-national course of action.

When you have taken a decision to have local manufacturing facilities overseas, you will find that setting up the factory becomes a highly specialised and skilled operation, and you will be advised to use specialists in this field. Some of the factors they will consider are:

1. The site of the factory.
2. The availability of raw materials.
3. The supply of labour.
4. The arrangements for distribution of the products.
5. The selling arrangements; for example, will a local sales company also have to be established?
6. The conditions under which the earnings from the factory may be remitted to the parent company.
7. The ability of local management and your own ability to work harmoniously with that local management.
8. The degree of control, in such areas as quality control, specifications, design and service arrangements, which you will need to exercise, and the amount of autonomy granted to the local people.

The tendency has always been for factories to be set up in a company's largest overseas market. British companies have relied mainly on Commonwealth countries, such as Australia, Canada, South Africa and India; only the largest have tackled the USA or Japan, or the larger Latin American countries such as the Argentine, Brazil and Mexico. Many, however, have, and are, establishing factories in Europe, and there is now a tendency to concentrate on Common Market countries in view of the growth of the European Community. That pattern will undoubtedly continue, with the addition of the major developing countries, since these can see the benefits of having production facilities provided by companies from the more developed world. Hence, if you aim to become one of the major world companies, you will have to consider manufacturing locally in some overseas markets as a part of your company's development.

Selling Know-How Overseas

Instead of exporting products you may export skills, or what is commonly called know-how. This entails your product being manufactured overseas by a third party. You can also sell the know-how of a service. There are several ways in which you may sell the manufacturing know-how, of which you should note:

(*a*) Establishing a manufacturing plant overseas and, having done this, taking no further part in the operation. This is often done in the Planned Economies, who like to buy the skills to manufacture outright, and do so for a cash sum.

(*b*) Establishing a manufacturing plant overseas, but taking a continuing interest in it by supplying raw materials or components for the plant. You may also agree to supply further skills, and for this you will receive royalties as well as an initial sum.

(*c*) Licensing a third party to manufacture and sell under licence from yourself, and for this you will also receive royalties, both on the manufacturing and sales sides.

Any such deals have to be negotiated with care for several reasons:

1. You must see that your product is manufactured to the same quality as in your own factory or your reputation may suffer, and sales of your product in other parts of the world be affected.
2. You must ensure that the rights to manufacture are not purchased with the intention of keeping the product off the market.
3. That your own patent rights are protected, although you will be selling those rights for the country concerned.

Normally licensing deals are negotiated on the principle of an initial down payment by the licensee, together with a minimum annual royalty on all sales made, plus a royalty of between 5 and 10 per cent of the actual sales. In return for this you will agree to supply any further skills if required, and the object of these kinds of agreements is that both sides shall in effect contribute towards the success of the project. For example, a pen manufacturer has found that he can sell in Sri Lanka by supplying skills and components to a local manufacturer, where the pens are sold under their original brand name. In this case the British manufacturer receives royalties for providing the skills, as well as making a small profit on selling those components which cannot be obtained locally.

You will appreciate, therefore, that the value of any licensing deal will be in direct proportion to the skills involved, the name and reputation of the manufacturer, and the importance of the brand name or mark, as well as the protection afforded by the patent. You are in effect selling your property, so that you should always make sure the patents are registered wherever you are likely to sell, or license anyone else to sell. You will need to register patents separately in each country of the world, but there is now a good deal of protection afforded to holders of patents on a worldwide scale. You will need the services of a good patent agent, which you can obtain from the Institute of Patent Agents, at Staple Inn Buildings, High Holborn, London, W.C.1. There used to be an International Bureau for the Protection of Industrial Property in Geneva, but this is now known as the World International Property Organisation, or WIPO. This organisation will help you to apply for registration of your patents in any other countries which subscribe to it, at the same time as you register the patent in the United Kingdom or within 12 months of that date.

When you sell a service overseas, you will probably be paid fees of some kind for helping to establish that service locally, but you may also operate on some kind of royalty system, where the use of a name or patented operation is involved. The areas where the sale of service skills are most important are transport, tourism, the construction industries, and the computer industry. Management training is another field where money may be made by selling service skills, and several countries require the establishment of information, export or even tax systems, and are willing to pay for experts to handle such work. A typical example of service selling is that of two quantity surveyors who sold a system in the USA which they had invented, which involved the tendering for construction work on the basis of a bill of quantities supplied by the quantity surveyor.

Clearly the increasing needs of developing countries in skills of all kinds opens the way for successful selling of services provided by those from the more developed countries, and you should concentrate on these newer, developing countries if you feel you have a saleable service skill.

Product Presentation for Export

The way a product is presented for sale overseas will play a significant part in its success, and the first thing you must always do is to ensure that your product conforms in every way to local technical specifications. The BOTB helps British exporters in this respect by paying half the costs of running the British Standards Institution, at 2 Park Street, London, W.1. The export side is handled by the BSI's Technical Help to Exporters section, known as THE, whose function is to guide you through a maze of local requirements which you may not realise even exist. If you wish to contact THE you may do so at Maylands Avenue, Hemel Hempstead, Herts.

The main areas you need to know cover local regulations and approval systems; overseas standards; test certificates; and inspection routines—all of which vary from country to country. THE publishes technical digests in many of these areas, as well as English versions of many of the more important foreign regulations and codes of practice. You may also become an associate member of THE.

Two other useful bodies are the Design Council, at 28 Haymarket, London W.1., concerned with the packaging and design of both industrial and consumer products; and the Research Association of the Paper and Board, Printing and Packaging Industries (PIRA) in Leatherhead, Surrey.

The main areas where you will be concerned with the packaging of exports are as follows.

The Company Name

While the country of origin of a product may become less important, the name of the manufacturer or supplier becomes increasingly important because of greater competition in all product categories all over the world. After all, a customer will gain confidence if the imported product he has purchased is from a company with a name he knows, both because this is probably a guarantee of quality, and because if anything goes wrong with the product he knows whom to contact to have it put right or even replaced. If you see the name of Heinz on a food product you know it is made by a company with a worldwide reputation. Likewise with the name Nestlé. There are innumerable examples of companies which have sold on the strength of their company names, Rolls-Royce being perhaps the most notable example.

When a company name is long or involved, the use of the initials can be most effective; few people refer to Imperial Chemical Industries as anything other than ICI. You may have noticed how Guest, Keen and Nettlefold have adopted the use of GKN as a company symbol. Even more advanced are nicknames, and you may have noticed the encouragement of Marks and Spencer in the use of 'Marks and Sparks' as a sign of almost affection.

Your aim should be to have your company name associated with a particular product. If, for example, you think of a diesel engine you would think of Perkins; if you think of pens you automatically think of Parker; and if you say aircraft for civil use you would probably add Boeing or Douglas. You should adopt a distinctive style of letter for a name or initials; the R.R. of Rolls-Royce and the GKN of Guest, Keen and Nettlefold are two examples of the value of special styles when using the company's initials.

The Product Name

Brand names of products are a feature of the modern marketing scene, but brand names for export markets are often a problem, because the name may have an unfortunate meaning in a foreign language. It may also be difficult to say. The modern tendency is to choose a word without any specific meaning, like Kodak, and attach to it the meaning of a product. Before deciding on a new brand name, have it checked for meaning and suitability in any country where it is likely to be used. One classic example is Ford's Mercury, nicknamed the Big M, which has a most unfortunate meaning in Spanish.

Where different models of a product are introduced, you may use numbers, which are easily translated into other languages. The Boeing 707, the Peugot 504, and the DC10 are typical examples of the good use of numbers as part of a brand name.

You may also encourage the use of nicknames, such as the Jumbo, but you must take care not to oversell a brand name or it may become used in a generic sense; the Jumbo jet is often taken to mean any large jet; the Frigidaire is often used to describe any refrigerator; just as a Hoover is used to describe a vacuum cleaner. Nevertheless, brand names are valuable marketing tools, Coca Cola sales having for years depended on the affection with which the name is regarded, even if it is often reduced to 'Coke', which in turn has now become a registered trade mark.

Trade Marks

In areas where literacy is low, a trade mark assumes great importance, and few people are able to forget the ICI 'roundel', or the mark in which the initials are placed. Ideally, trade marks should consist of familiar signs of some kind, although most of these have already been used.

Both trade marks and trade names can, and should, be registered. You should contact the Institute of Trade Mark Agents at 69, Cannon Street, London E.C.4, for the name of a good trade mark agent.

Packaging

The number and variety of products which are now packaged continues to grow, as customers demand that products shall be both protected against dirt and damage, and at the same time be instantly recognisable. You may need to vary the amount of protection given to a product according to climatic conditions, especially extreme heat or humidity.

You may also need to vary the wording used on packages to suit local languages. You may have to alter the colours, because some countries have strong prejudices for and against certain colours. Gold is a lucky colour in many parts of the East, as is red.

When the size of the unit of sale varies, so will the package, as you have already seen with the case of razor blades. Aspirins are often sold in one's or two's, and must be packaged accordingly.

Remember that in many of the poorer parts of the world packages have a value in themselves. A glass jar with a screw-top lid, for example, is a valuable container, so a product may well be bought because of its package. When a package for export is designed you should consider its re-use value as an additional selling point.

Legal Requirements

All packaging will generally be subject to local legal regulations, especially in the case of food and pharmaceutical products. In Spain, for example, all imported food packages must show clearly on the label the country of origin, the contents, the nett weight of each ingredient, the date of preparation, and the factory of origin. All lettering must be in Spanish, and of a readable size. In most cases packages have to be submitted to the local authorities before they can be sold, so that you must always check to see that this has been done before allowing a packaged product to be sold in another country.

If you look at your product through the eyes of the local customer overseas you will appreciate how important presentation is in all its aspects, because the customer may not be especially interested in your product, but is generally prepared to be if you have made it as attractive as possible. The protective aspects of packaging are today generally taken for granted. It is the appearance that matters. So make sure that your company name, the product name, the trade mark, and the package are all both suitable and familiar in every demand market.

Price and Local Environmental Conditions

You will recall that the export price of a product was first examined as far back as Chapter 3, and that it has been modified in subsequent chapters. So far, however, no attempt has been made to consider the final export price, and this cannot be done until the preparation of the final marketing plan.

So far the factors affecting price have been as follows:

1. The basic costs of producing the goods, depending on the quantity manufactured, and the minimum contribution to the company's profit the product is expected to make, if it is to use company money to advantage, as set out in Chapter 3.
2. The administration costs of an export office, dealt with in Chapter 4.
3. The transport and documentation costs to be taken into account, as set out in Chapter 5.
4. The costs involved in seeing that the goods are insured in transit, as in Chapter 6.
5. The costs involved in obtaining payment from overseas for the goods; the cost of credit; insuring against non-payment; and the use of company resources, as in Chapter 7.
6. Allowances for possible legal costs, as shown in Chapter 9.
7. Costs involved in obtaining all the required information about the local environmental conditions, as dealt with in Chapter 11.
8. The possible costs involved in modifying a product or its presentation, as shown in this chapter.

However, you will still have to consider:

9. Selling and distribution costs, as set out in Chapters 13 and 14.
10. Promotion costs, as shown in Chapter 15.

In the meantime, you need also to add some consideration of what the local demand market will bear, because this will tend to show you the maximum and minimum extents of your export price range. And this range will probably vary from market to market, your object being to attain the maximum price whenever possible. To arrive at these maximum and minimum price ranges for any one demand market you must consider the following points.

Competitive Prices

You must be able to assess your chances of success against the competition in respect of:

(*a*) The merits and de-merits of the product itself.

(*b*) The terms of delivery of these products, as well as the method of distribution.

(*c*) The payment terms you offer, which may make it easier for your customers to buy from you than from your competitors.

You may be able to obtain a higher price than that charged by the competition because of some product advantage, better terms of delivery or payment; you may try to undercut the competition by means of a lower price. But competitive prices will help to indicate the range within which your prices must fall.

Local Purchasing Motivations

Where purchasing is based on necessity, your product may command a lower price than when it is in the luxury class. Where a motivation includes status, then again the price may be higher. But where there is a wide choice, and motivations depend on other factors such as habit or brand awareness, your price may fall within varying ranges.

Local Purchasing Habits

When products are continually being purchased, prices tend to become keener; where less frequent purchases are made, then price is often less important than design or technical specifications.

The three areas which affect the price a market will bear in any given environment, as affected by local purchasing habits, are:

(*a*) The degree of bargaining practised and the amount of leeway which must be allowed in the price itself. In many parts of the world bargaining is a way of life, and considerable latitude must be given in any export price to allow for the game of bargaining to be played to the full.

(*b*) The time buyers take to make up their minds. This varies considerably, and will affect the actual selling costs. In most Latin American countries, for example, sales negotiations take an interminable time, as they do in the eastern half of the world.

(*c*) If inducements have to be allowed for in the price. In many parts of the world inducements are common practice and need adding to the price, whether they are paid in cash or kind. You should always handle any form of inducement through a third party, but unless you have a strong moral feeling that you will not do business with those who demand them, inducements will figure in many business deals overseas. They might be taken as a variable selling cost.

You will appreciate now why fixed export prices for all demand markets are probably not the best way of maximising profits from export, and why what the market will bear should play such an important part in finally deciding any export price.

Revision

Cover the page with a sheet of paper and uncover one question at a time.

Answers	*Questions*
	1. How may you define a product?
1. The result of using a skill.	2. What is an alternative to manufacturing a product for export?

Answers	*Questions*
2. Selling manufacturing know-how.	3. What do some people overseas consider a radio set to be in addition to a means of entertainment?
3. A status symbol.	4. What are the normal rates for royalty payments?
4. Between 5 and 10 per cent.	5. What is ICI's trade mark called?
5. A roundel.	6. Who makes world-famous diesel engines?
6. Perkins.	7. What does a package often have in its own right?
7. A re-sale value.	8. How are inducements usually paid?
8. In cash or kind through a third party.	9. When can you finally fix the export price?
9. When the marketing plan is prepared.	10. Give an example of a British product which hardly needs modifying for export.
10. Maggots, a Union Jack, a bowler hat.	

Exercises

1. What reasons would you consider important in deciding to manufacture your product overseas?
2. What skills does your own company, or one that you know, possess, and in what other ways might they be used?
3. In what ways might a product need to be modified to make it suitable for overseas demand markets?
4. What do you understand by 'presentation for export'?
5. How would you set about calculating the price the market will bear for an export product?
6. Discuss the local environmental conditions which might affect the packaging used for an export product.
7. What is your personal attitude towards inducements and how would you deal with a request from an overseas buyer for them?

13

CHANNELS OF DISTRIBUTION

In Part 2 you saw how goods may be physically transported to your customers overseas. But these customers may not be the final users of the goods. If you export biscuits, for example, you are unlikely to sell them to the people who finally eat them. Moreover, the biscuits will probably have been bought in a store, which in turn may have been supplied by a wholesaler, and he may have bought them from your importer. If you export industrial goods such as machinery, you may have exported direct to the final user, or to someone who has sold to the user.

Hence when you export you may well need the services of some kind of intermediary to ensure that the goods reach the final user, and you may directly or indirectly employ several kinds of intermediary. On the other hand, you may feel that using intermediaries is not the best way to service your overseas customers, and that it would be better to set up your own sales organisation in certain parts of the world to carry out some or all of the functions of intermediaries.

You may indeed prefer to consider this is an area where you would do better to subcontract all the work of supplying customers overseas, and sell only to people in your own country, leaving them to arrange distribution of the goods to customers overseas.

The extent to which you make use of various channels of distribution will depend on how far you feel it desirable, or necessary, to become involved with them. You may in certain cases deal direct with the customers who are the end users, and you may also sell direct to these users, which would be the case if you were selling to a small number of people around the world. In this case, however, you would be concerned with personal selling, which will be covered in the next chapter.

For most exporters it is necessary to make some use of some sort of intermediaries, whether they belong to you, or are outside companies. Hence this chapter has been divided into the following sections:

1. The functions of intermediaries in export
2. Overseas sales intermediaries
3. Overseas sales companies
4. Local channels of distribution
5. Domestic sales intermediaries

The object of using these various channels of distribution is to have your goods distributed to the final users as quickly and effectively as possible, and to sell to them, either directly or indirectly.

The Functions of Intermediaries in Export

There are four main functions that any intermediary will be required to perform for an exporter, or which he may in certain cases carry out himself. These are as follows.

1. Buyer Negotiations

The most important function of any intermediary is to sell, so that you would employ one primarily to secure business for you. To do this he would have to know on what terms you will accept the business—that is your terms of delivery, as set out in Chapter 3, and your terms of payment, as shown in Chapter 7. The intermediary can keep in touch with potential buyers overseas, and actively secure orders for you, or sell your goods himself.

2. Supplying the Market

Any intermediary is concerned to ensure that your goods are available in the local market, either by having you supply direct or by his supplying from stock. Normally, in the case of industrial products orders are sent direct to the users; in the case of consumer products the supply will usually be from locally held stocks. But an intermediary will be expected to see that any other links in the chain of distribution, as in the case of the biscuits quoted earlier, are also kept supplied at all times.

3. Providing After-Sales Service

Where a product requires an after-sales service to be provided locally, and where the possibility of replacements occurs, an intermediary will generally be employed to handle this work. This is an area often neglected by exporters, who fail to appreciate that anyone buying an imported product is likely to be more concerned about the degree of service he can expect from the manufacturer of another country, than from one in his own country, with whom it may be easier to get into contact. But you must, if you export goods which require a service, be as careful to set up such a service as you are to secure the business, and you should always provide the service facilities at the same time as you begin to sell your product.

4. Information and Promotion

An intermediary will normally be expected to supply information about a product to the local buyers, and to pass on what he learns of their reactions to the exporter. Note here that for products of high technology, the problem of keeping any intermediary up to date with essential information may prove difficult, so that the decision whether to use one or not may be influenced by this consideration.

Whether or not an intermediary should also be concerned with such forms of promotion as advertising is discussed more fully in Chapter 15. Many exporters take the view that it is their responsibility to create a demand for a product overseas, and the intermediary's to supply that demand. Others hold that all forms of promotion should be handled by the intermediary. The best solution is a combined operation, but you may find difficulty in deciding how far each side is to go.

Information is also a matter of local conditions being made known to the exporter and here the intermediary is expected to provide it, although if this becomes too burdensome a task, then he will expect to be paid additionally for the work involved. But clearly one of the main advantages of having someone acting for you in an overseas market is that you have access to information on a continuing basis. Whichever form of local representation you decide is most suitable for you in any export market, you can see how valuable it is to have someone on the spot looking after your interests and advising you how to proceed.

These four main functions represent the work that requires to be done to ensure that your product is made available to the various channels of distribution, and on to the final user. So you must decide which kind of intermediary best suits your product, your company and the markets concerned.

Overseas Sales Intermediaries

It is customary, but inaccurate, to refer to local sales intermediaries as 'agents'. You should, therefore, be more precise in defining what you mean by an agent, so it is better to consider the two main types of agents as follows.

1. Commission Agent

A commission agent obtains orders on your behalf, which you then execute direct to the buyer concerned. For this work the agent is paid a commission, usually on all the business received from the area in which he operates and to which he has been appointed. The reason for his receiving commission on all the business is that he may well have influenced sales, even if they come direct from the buyer to you. Rates of commission vary, but are usually between 2½ and 15 per cent of the value of the business, although on large contracts commissions as low as 1¼ per cent may be paid.

If a commission agent has to supply a great deal of information and provide an after-sales service, he will naturally expect to be paid more. If he has to take the credit risk on behalf of his customers, he will also be paid a higher rate of commission, and will be known as a 'del credere' agent. When agents are referred to as 'sole' agents, this merely means that they are agents appointed for particular territories, whereas in large overseas markets it is not unusual to appoint more than one commission agent to cover a certain section of the market. You might do this in the case of the US market, whereas you would probably only have one commission agent for a market like Thailand.

A commission agent generally follows up orders, sees there is no problem with the exporter's documentation or transport arrangements, and that payment is made in accordance with the agreed terms. He is in effect your representative in the market, and you will refer any enquiries or queries you receive to him. Because he does not carry stocks he will generally act for companies making industrial or capital goods, or any products which are supplied by the exporter from his own country, and which buyers obtain direct, not via local stockists. Commission agents seldom handle competitive products, but generally operate in well defined fields—for example, the construction industry or the heavy engineering industry—and they tend to specialise in certain fields.

2. Distributors

While a distributor also acts as your 'agent', his usual task is to stock your product and supply local buyers on demand. Usually he buys the product from you, and re-sells it at such a price that he makes his profit from the difference between what is called his landed cost (i.e. the cost of the product delivered into his warehouse) and his re-sale price. It is customary for an exporter to fix the distributor's margin of profit, or at least to see that it is an adequate one.

A sole distributor is one who has the exclusive importing rights for a particular territory, and all buyers are referred to him for their supplies of the product. He is the local stockist, and he also carries out the job of representing your interests in that market, providing after-sales service if necessary and sending back information. Because consumer products usually need to be stocked locally and pass through various local channels of distribution before reaching their end users, distributors normally handle consumer and consumer durable items.

There is a variation of this method of operation when a distributor does not actually pay for the goods he receives from the exporter, but has them on consignment. In this case the stocks remain the property of the exporter, and the distributor is only responsible for selling them and then accounting to the exporter for the value of those goods he has sold. The weakness of this method is that the exporter's money is tied up in stock held overseas which has not been paid for; the advantage lies in being able to offer for sale stocks of a product which is new or not yet in demand, so it may be the only way to break into a new demand market.

There is a third type of 'agent' which you should remember, namely the franchise agent, who operates on behalf of an exporter in another country, working on his own account, but being granted the franchise for selling that product, which he may even produce himself or from components he buys from the exporter. There are many examples of franchises, Wimpy bars being one. Another is the rust-proofing system, Ziebart, which allows the local franchise holders to offer the rust-proofing locally, in return for which they pay the company a royalty but receive the know-how of the system in exchange.

Finding and Selecting Commission Agents and Distributors

If you decide that you wish to appoint a commission agent or a distributor to represent you in a particular market, to obtain a list of possibles you should:

(*a*) Approach the Export Services Branch of the BOTB.
(*b*) Ask the banks.
(*c*) Enquire from local embassies.
(*d*) Tackle your own trade association.

You will occasionally see advertisements in the Press from local companies seeking agencies, while you may run across them at a Trade Fair. Other exporters may be able to help, which is why joining an Export Club or going to meetings organised by the Institute of Export is so helpful.

Having obtained such a list, and having decided what functions you require to be carried out locally, you will have to visit the intermediaries in their own countries to make a final choice. This is something that it is unwise to attempt to handle by correspondence. It is almost impossible to judge a local company's competence by mail. Since your company will be represented locally by whoever you choose, you must take care to appoint someone in whom you have every confidence, and who you know will do a good job for you.

The following are the main points you should include in any check on possible commission agents or distributors:

(*a*) A precise indication of the business in which they are engaged.
(*b*) Their standing in the local market.
(*c*) The principals for whom they already act.
(*d*) Their financial standing.
(*e*) Their contacts in your particular trade.
(*f*) Their ability to carry out the functions required of them.

So go and see them, judge for yourself how suitable they are, and make your final choice accordingly, This is often a tedious task, but in the hope that the relationship will be a lasting one, it is worth taking immense pains to make the right choice from the outset. It is normal practice to have a trial period to see if both of you find the relationship satisfactory. Once this is over, and assuming all to be well, you will need to make some form of agreement with them.

Agency Agreements

Agency agreements need be neither lengthy nor complicated, but because they are a form of contract they should be embodied in a legal document, containing the following essential clauses:

1. The **names and addresses** of both parties to the agreement.
2. The **purpose of the agreement**; for example, one party agrees to appoint the other to act as sole distributor, subject to the terms and conditions as stated hereunder.
3. A **description of the goods** involved, including any which are specifically excluded. It is also important to say whether any new products the company might produce are to be automatically included.
4. The **territory** to be covered, which should be precisely defined.
5. The **duties of the agent**; for example, to promote the sale of the product to the best advantage, according to the terms as set out later. In the case of a distributor a minimum stock-holding may be specified.
6. The **duties of the principal**, such as supplying technical knowledge, helping to train salesmen and so on.
7. Any **restrictions** imposed on either party, such as not supplying the goods to any other importer, or to any other territory.
8. The **prices and terms** which are to operate, such as buying on F.O.B. or C.I.F. terms, with payment by means of drafts drawn at so many days, as the parties agree to work.
9. The **remuneration of the commission agent**, probably expressed in terms of so much commission, payable quarterly; the remuneration of the distributor is probably expressed in terms of the amount of profit he is allowed to make when he re-sells for his own account.
10. The **payments, if any, for additional work**, such as providing information, carrying out promotion; and if advertising is included, the basis on which this is to be done (see Chapter 15).
11. The **starting date** of the agreement and the extent of the notice to be given if the agreement is to be terminated.
12. There are three legal points to be included as follows:

(*a*) That the **ownership of trade marks**, patents and names rests at all times with the principals;
(*b*) A **choice of law clause**, indicating the law under which the agreement is to operate (see Chapter 9);
(*c*) The **arbitration procedure** to be followed in the event of any disputes between the two parties.

You should note that there are certain implications in any agency agreement, under which it is presumed to operate. These are that both sides will give sufficient time and attention to the tasks involved and that neither will ignore them. This ensures that the agent will not fail to try to sell his principal's goods, and that the principal will not fail to supply them or pay attention to the market needs.

When making agreements within the EEC, however, there are some Community prohibitions, which are currently as follows:

1. No agent or distributor may be prevented from supplying a customer outside his territory, although he may not actively seek such business.
2. No agent may be prevented from supplying a third party, even if he knows that party will sell the goods in another part of the Community.
3. No distributor may be instructed to sell goods at a certain price.

Community rules are changing daily, but you should remember that it is the intention of the Community that it shall be a Common Market, and not a set of nine member states. Hence you may feel that arranging local representation within the EEC calls for rather special or different treatment, a point already made when considering the set-up of an export office in Chapter 3. Organising channels of distribution within the Common Market has really only just begun, and many companies are finding that they have to consider this separately from the rest of the world.

You will appreciate, however, that when you appoint commission agents or distributors to act for you overseas a great deal will depend on how well you treat them, and how much you get out of them. Hence you must adopt the attitude that they are part of the company, are entitled to its confidences, and are to be encouraged as if they were company employees. They must be visited regularly, encouraged to visit their principals, and given every help possible, otherwise you will find that they do not give your problems the time and attention they should. Hence it is important that once they have been appointed, they be treated as friends.

Overseas Sales Companies

You always have the option of not using any form of intermediary to sell overseas for you or to ensure the smooth distribution of your exports to the final user. Hence you may decide it is preferable to do this work yourself, and while this may be carried out in several ways, there are two basic types of local sales operation.

1. Using your own Company Salesmen

There are two areas where using your own export salesmen may be to your advantage. One is for products with a high technology, because it is difficult to impart the technical knowledge necessary to sell this type of product to a third party.

The second is to use your own salesmen to supplement the work of your intermediaries, particularly if you operate in specialised fields. For instance, in selling medicines and drugs to the medical profession you might use your own salesmen to call on doctors and hospitals, leaving the intermediary to concentrate on supplying the products.

But you may prefer to sell as a company, by having your own salesmen who may operate from your domestic base or be stationed more or less permanently overseas. This is often done when you are working on a specific area in the world, such as the Caribbean or the Middle East. You can see here the possibilites within the EEC, because your salesmen could cover it from Britain until such times as they obtain enough business to be stationed permanently on the other side of the Channel. No export sales manager ever has time enough to visit all the overseas markets as often as is necessary, so the use of export company salesmen is common practice, if only to supervise the work of the local intermediaries. You can also see how a company salesman could oversee certain defined demand markets, especially if these are not confined by national boundaries.

2. Setting up a Local Sales Company

In major overseas markets, in addition to having a local manufacturing facility, you may also set up local sales operations. You may do this on your own or you may buy an existing intermediary and turn him into your own sales company.

In practice, such companies are usually set up, as you would expect, in the major overseas countries, such as Canada, the USA, Australia, and many of the Western European and Latin American markets. Once an exporter begins to set up local sales companies he is embarking on a multi-national operation, so that fairly large resources are needed to accomplish this. But the main advantage is that it is your own personnel who are involved, so that you may insist on things being done in exactly the way you want them, as opposed to having to persuade an intermediary to see your point of view. Should you consider the establishment of sales companies overseas you should bear in mind the following:

(*a*) The **site of the company** within a particular area. For example, you would have to decide in Australia whether to have the company in Sydney, Melbourne or Brisbane, and whether you also need branches in Perth or Adelaide.

(*b*) The **personnel** required to run the company. Should these be local nationals or should some senior posts be filled by expatriates? Some countries have strict laws governing the employment of expatriates, and you may feel that local nationals are in any case likely to succeed to a greater degree than people who are unfamiliar with local conditions.

(*c*) The **system of management** to be used in the company, because management practices vary a good deal throughout the world. Financial accounting practices vary, as do such things as staff recruitment, and you may need to allow the local company to operate in quite a different way from its head office.

(*d*) This raises another problem: namely, the **degree of supervision** to be exercised on the local companies by head office. You have to steer a careful line between insufficient supervision and too strict a control, which in practice often leads to considerable problems.

(*e*) When you establish local sales companies overseas, you will have to adapt your head office structure to accommodate this new set-up. You must decide what services are to be provided by your export office, and what information is to be sent back to head office from the local companies.

(*f*) You will also be concerned to ensure that, as far as possible, you present through each of your companies a uniform and recognisable company image, and that none of the local companies in any way impairs your company reputation.

You must weigh up the advantages and disadvantages of dealing through some form of intermediary overseas, and going it alone. Clearly costs will be a deciding factor, as well as the extent to which you wish to become an international company. This will involve your deciding on a strategy of overseas development, which will be considered in Chapter 16. But before you can arrive at any such decisions, you must consider the effect of local channels of distribution on your own selling strategy.

Local Channels of Distribution

So far you have been concerned with the importer of your goods, whether he acts as your intermediary or whether you sell to him as a customer. But since the importer is often not the final user, you will to some degree be concerned with local channels of distribution. While this is generally more important in the case of consumer and consumer durable goods, there are many instances where the importer of industrial goods is not the end user. Hence most exporters need to identify and have a policy regarding the channels of distribution through which their goods pass to the final users.

The main factors with which you will be concerned in this respect will be as follows.

The Functions of the Channels of Distribution

These vary considerably in different parts of the world. In Britain, for example, a chemist not only sells patent medicines without prescription, but makes up prescriptions provided by a doctor. He also sells cosmetics and a range of toiletries. In Europe, however, there is a distinct difference between the functions of what is loosely called a chemist and different outlets which often only handle one type of product in this field. On the other hand, in Belgium, in the grocery field, you will find small stores selling not only groceries but a wide range of toiletries.

The functions of a wholesaler and a retailer are generally well defined in major markets, but in smaller ones these functions are often handled by the same people, who may even act as importers. In the USA, factors handle the distribution of many industrial goods but seldom are the actual importers.

Identification of Local Channels of Distribution

You will find that names are used in many markets which bear little relation to those in other markets. A pharmacy is seldom the same as a druggist, and neither necessarily bears any relation to a drug store. A supermarket is often no more than what you would call a self-service store. So you must be careful to define the names used in any overseas market, and use them only in accordance with the local environment.

The Links in the Chain

The relative importance of each link in the chain of distribution will vary. In a small country with good transport facilities, there is a tendency for wholesalers to be powerful because they can offer a service to retailers of fast deliveries, in small lots, at frequent intervals. In countries with poor communications, retailers often act as their own wholesalers, and prefer to buy direct from the importers, or even from the exporter in large quantities, to ensure some continuity of supplies.

The Size of the Distribution Outlets

Sizes vary from American and European hypermarkets to individuals peddling goods in the street and selling, as you have seen, articles like razor blades or cigarettes singly.

The Appearance of the Outlets

This can be a confusing problem because you cannot judge the worth of any outlet merely by its appearance. In India, for example, a dealer in something like electrical goods may have his headquarters in a shed, crammed with merchandise worth thousands of pounds, whereas to look at it you would not imagine he could afford to pay for a quarter of the goods stocked. This appearance problem also applies to offices; some are so poor that you hesitate to enter, whereas in fact the reason for the poor appearance may be due to a reluctance to let the local tax authorities think that the owner has any money. A store in Europe is fairly recognisable, but in many parts of Africa it may only consist of a collection of wooden crates.

Margins of Profit

In some markets the margins of profit expected by each link in a distribution chain will be clearly established, so that you will be able to set up a well-defined price structure. In others, margins appear almost non-existent, and will depend on whether the product is in short or full supply.

When you deal with local channels of distribution you may need to vary your packing, and even your methods of transport, to suit these local conditions. Hence you must always examine what happens to your exports after they arrive in a market, and on this you will be able to decide whether or not you need intermediaries to act for you; what kinds of intermediaries will suit your product best; and how you should supply your goods in the first place. The only way to do this is by a personal visit to the market concerned, and it is impossible to generalise about local conditions because they vary so considerably from country to country. This is another area where the practice of export is closely connected with export marketing and where you may need to amend your methods of supplying the market to suit the various channels through which your goods pass, until they reach the end user.

Domestic Sales Intermediaries

So far you have been concerned with exporting on a fairly large scale, in the sense that you can follow your goods right through to the customer at the end of the chain. But you may, if you are in export in a much smaller way, feel that having produced products suitable for export, you are not large enough to handle their distribution overseas, and that you would prefer to subcontract this work to others. It is possible to do this, and export without in effect leaving your own country. There are several options open to you, of which the following are important.

Confirming Houses

In essence, confirming houses are agents for overseas buyers. Their function is to place orders on behalf of their principals, and they may in addition not only place the orders, but arrange their shipment and even pay for them. They may buy from suppliers named by their principals, or be left to find the most suitable suppliers. They are usually paid a commission by their principals for the work they do. Hence you are often relieved of both shipping and payment problems, and can concentrate on the production of goods for export rather than having also to sell them overseas. Confirming houses act for the principals in most countries, and are particularly active when buying for customers overseas who deal in a large variety of goods and who require regular shipments on a combined basis at regular intervals. Customers in smaller overseas markets such as the Seychelles, who are buying smallish quantities of many kinds of goods, also often use the services of a confirming house. So you will, by supplying them, be able to do quite an appreciable amount of export business.

Export Merchants

In general, export merchants operating from a domestic base usually buy for their own account, attend to the shipping, and pay the supplier in his own country for the goods. The merchants then re-sell the goods at a profit. These merchants came into being many years ago, when their primary function was to buy raw materials from overseas, a role many of them still play. Being the direct descendants of the merchant adventurers of Elizabethan days, they realised the advantages of being able to get back the money they had paid out for the raw materials by selling goods which they brought with them.

As with confirming houses, the exporter is relieved of having to ship the goods, while being paid in this country in sterling. But while this also is a good way to export, remember that the merchants will only buy what they are sure they can re-sell, so that you may find it difficult to break into new markets or launch new products.

International Agencies

There are several international buying agencies, one being the Crown Agents, who act for a number of overseas countries, buying on their behalf, paying for the goods and shipping them overseas. Their main expertise is handling major contracts, and if you are in this field you should be on their list. Another international agency is the United Nations, which buys a wide variety of goods for developing countries, although the UN will usually expect you to ship the goods as requested. Payment, however, is no problem. There are many UN agencies such as UNCTAD/GATT; the World Food and Agricultural Organisation (FAO); the World Health Organisation (WHO); and the United Nations Education and Scientific Organisation (UNESCO). OECD does not buy a great deal, but occasionally arranges for supplies to be sent to certain developing countries.

Local Buying Offices

Many overseas companies maintain their own local buying offices in Britain, especially department stores such as the T. Eaton Company of Canada, Myer's in Australia or Macey's of New York. These buying offices place orders here in Britain, and will both pay for and ship the goods overseas. You will find details of many of these outlets in the BOTB's *Export Handbook*.

As you have seen, inward trade missions are encouraged by the BOTB and you should try to get on the list for being visited, because this is another way of being put in touch with buyers from overseas. But you can, by concentrating on making or supplying goods for export, find customers in your own country, and this is another way of arranging your distribution for export. Much will depend on the way you wish to develop your export trade, and this will depend on what kind of strategy you employ, which will be considered in Chapter 16.

Other Export Sales Methods

There are a number of other ways by which you may export, and you should also consider these before finally deciding how your goods can best be distributed to customers overseas.

Export Concessionaires

There are companies in Britain which have been set up to handle all the shipping, documentation and payment problems of exporters, and which will also go out and obtain export business for them. Such companies often specialise in certain parts of the world, such as the Middle East or America, and act in effect as the exporter's own export department. For small producers who wish to concentrate on supplies or for those exporters who lack the resources to expand their export trade themselves, these concessionaires provide a valuable service.

Group Selling

For many years the idea of group selling for export has been suggested, the intention being that a company well versed in export should help a company lacking that expertise by taking over the exports of the smaller company. It was always envisaged that the two companies would be in similar but non-competitive fields, and in certain instances the idea has worked. But it would seem that in practice this method of exporting has not been so successful as was originally believed, mainly because it is difficult to find companies compatible with each other, and because there is always the fear that the smaller will be ultimately taken over by the larger.

Other Domestic Manufacturers

Many companies are more involved in export than they often realise, because they concentrate on supplying parts or raw materials to companies which then export the finished product. This is common practice in the automotive industry, for example, and you may find that in your own case it is better to concentrate on this aspect of export. Of course, the logical extension of this method of operation is later to consider supplying similar manufacturers in other countries, and many foreign vehicles are, for example, composed of parts supplied by exporters of other countries. In the food industry suppliers of 'own brand' products are often involved in this way with export, while you will find many examples of companies working in the textile or fashion industries who export at secondhand, so to speak.

Tourists

Because export basically involves the earning of foreign currency for the country, those companies which concentrate on supplying tourists who visit this country are also involved in export. The advantage is that you are paid in cash for the goods, but you will need to observe the same principles of having the goods made to the tastes and needs of visitors as you would if you were selling to these customers in their own countries. This involves the shopkeepers and even street traders in export, a field which is rapidly developing as improved travel facilities increase the number of tourists. Tackling the tourist trade is also a way of having your products become known to people from other countries, which means you are promoting your business overseas to some degree.

Consortia

There is an increasing demand overseas in major projects for what may be termed 'packaged deals'. These take many forms, such as installing complete factories, building hospitals, hotels, and schools, the work involving many suppliers. Hence by joining in a consortium concerned with such projects you may obtain good export business. Moreover, these consortia also need services such as those provided in the engineering and building industries, particularly when feasibility studies are involved. Hence firms of architects and surveyors often make it a practice to join consortia, and profit from their handling of contracts overseas.

Logistics is the word now applied to any activity connected with getting your goods to your customers, so that deciding which channels of distribution to use is an exercise in export logistics. You will of course include the transport of your goods in any such exercise, so that logistics is concerned with both the practice and marketing of exports. Naturally you will, when deciding the costs on which to base your export prices, include some allowance for the costs of distributing your exports. These costs will include those incurred in finding and selecting intermediaries in other countries if you decide to use them; visiting and looking after them; and, of course, setting up local sales companies or using your own export salesmen. Normally these costs are taken as a whole and counted as part of the export operation's overheads. But where a local company is set up, then the costs can be charged to that particular country. If you use concessionaires or concentrate on selling to buyers in your own country, or even to tourists, then you will have to include the costs involved when fixing your prices. So you will need to know your distribution costs, and devise a method of seeing that they are charged against export revenues.

The work of arranging distribution in export is normally handled by the export manager, who must decide which channels of distribution are most suitable for the company and then ensure that these channels are used to the best advantage.

Revision

Cover the page with a sheet of paper and uncover one question at a time.

Answers	*Questions*
	1. Which are the two main kinds of overseas intermediary?
1. Commission agents and distributors.	2. What is an intermediary who takes the credit risk called?
2. A del credere agent.	3. When does a consignment agent pay for the goods?
3. After he has sold them.	4. What does a confirming house do?
4. Confirms the orders of its principals overseas.	5. What is implied in an agency agreement?
5. That both sides shall give sufficient time and work to the tasks agreed.	6. What are logistics?
6. The activities connected with the distribution of goods.	7. What is FAO?
7. The Food and Agricultural Organisation of the UN.	8. Name an example of the work of a consortium.
8. Building a hospital, school or factory.	9. Which is the best way to select an intermediary overseas?
9. Go and see him in his country.	10. What does an export concessionaire do?
10. Handles the exports of a supplier.	

Exercises

1. Discuss the functions that an exporter usually requires from intermediaries overseas, and say why these are important.
2. How do you think after-sales service can best be provided overseas?
3. What are the essential clauses in an agency agreement?
4. What do you think are the main advantages of having your own sales company in an overseas market?
5. How would you set about finding a sole distributor in a country like Algeria?
6. You can export without leaving your own country. How?
7. How do local environmental conditions affect local channels of distribution?

14

PERSONAL SELLING OVERSEAS

Any efficient exporter will at some time have to travel overseas. There are many reasons for undertaking travel, in addition to making a sales visit. You may wish to explore the possibilities of a demand market. You may have to find and appoint a commission agent or distributor. You may be concerned to set up a factory. You might wish to take part in a Trade Fair, appoint an advertising agency, or organise a local advertising campaign. But in order to achieve success you must set about any overseas travel in an organised way. It may sound glamorous to dash off at a moment's notice, but from personal experience I can assure you the value of any visit is generally in direct proportion to the amount of planning that you have put into it.

While selling in other countries to people of different nationalities depends to some degree on the salesman's individual style, there are certain areas where you may profit from other people's experience—for example, in the art of travelling. Theoretically, buying a ticket more or less guarantees you will arrive, but the better you travel the more you will be able to profit from your visit when you have arrived. The main value of any travel is often after you have returned, when you make use of what you have learned and justify the costs of the travel.

Because much of the art of successful travel and selling overseas is highly personal, in some cases I have quoted my own preferences, and have used 'I', which has seldom been done in other parts of this book. But you should always try to develop your own style of travelling, because no two travellers ever approach things in quite the same way. Hence this chapter has been divided into the following sections:

1. Planning a visit overseas
2. The art of travelling overseas
3. Selling overseas
4. Making the best use of an overseas visit.

Planning a Visit Overseas

Before you make a visit to an overseas country there are several things you should consider.

The Object of the Visit

Every visit should have a clearly defined objective. It may have more than one, but each must be stated. This will to a major degree also serve to determine the length and scope of the visit. It is not enough, for example, to say 'I think I'll go and have a look round', because if you do you are likely to return home with poor material.

The Cost and Likely Returns of a Visit

You must first calculate the costs of a visit, and then estimate what returns you are likely to obtain from the expenditure. Suppose you make a sales visit to a demand market producing £3,000 p.a. You believe you could increase this to £5,000. The estimated cost of the visit is £250, so that if you are successful you will have incurred an expenditure of 5 per cent of the turnover. Normally, travel overseas is reckoned to cost between 1 and 5 per cent of sales turnover, and in this case the costs can be debited to the market concerned. If visits are made for other reasons then the costs must be debited to other activities, such as research, promotion, distribution and so on. But you will of course take these costs into consideration when arriving at your export selling prices.

How the Work is to be Handled in your Absence

Some form of delegation is required, while the measure of responsibility of those who handle your work while you are away must be decided. But your office must be able to contact you at all times, especially if an unexpected problem arises.

What Information is to be Obtained

In any overseas visit some information will always be obtained, but you must decide what this is to be. In the case of a sales visit, for example, you would probably need to up-date customer records, but you would also probably be concerned to examine transport, finance and Customs problems, as well as check documentation procedures. Here you should make sure everyone in the company has an opportunity of asking you to look at a problem while you are away; it is a waste of money to sneak off without saying anything to anyone.

What Information You Need to Take Away With You

In the case of a sales visit you must take all the information about the customers you plan to visit, which is where customer cards are so useful because you can photocopy them, and then up-date them during the visit. But try to keep some law and order in the selection of paper you take, as I can assure you that after a few days or weeks your paper is likely to become muddled and untidy unless you keep to a system.

Do not forget your visiting cards, and make sure your own title is as high as you dare make it, because people overseas always like to feel they are meeting someone senior in the company. I once promoted myself to be the President of the company, with excellent effects, when visiting Latin America.

If you use a tape recorder make sure you take spare tapes; arrange a system for sending home tapes and having them transcribed in your absence. You can do the same with copies of customers' cards, and also with written reports.

An Immediate Action Routine

When you are overseas you will need to promise action, especially in the form of quotations, sending samples, preparing literature, and so on. If this has to be done at home, you must arrange that your office takes the necessary action at once on your instructions. Buyers overseas quickly get fed up with salesmen who promise action and then forget to ensure it materialises. I have always found it pays dividends to get this part of an overseas visit highly organised in advance.

Planning the Visit

When you plan a visit overseas you must consider several things:

(*a*) That the people you wish to see will be available and not on holiday or away on a business visit themselves. I once failed to meet someone because, unbeknown to me, he was calling on my office at home while I visited his overseas.

(*b*) Avoid possible public holidays. The *Hints to Businessmen* series of booklets and many diaries give the necessary information.

(*c*) Check when offices will be open, because office hours vary considerably from country to country.

(*d*) Allow enough time to see everyone, yet also allow for unexpected delays in travelling, meeting people, and negotiating with them. In North America business moves at fast pace; in the Middle East at a much slower rate. My own solution is always to travel at the weekend and be able to work the remaining five days, but make sure you know which days are weekends, because they are not always Saturdays and Sundays. I also always allow at least one spare day everywhere, to cope with the unexpected, such as getting an exit visa or tax clearance, and even taking a day off if the visit is a strenuous one.

Arranging your Home Affairs

You owe it to your family to arrange your affairs so that problems do not arise while you are far away. You owe it to yourself to avoid personal problems while you are overseas, because worrying about them is bound to affect the quality of your work. One way is to cable or telex your family when you arrive at a new place and have them advise the office; in this way everyone knows where you are.

If this all sounds like a formidable list of things to do before you leave, I can assure you that with practice you will tend to do all these things almost automatically, so that you can leave at a few days' notice if you have to, such as when you hear of a major contract you wish to go after before the competition gets wind of it.

The Art of Travelling Overseas

An experienced overseas traveller is never at a loss under any circumstances, because he has devoted a great deal of care and attention to the art of business travel around the world. May I suggest you cultivate this art, and that you think in terms of the following.

Booking the Travel

Never try to do this yourself except for the simplest of visits. Always use the services of an experienced travel agency that specialises in business travel.

I always prefer to use the airline which originates from where I am leaving, to avoid delays. I always work out alternative ways to travel if delays occur. While I never travel by sea because of the time involved, I do use trains and a car in Europe, because they may be quicker. I always try to get around a country by car, or public transport, because this is one of the best ways of learning about the local scene. I also walk a good deal in cities, because you will not sell much from the back of a taxi. But I take care to book my travel as far as possible in advance.

Travel Documents

Never allow your passport to expire when you are overseas, because renewing it can be both costly and time-consuming. Never set out without all the necessary visas in your passport, and make sure there are enough blank pages in it for the entry and exit permits, which can take up a great many pages. Always carry with you a set of passport photographs, because immigration officials seem to love to collect them. Always know your passport number off by heart; it saves time when filling in forms or checking into the hotel; and if you unhappily lose your passport it will help having it replaced.

Make sure you have all the necessary health documents and that your inoculations are up to date. You may not care to be vaccinated in a strange country by a doubtful-looking doctor.

Keep all these documents on you at all times; police checks are not infrequent in many countries. And carry an international driving licence if you are going to hire cars locally or take your own.

Hotels

These days hotel accommodation is often as hard to obtain as air tickets, so as far as possible book your hotels in advance. Here the chains of international hotels are a great help. But you may feel, as I do, that a good local hotel is better than an international one if you wish to learn something of local conditions. Hotels are much a matter of personal choice, and you will develop your dislikes and preferences as I have done. Always tip when you enter a hotel, especially in the Planned Economies countries, because this ensures that your hotel reservation will be honoured. Keep on good terms with the hotel manager, who can be of great help to you, and after all, you may be going back one day on another visit.

Money

You should always take some loose change in each currency you are going to use to pay for entry visas, airport charges, local transport and so on, as well as being able to tip, which saves you the problem of having to change money as soon as you arrive. I always keep back about five pounds of change in local currency after each visit, ready for the next time. Strictly illegal? Maybe, but sensible.

Most people seem to prefer to carry most of their money in travellers' cheques, but make sure when you buy them that the issuing bank is known in the country concerned. Bank of America cheques are generally acceptable everywhere, as are those issued by American Express. If you think the rate of exchange may go against you or that sterling may weaken, buy your travellers cheques in local currency. You will also need some sterling for the return journey. You will have estimated how much to take in advance, but be on the safe side because having money sent to you overseas causes problems, so keep a small reserve.

Clothes

Shoes should always be in good repair because it always seems to me that buying a pair overseas to fit is difficult, whereas clothes can more easily be replaced. You must take the correct weights of clothing, and here the *Hints to Businessmen* booklets are of great help. As a visitor you are expected at all times to be well dressed, and while you need to keep the amount of clothes to a minimum, they must be of good quality and suitable for the occasion.

Thanks to the odd embarrassing experience I pack a small wallet containing needle, thread and buttons so I can carry out running repairs. Except in tropical climates I prefer to do my own washing so I tend to rely on drip-dry shirts and so on. I include a small towel, soap and shoe-cleaning materials, and the odd spare shoelace. If you wear spectacles or false teeth, be sure to have a spare set with you.

Baggage

One large suitcase is plenty and as much as an economy-class ticket allows. One large brief or attaché case is enough for your papers, but pack this with care. I include pins, clips, paper, envelopes and plastic files, so that I can work wherever I happen to be, even when travelling. Keep a firm eye on baggage, especially when it is being labelled at airports. You may not lose it, but remember some baggage labellers seem illiterate.

Health

Without in any way appearing hypochondriac, I pay great attention to health, because a visit overseas can be physically exhausting, and being ill in another country is costly, as well as a waste of the company's time and money.

In addition to all the normal inoculations—and have them all as you never know when an unexpected epidemic will break out—I take with me my favourite stomach remedy to minimise the effects of the various 'tummies' you are almost certain to attract. (It's the same illness with different names.) I include aspirin and a tube of disinfectant cream, and take extra care to wash my hands regularly. I also take some sticking plaster, because odd cuts are not infrequent. Avoid uncooked vegetables, and be wary of salads. Make sure fruit has been washed, and try not to eat anything unpeeled. You will have to eat a good deal of unusual food—unusual, that is, to you—but if you eat moderately you should come to little harm. Moderation also applies to alcohol, which will slow you down if you go overboard on it, merely because it is available to you personally for free. Remember that drink is a weapon some customers use to extract better terms from you.

Relaxation

This is one of the most difficult things to achieve successfully. Flying on a Saturday and having Sunday off is one way of relaxing. Another is to take an entire weekend off and lie on the beach if there is one handy. Books to read are essential, and if you have a hobby like photography, collecting stamps or looking at old buildings this is a good way to take your mind off business for a short while. Being entertained is part of the whole operation, but you may find this more a case of 'singing for your supper' than relaxation. The best way to relax I know is to learn to 'cat-nap'.

Insurance

In the interests of your company, yourself and your family, make sure you are fully insured, both for travelling and for all the time you are out of the country. Insure your baggage, and you can relax with the confident thought that if anything unhappily occurs, then you, or your family, will not be the losers. All such insurance should be a company expense.

Much of the art of good travel comes from experience. But listen to other travellers and profit from their experiences as well. Moreover, there is an intense satisfaction to be gained from a well-run business visit, which should not exceed about six to eight weeks if you are to remain at full pitch.

Selling Overseas

When you sell in any overseas environment you will need to adapt to that environment without losing any of your own personal qualities. But to sell successfully overseas you might bear in mind the following points.

Language

If you can speak the local language so much the better. If you cannot, you must use an interpreter, generally available from a hotel or from the local business community. Unless you speak the language fluently do not try to negotiate in it, as you will undoubtedly end up in disaster. All export personnel should be fluent in one language besides their mother tongue. But you should also be able to say a few words in most foreign languages, so a phrase book is essential. This will at least show your customer you are trying, as well as making travel that much easier and more pleasant.

Time

You must be prepared for varying concepts of time when you negotiate in other countries. In the USA you can make your sales pitch as fast as you wish. In the Eastern part of the world you must go more slowly. In the Middle East there is a word *bukha*, which is said to be the equivalent of *mañana*, but without its urgency! In France, or any French-influenced country, you are expected to spend some time exchanging the pleasantries of life. In Japan you must never allow a customer to lose 'face', so you proceed slowly and humbly.

Titles

You must learn people's titles and use them, because in many parts of the world they are important. In countries like Switzerland and Sweden to be a doctor or an engineer carries status, and the title is always used. Even if the customer is only a buying director he expects to be called director. Names are all-important, and hence the value of visiting cards.

Sales Material

You will automatically take with you all the sales material in the form of literature, specimens, and samples you need, and make sure everything is in the local language. Where you cannot carry a sample, take a film of the product and show it in action. Many companies have projectors, and if you have the commentary in the local language it shows you have taken the trouble to prepare for the visit and are serious about doing business. If you are on a long trip have material sent to you at each stop, to cut down on your baggage. Photographs are useful, and I always advocate the use of a prepared 'book', setting out the sales story. You will need a list of prices, and a 'crib' showing the cost of credit, so that you can offer discounts without having to work them out on the spot (see Chapter 7).

Basically you must enjoy trading, or bargaining, and be prepared to be patient. Good humour is another ingredient essential to good negotiating, and having exactly the right material in front of you will help you to present your story in the best possible manner.

Inducements

Inducements were considered in Chapter 12, and you will have to adopt a definite policy towards them. I take the view that I play the game according to the local rules, and that I will always pay for services rendered, but not for promises or expectations. Small presents are a useful way of generating good will, something like a ballpoint pen or a ruler. Someone I know gave away replicas of the company's flag, which soon found a place of honour on buyers' desks. Duty-free cigarettes and liquor are useful, but avoid liquor where religion prevents its acceptance.

Conditions of Sale

You will remember that in Chapter 3 conditions of sale were considered, and you must know these by heart. But avoid hidden conditions and always be completely honest with customers, who will never forgive you for pulling a fast one on them. At the same time, use your knowledge to the best advantage, and the more you can learn about what the competition is offering the better, so it is not a bad idea to spend the first few hours sizing this up.

Social Contacts

You will find business easier to obtain if you can cultivate your customers socially, and you should be prepared to spend both time and money doing this. Accept invitations with pleasure; take a genuine interest in people's families; and join in any local activities, such as racing, picnics and so on. I always carry photographs of my family with me because this makes a good talking point. I also discuss the Royal Family, about whom I know little, because people overseas are generally interested in them. You must be prepared to enjoy unusual food, and visits to local homes. I have always rated the social side of selling as highly as the ability to negotiate formally.

In all this you can only basically be yourself. But I suggest you can also adapt to local environmental conditions, and this is what, in my opinion, a good international salesman always does.

Making the Best Use of an Overseas Visit

Your return is, as you know, when you really obtain the best value from most overseas visits, and in order to achieve this you should bear in mind the following points.

Time Off

Ideally you should always take some time off when you return. This is in practice often difficult to do, but you should resist the natural temptation to rush straight into the office. The only solution I have found is to fly back, not to London, but to somewhere near, such as Paris, Brussels or Amsterdam, and have my wife join me there. Arriving on a Friday evening I then spend Saturday and Sunday with her, catching up on the news, etc., and fly back to London on the Sunday evening. I am then happy to go into the office on Monday morning. It is the only way I have been able to avoid the inevitable tired feeling that follows a visit overseas.

Urgent Action

My first task is always to check that all urgent action requested during my visit has been taken. It is these follow-ups which count for so much in selling overseas, because orders are seldom handed out on the spot.

Thank You Letters

I have always made it a rule that everyone I have seen during a visit overseas receives at least a thank you letter. Hence I keep a careful list of all the people I meet and add in any personal points, such as what they did for me, what their families are doing and so on. I then dictate personalised letters to those I have met, and I have found their effect is out of all proportion to the time and effort involved.

Reports

While there is often a temptation to leave these for the time being, reports should be written as quickly as possible while the events are still fresh in your mind. They need to be written systematically, and include details of travel for future reference.

For those new to export and concerned to interest the company in export, sending home a weekly diary during the visit is an idea I have used successfully. It serves to focus attention on the travel, and to involve the company with overseas customers.

Following up Contacts

In addition to thank you letters, following up the contacts you have made is a must after you return. You must tackle this work before you start to plan another visit, and you must put on the pressure to show that you are genuinely keen to obtain the business.

Evaluating a Visit

You will need to prepare a report showing in detail the visit, its costs and its results. You will need an assessment of how well your objectives were achieved. Travel overseas is an investment and must be evaluated as carefully as any other form of investment. Its cost must be included in the export costs, and charged as you have seen to the appropriate sector of export activities.

If I had to summarise a lifetime of travelling around the world, I would say that you must always enjoy it and start off with some sense of excitement.

Nothing can ever replace the value of personal contact with your overseas customers, and nothing will teach you about local environmental conditions—or show you the mistakes you are making—as well as visits overseas. Of course you get weary, jaded and travel-worn. But this soon passes and you are eagerly looking forward to the next visit. But as you have seen, there is an art to this side of export work. Like everything else in export it has to be learned, and it has to be practised in a professional manner. For myself it has brought all the rewards I ever hoped for, not least the countless friends you make, and whom you meet again when they visit your country.

Revision

Cover the page with a sheet of paper and uncover one question at a time.

Answers	*Questions*
	1. What are the normal amounts spent on overseas travel?
1. Between 1 and 5 per cent of sales turnover.	2. Where can you find information about public holidays and office hours?
2. In the *Hints to Businessmen* booklets and many diaries.	3. What is your own passport number?
3. Well?	4. When is it a good plan to tip at a hotel?
4. On arrival.	5. What should you avoid in the way of food?
5. Uncooked food and unpeeled fruits.	6. What should you know in all foreign languages?
6. Simple, everyday phrases.	7. If you cannot take a sample of your product with you, what can you do?
7. Take a film.	8. What should you send off as soon as you return to the office?
8. Thank you letters.	9. What is the best way to relax?
9. To cat-nap.	10. What does *bukha* mean?
10. The same as *mañana*, without the urgency.	

Exercises

1. What sort of objectives might you have to justify a visit overseas?
2. When you pack your baggage what would you be sure to include?
3. What local conditions affect the way in which you have to negotiate in overseas countries?
4. How can you minimise the strain of a long overseas visit?
5. What would you do before setting off for a sales visit to Canada?

15

PROMOTION

Every company which exports has to make use of some forms of promotion, although this side of exporting has been greatly neglected by many British exporters, who have been generally loath to promote themselves or their products overseas because in many cases they have had protected Commonwealth markets and because of some kind of innate reluctance to publicise their products on the grounds that a good product sells itself. It does not. Yet it is much easier to sell personally to a customer who knows you, instead of working in an atmosphere that can be expressed as, 'Why should we buy, from an unknown overseas supplier, a product about which we know little, and on which we have no idea if we can rely?' This lack of appreciation of the use of publicity stems from the same thinking that produces remarks like, 'Export is unprofitable. It is only a means of selling additional production.' Moreover, many British people still believe publicity, or promotion, is akin to boasting, and that it is traditionally a somewhat un-British activity.

Promotion, or publicity if you prefer the word, aims to provide customers with a knowledge of a product and of the company that makes it, and it also aims to persuade people to buy, particularly in the face of competition from other products made by other companies. Since you can seldom, if ever, hope to sell personally to all your possible customers, you will need some form of promotion to reach all those who buy or who influence purchases. To use promotion in export you will need to consider the following five areas, into which this chapter has been divided:

1. How promotion may be handled overseas
2. Export promotion budgets
3. Promotion media
4. Export sales messages
5. Export public relations

Because you export against your own national background you are entitled to some help from your government, and some indication of the help British exporters receive has already been given in Chapters 7 and 11. In Britain, national export promotion is the responsibility of the **COI**, or **Central Office of Information**. Their task is to promote a favourable image of Britain and its products in the rest of the world, and they also have some responsibility for helping exporters with their own promotion.

All you need to do is to provide the COI with information about your company and what it exports, and the COI will disseminate it through the Press, radio, television and other communications media overseas. Because of their standing, the COI can generally obtain a greater coverage in these media than you would as an individual exporter. The COI are also actively concerned with major trade fairs overseas, mounting exhibitions which seek to promote British exports as a whole. If you use films as a means of selling, the COI will arrange for these to be shown to selected audiences in other countries, and they arrange visits to commercial establishments in this country.

The services of the COI are free to exporters, and it is a pity that more do not take advantage of them. Hence you should, as an exporter, make sure you are in contact with the COI and see what help you may obtain from them.

How Promotion may be Handled Overseas

Your first task is to establish who in your company is to be responsible for export promotion. A large exporter can afford to have publicity experts specially for this task, but medium and smaller exporters may only have on their staff domestic publicity experts, who do not know enough about overseas conditions to handle export promotion effectively. If, however, the work is left to the export sales or office staff, they may lack sufficient knowledge of promotion. This is another reason why many exporters fail to carry out promotion effectively.

Ideally, there should be at least one person in any export set-up responsible for the promotion of exports, and that person should be both knowledgeable and experienced in export and publicity. He or she may work in either the export or publicity department, but because of the complexity of the work in many cases, it should be looked after by a specialist. Having established the responsibility for the work, you then have three main options for handling promotion in overseas markets:

1. Leaving Everything to the Local People

It has for long been a concept among many British exporters that, because effective promotion depends so much on local environmental conditions, the local people, in the form of intermediaries or representatives, are the only ones qualified to handle it. Yet this is often an erroneous view, because an intermediary is usually sales-oriented, and that does not necessarily imply he is publicity-conscious. Moreover, there is often a tendency for the intermediary to promote himself rather than the interests of his principals. Hence much of the money spent is often, from the exporter's view, wasted. So if you decide to entrust promotion moneys to local people you must exercise strict control over what is done, not only to ensure that it is not wasted, but also that your company and your products are suitably promoted, since it is you who will suffer most if it is badly done.

2. Doing It All Yourself

This system, in direct contrast to the above, will work well only if you have people in the company competent to handle the promotion overseas. In practice this nearly always means that some local knowledge is lacking, because however much you may learn about any overseas environment you will never know as much about it as the local people. In such areas as buying motivations, the use of the local language, and the coverage of local media, you will almost inevitably find that your knowledge is too limited.

3. A Combination of Company and Local Expertise

It would seem, therefore, that the best way to handle promotion overseas is to use all the company's export experience in conjunction with the best local advice. The exporter must take the final responsibility for what is done, and should always approve any publicity campaigns. But their preparation and execution may be left to local people; or if they are handled from the exporter's country, then the local people should have the opportunity of approving the proposals. This method is, of course, in line with the close cooperation needed between you as an exporter, and your intermediaries on the selling side, and it will also help to preserve that essential link between sales and publicity.

When you examine various forms of promotion you may divide them into advertising and non-advertising media. The responsibility for the non-advertising media usually rests with the exporter, while that of the advertising may rest locally, as well as with the exporter. Here the position becomes a little more complicated, because advertising is usually handled by an advertising agency. Hence you have to decide which agency is to be used, and here you have three basic choices:

(*a*) **A local advertising agency** in the country concerned. The advantage is that it should know as much about the local conditions as anyone; the difficulty is that it may not be effective, because in some areas local agencies are involved with local media, lack good creative staff, and require strict supervision if any worthwhile results are to be obtained.

(*b*) Use the **branches of an international advertising agency**, particularly if you use such an agency for your domestic publicity. This limits the field to some degree to the larger advertisers, but you have the advantage that you know the agency and it knows you. But all its branches may not be of the required standard, and there will probably be areas where it does not have any branches at all, because most international agencies tend to set up branches where the business is greatest. So your ability to use them will be limited to the major markets.

(*c*) Use your **domestic agency**, provided it has some facility for handling overseas business. This limits the field a good deal, because too few British advertising agencies have developed an ability for export work, largely because exporters have not bothered to demand the service. But of course you run the risk, by this method, of acting incorrectly locally, or of upsetting the local people.

There is no absolute answer to this problem. It will depend on many factors, including the facilities in the markets concerned, the degree to which your intermediaries are autonomous and the attention you pay to both promotion and the advertising side of the work. But do not let this work go by default; compare the relative merits of local, international or domestic advertising agencies in each case.

Export Promotion Budgets

If you refuse to consider any expenditure on promotion you might as well forget about exporting, because you will never be successful unless you make some effort to tell people about your export products or services. Few exporters are so shortsighted as to take this extreme view, but many are unsure how much should be spent or in what way a budget should be calculated. There are six main ways in which this may be done.

1. By Guesswork

You may be surprised to know that some 4 per cent of exporters adopt this method. But it is not one to be taken seriously, or recommended.

2. By What can be Afforded

Some 6 per cent of exporters seem to use this method, treating promotion as a company investment and deciding it in the light of all the investment the company proposes to make in export. The results are often surprising. One is to use the same figure as was allowed in the previous year. Another is to halve/double it because times are bad/good. Yet in bad times more promotion is needed, and in good times you may argue that you should exploit a success, not cut back. In most cases the answer is that too little can be afforded, and this method tends to merge into the first one. Hence it is not to be recommended.

3. As a Percentage of the Previous Year's Profit or Turnover

Some 30 per cent of exporters use this method, and opinion seems equally divided whether to use profit or turnover as the yardstick on which to base the percentage. The main problem, however, is to decide on the percentage figure, which then has to be built into the product costs and hence into the export prices. Exporters of industrial goods usually reckon on between ½ and 5 per cent; exporters of consumer goods on anything from 1 to 50 per cent, depending on the product. The advantage of this method is that it relates expenditure to sales; the weakness is that it is a static approach in that it produces money for flourishing markets, but ignores those which are small or poor, and leaves out any consideration of tackling new markets when the demand is there, provided it can be developed.

4. A Percentage of Expected Profits or Turnover

This is an improvement in that it relates expenditure to what the exporter hopes to achieve, and is a method favoured by some 40 per cent of exporters. It relates expenditure to anticipated results, and if the money is properly spent, then the results will follow. But it ignores the facts that promotion costs different amounts for the same result in different overseas markets, and that advertising is not something you turn off and on like a tap if you want any lasting results. Moreover, it relies far too heavily on the sales forecasts of the export department, which may in individual markets be inaccurate.

5. To Obtain Parity with a Competitor

Some 2 or 3 per cent of exporters like to spend what the competition is spending, on the basis that they are as likely to be as right as themselves. There is some truth in this, as you should always take note of the competition in all export areas. But the weakness is that this method nearly always results in an upward trend in expenditure as each exporter tries to outspend the other. Besides, it is not necessarily true that because one company acts in one way, that is the best method for another.

6. To Take Advantage of Market Opportunities

Some 10 per cent of exporters now use this method, which seems to be the best, because it allows you to spend what is required to produce a given result. It allows you to exploit an opportunity, and it also makes allowance for varying costs of promotion in different parts of the world. The use of decision models is probably the best way of arriving at a promotion budget for overseas, which means you can construct various models of options based on varying circumstances and decide which is the best one for your purpose. This has been called the 'task' method, but is better described as taking advantage of market opportunities. Of course, you must relate your expenditure in some way to the amount of money earned by exports, but this is merely allowing in your total costs for this expenditure, as you do for all other expenditures incurred. The point is, however, that you start by calculating what you require to carry out a given task, and then work backwards to your price, instead of arbitrarily arriving at a sum of money and then deciding how you might spend it.

If you are tackling a new export market or launching a new export product, you may treat this as an investment, and not relate the costs of the promotion to the initial results. Hence you may write off the initial launching costs, in the same way as you may write off the costs of providing a new factory and machinery to build the product. But after an initial launch the product should of course earn its keep.

Many exporters adopt a rather different system where they put up a certain sum of money for a market and then expect the local intermediary to contribute an equal amount. This has the merit of involving the intermediary, and the argument is that he will see the money is not wasted because some of it is his. In some cases it can work well, but you will need to allow the intermediary a higher rate of commission or a larger profit on his re-sale prices if you expect him to contribute to a promotion budget, because he can hardly be expected to pay out of his profits if these are no more than reasonable. But for most exporters it is not a method to be recommended, because it is usually a device for subrogating the exporter's responsibility for promotion to his intermediaries, and this a serious exporter will seldom do.

Promotion Media

Having decided what money is to be spent and how it is to be handled, you must then decide in which directions it is to be spent. Note here that promotion takes longer to arrange overseas than at home, so you should plan farther ahead in export than on the domestic scene.

When you schedule expenditure you must have defined your marketing objectives, and you must adjust the amounts to be spent according to these objectives and relate them to the total amount available. The preparation of marketing plans is dealt with in the next chapter, so your concern here is to become familiar with the various means of promotion available to you. You may start by dividing them into two main types: non-advertising media and advertising media.

1. Non-advertising Media

It is convenient to consider all non-advertising media together, although this is a somewhat artificial division in that all promotion media are designed to put over sales messages. But as you have seen, there is a tendency for advertising media to be handled by advertising agencies, whereas the exporter will usually handle most, if not all, of the non-advertising media himself. The main types of non-advertising media of interest to an exporter are as follows.

Sales Literature

Almost every exporter will require some kind of sales literature in the form of price lists, catalogues, leaflets, operating manuals and so on. You may produce this material yourself, or you may, to save heavy import duties overseas, have it produced locally. How it is produced will be dealt with later, but you must ensure that whatever is printed must actually be used. There is a tendency for exporters to have various kinds of sales literature, but then not insist that it is used overseas, so much of it is unfortunately allowed to rot away on some intermediary's shelves. You must produce it for a specific purpose, and see that it is used for that purpose.

Sales literature is today normally produced in a standard ISO paper size, and the most widely used is the A4, one of the A series, standard wherever the metric system, on which it is based, is in use.

Direct Mail

For many products direct mail is a valuable promotion medium, because it enables you to send a sales message direct to selected potential customers. But its use is limited to the extent that it can only be effective where literacy is high and the postal services adequate, so it is generally used in the more developed world markets. It is usual for direct mail campaigns to be handled locally, because it costs more to post from overseas, although you may find that a letter or package with an overseas stamp commands more attention than a local one. Its success will depend on the quality of the mailing list and on the kind of literature used. Most mailing lists available locally are of good quality, and may be obtained from specialist agencies in this field.

There are a few companies who specialise on handling this work on an international scale, and these companies have developed what might be called a combination of direct mail and mail order—namely what is called 'direct marketing', which means actually selling, as well as promoting, through the use of mail services.

Trade Fairs and Exhibitions

There are literally hundreds of exhibitions held virtually all over the world, covering specialist trades and industries, and in some cases defined marketing areas. For example, you have the Cologne Furniture Fair, concentrating on furniture, whereas you have the Izmir Fair concentrating on the eastern Mediterranean countries, but covering all kinds of industries.

Your first task is to select those fairs which will give you the coverage you need, and you will find lists of these in publications like *Trade and Industry*, the *Financial Times*, etc. You must have a clear objective in spending what will be a not inconsiderable sum of money on exhibiting at a trade fair, because it is useless trying to do anything of this kind on the cheap. You may obtain assistance, however, from the BOTB in certain cases. You must plan well ahead, design your exhibit carefully, arrange to handle visitors to your stand by giving out literature in the appropriate languages, and having people there who speak the languages involved. You must above all arrange to follow up all the contacts you make, because it is seldom that orders are placed directly on a stand. They usually come later, but many exporters depart without ensuring that every contact is subsequently followed up, a task which is often left to intermediaries with disastrous results.

You may arrange your own local exhibitions overseas—for example, in a hotel room—and this is a much cheaper way of showing your products, albeit to a smaller audience. You may also design a travelling exhibit, mounted on a truck, train, or even a yacht. The essence of all exhibition work is demonstration, because you can show your product in action and in use.

Films

You have already seen that you may use a film to sell overseas if you cannot take a sample of the product with you, perhaps because of its size. Hence films can be used to sell, and they can also be used to project the image of the company, in which case they will probably become part of its public relations activities, which will be dealt with later in this chapter. But films are increasingly being used by exporters because they can be used to put over specific moving messages to carefully selected groups of people.

Gifts and Samples

Samples are used to persuade people to try a product, and are commonly used in the food, confectionery and medical fields. Free gifts attached to existing products are used in what is called 'below-the-line' promotions—that is, promotions carried out in stores to attract the customers by means of some special offer. But many markets have strict regulations about the use of gifts and samples, and you must check before you think of using this form of promotion overseas that you are allowed to do it, and if so in what form.

Gifts made without any purchase are a different matter, because you will always be faced with the problem of deciding whether it has resulted in any business or not. Gifts range from calendars and diaries to cases of Scotch whisky, and are demanded by customers on many occasions. Should you provide them? As a means of promoting goodwill, there is some justification. But you would be advised to spend as little as possible on gifts, because they cost money and it is difficult to see what return in the form of sales they actually bring to the exporter.

Display Material

If you are in the consumer goods business, you will need to supply some forms of display material, both as a means of reminding people of your product when they are about to buy and ensuring that the product is available in the store, because display material is often linked to some form of container for the goods. If the costs of producing stands or receptacles become high, you need only distribute them provided the retailer has bought a certain minimum quantity of the product, and you may adopt the same attitude towards importers, who often request material and then never use it.

2. Advertising Media

The range of advertising media available all over the world is considerable, so you will need expert advice on which kinds of media to choose, particularly local help, because advertising media vary with the local environment. The main types of advertising media you will find in different parts of the world are as follows.

The Press

This comprises newspapers and magazines, produced according to language, religion, politics, trade and a variety of special interests such as sport, hobbies, women's interests and so on.

Newspapers are most successful in those parts of the world where literacy is high and populations are fairly concentrated, because papers need to be distributed quickly. They are read for their politics, their religious backgrounds, and also for their news. In Britain we have a national morning Press, but this is unusual, most countries having a much more localised press. The USA, for example, relies on the major newspapers in the main cities. Some countries have newspapers according to the languages spoken, so that in Malaysia you have papers in English, Malay and Chinese. Many countries have newspapers divided by religion, such as the Netherlands, where there are both Protestant and Catholic papers. Other countries have racial divisions, with special newspapers for different races. And in some countries you will find the circulation figures bear little relation to the number of copies printed, although each copy may be read by several people. Newspapers are published daily, weekly or bi-weekly, but not necessarily every day in the case of a daily paper. They come in various shapes and sizes, and are still, for most people in the world, the main source of news.

Magazines are also divided in much the same way as papers, and appear at weekly or monthly intervals. There is a virtually infinite number of magazines published all over the world, and as an exporter you should take note of three kinds in particular. First, there are the specialised trade magazines, appealing to people in specific industries, and hence of value especially to exporters of industrial goods. Second, there are the consumer magazines, appealing to housewives, children, young men and so on, of immense value to exporters of consumer goods. Third, there are the major international magazines, which cover a number of countries and appeal to the wealthier and more influential people, both on the industrial and consumer sides of business.

You must, therefore, define your demand markets and choose those newspapers and magazines which reach as many of your potential customers at the cheapest possible price. You buy space in newspapers at so much a column-inch, centimetre, or line, with discounts given for the amount of space bought, and additional charges where colour is available. The rates are based on the number of readers and the economic assets of those readers. Space in magazines is generally bought in units of a full page, half page, quarter page, etc., with rates based on the extent and quality of their readers. As you may know, advertising agencies obtain a discount from the Press, which they keep as their remuneration, this discount not normally being available to advertisers.

There is no such thing as a standard Press pattern anywhere in the world, so that you must tackle each overseas market on its own, and decide how a Press advertising budget may be spent to the best advantage in your own particular case.

Television

Most countries have television to some degree and most allow advertising on it, the notable exceptions at present being the Scandinavian countries and South Africa which forbid television advertising. The power of television as an advertising medium is intense, allowing a product to be seen, demonstrated and promoted visually and by sound. Its effectiveness is, however, limited to those parts of the world where it is available to large audiences; and its major disadvantages are that it is costly and reaches such a wide audience that you are buying a coverage which is usually too wide for most products, except those with general consumer demand.

There is a division between television systems which allow the advertiser to sponsor the actual programmes, as well as put over a commercial message, as in the USA, and those where the advertiser may only put on his message or commercial in the breaks between programmes which are produced by the stations and over which the advertiser has no control, as in Britain.

Time is booked at so much a quarter, half or full minute, the rates depending largely on the estimated number of viewers and the time at which the commercial appears.

Radio

Most countries allow advertising on their radio stations, and similar rules and regulations apply as for television. The use of radio as an advertising medium, however, is limited mainly to those products which do not require a strong visual impact and which are already well known enough not to need much explanation. Hence most advertisers on commercial radio are producers of well-known proprietary consumer products. But note that radio can reach illiterate audiences, especially those outside the reach of television programmes, due to the wide use of cheap battery transistor radios. It is especially suitable, for example, for reaching country audiences, and has been most successful in markets where life is lived out of doors, as in many African countries.

The Cinema

Despite a fall in worldwide cinema audiences, due probably to the competition from television, the cinema in many parts of the world is the main means of entertainment outside the home. Hence by using the cinema you can reach a vast audience in many world markets, and appeal to it visually as well as in sound. Many developing countries have open-air cinemas, attracting audiences of thousands at a time. You can buy time at so much a full or half minute, the advertising filmlets generally being shown in the breaks between the films. You can also buy time to show cinema slides, although these are generally used by local tradespeople. The rates for slides are usually based on so much per showing.

Posters and Outdoor Signs

There is an immense variety of outdoor and indoor signs, posters being used in temperate climates and signs in tropical ones. The value of signs is the constant reminder of the name of a product. Opportunities exist on all forms of transport, such as at bus and railway stations, inside the transport, and in areas of cities and towns where there are concentrations of population. Some countries have tried to control the erection of signs along highways and in urban areas. But if you have one single name or thing to say about a product, you can reach many people over and over again by using some form of poster or sign medium.

You will appreciate that with such a wide choice of advertising media available to an exporter, you must take expert advice when making your own choice. Media buying is a specialised field of advertising activity, and you will need to know the local environment well to make the best choice. You should remember that most exporters get the best results when they concentrate their efforts in a few media that match their demand markets as closely as possible. But you will need the help of an advertising agency, and for any help with finding agencies you should contact the Institute of Practitioners in Advertising, at 44 Belgrave Square, London, S.W.1. On the media side, many newspapers and magazines in overseas countries have representatives in London, while the COI will also provide information on various types of media in other countries.

Export Sales Messages

While choosing which advertising media to use in overseas publicity campaigns may be difficult, you must also pay careful attention to the sales message you put over, otherwise your money will be largely wasted. This also applies of course to the message you put over in any non-advertising media. And the way any sales message is presented will depend, as you might imagine, on the local environmental conditions in the market concerned.

Your main aims when preparing any sales message must be to inform and to persuade, which means that the message must be seen or heard, believed, remembered and acted upon. It must also be entirely suitable for the local environment. There are four main areas with which you will be concerned when you produce sales messages as part of your export promotion activities.

1. The Theme of a Sales Message

Most successful sales messages are based on a simple, yet instantly recognisable, theme. You probably remember some, such as the 'Tiger in the Tank' campaign by Esso, or the famous film-star appeal put out by Lux Toilet Soap. In the industrial field you have probably all seen advertisements by ICI or IBM, and the campaigns exhorting you to fly on a Boeing or Douglas aircraft. In the field of services the Chase Manhattan Bank have a series about 'Our man in . . .' which has a truly international appeal, while on the television and radio side you will all remember the famous Coca Cola theme song, about teaching the world to sing, which became a best selling pop record.

Hence you should aim to use a theme which will become known all over the world, and with which your company or its products is instantly associated. However, this is not easy, especially as so many themes are not universally acceptable. For example, if you base a sales message on the idea that your product will bring the user a marriage partner, you would be unable to use it in markets where marriages are arranged by the parents, as happens in many Latin American countries. If you use a theme for an industrial product which shows how labour may be saved by the use of a particular product, you would find this quite unacceptable in any market where labour is both cheap and plentiful. Moreover, themes often have to be varied to suit local buying habits. If you present a sales story to a German, for example, he wants it put in strong, hard-hitting and factual terms. When selling to the French or Italians you need to be more emotional, and less hard-hitting. Hence even if you can find a theme which appeals on a fairly international scale, you may well need to vary its presentation to suit local conditions. Even the Esso Tiger campaign had to be altered in countries where there was no easily usable word for tank.

2. The Wording of a Sales Message

Since most sales messages will have to be put into other languages, you will be concerned with what are often called 'translations' but should more correctly be termed 're-writes'. You cannot easily translate a sales message, but you can re-write it in other languages and still retain the original thought. This is highly skilled work, and you must not, for example, use a secretary to turn your sales leaflets into French or Dutch merely because she happens to speak those languages. You must not use translators as such, because you will get literal renderings of the original which will never have the same informative or persuasive power. All re-writes must be done in the country concerned, by people skilled in this type of work; who have a good knowledge of the trade in which you are engaged. This costs money, but it is better to spend money getting the message right in the first place, than to waste all the money you spend using the wrong words, which you will do if you put out inadequate sales messages. And always have any re-writes put back into English, to check that no mistakes have been made.

When you prepare an original sales message in English, for example, try to use simple and uncomplicated words. Avoid any play on words, and do not use words which have acquired special meanings. Hence avoid the use of slang expressions and colloquialisms. If in doubt, remember that many people have been educated by missionaries, so that English words in the Bible are generally familiar.

If producing material for use in other English-speaking countries, you must be careful to re-write this, because the Americans and Australians, for example, do not use the same version of the Queen's English as is used in Britain. Many languages, especially the older ones, lack the equivalents of modern technical terms, and you must add explanations of these where this occurs. Two other points are important: first, languages like Arabic read from right to left, which means the flow of the eye is affected as regards the words used; second, languages like German require more space for the same amount of wordage than English.

You should appreciate that leaving this kind of work to local people can result in mistakes being made which may be detrimental to your sales messages. You will doubtless recall instances when you have been in another country of seeing your language mistreated. 'Swits to order from the troley' is one. You may smile, but you would not wish your sales message to be the occasion for amusement. So make every effort to ensure that the words you use in a sales message are those which the local people would use themselves, and that these words put over your message in exactly the way that you wish and appeal to the motivations of the people reading them.

3. Illustrations in a Sales Message

As much care and attention must be paid to the illustrations in a sales message as to the words, and this is especially important when preparing material for television or the cinema screen. You must present your audience with scenes which are familiar to them, and this at once raises problems. Physical characteristics, dress, settings and general appearance vary a good deal throughout the world, and you must take local advice before you choose an illustration of a person. If you use photographs, make sure they represent the right type of people. If you use drawings, avoid giving offence by allowing the artist to add in, for example, a few lines on a face, thereby possibly indicating people of a certain tribe, which might offend those of a different tribe. It is all very well to say that Turkish women, for example, wear baggy trousers, but this is true mainly of the poorer people and those in the villages; it does not apply to the better-off Turkish women and would be downgrading to them.

In addition to people, backgrounds are important, because scenery varies so much around the world. The vegetation in hot climates is quite different from that in colder climates. Houses come in an infinite variety of shapes and sizes, both from an interior and an exterior point of view. Even a simple thing like perspective may be misunderstood, and you may know the story of the poster showing a picture of a huge fly with the message that since flies carry dirt and disease, you should keep them off food: the message failed because no one could believe that flies existed of that size. The setting to an advertisement must therefore be as carefully chosen as the words which are used. You may of course show internationally known scenes, but only to an audience which knows and appreciates them. And do not forget that in many parts of the world familiar things like the sea, snow, the desert even, are often quite unknown locally.

4. Production

Having chosen a suitable theme, the right words and the most apt illustrations, you still have the problem of turning these into type or film. Mistakes can be made here—for example, when the words are broken at the end of a line in the wrong place. Misprints are easy to make in any language, and easier still in an unfamiliar one. If you have type set in your country, make sure the proofs are also checked locally for hidden mistakes. If you have film material processed, make sure you show it, before it is used, to the local market, and have it checked. If you are making a radio commercial, check that the voice is suitable and understandable locally.

Hence the practice of having sales messages conceived, prepared and produced entirely by the exporter, or by the local people, seems to lead to many possibilities of error, which is why most experienced exporters prefer to control the execution of their promotion, but use the best skills of those in their own company allied to those of experienced local people. The whole purpose of any sales message is to create and motivate a demand market, so that you must know the characteristics of these demand markets thoroughly before you start to prepare the promotion material.

Export Public Relations

In the widest sense, public relations is a means of using any form of mass communications to create a favourable image of the company and its products, without actually buying space or time in the media. Hence it differs from advertising, where the company buys the right to say, within reason, what it wishes, subject only to the restraints placed on advertising by the law.

Public relations is concerned with several 'publics', whereas advertising is mainly concerned with the company's customers. Public relations is also concerned with the company's customers, but to the extent that the more favourable an image of the company and its products the more likely are people to buy the product. Product publicity in this case is a sales weapon, and a means of backing up the work of the salesmen. You can appreciate the value of publicity to a product given by means of an appearance in a television play or documentary, or in articles in the Press. Hence product publicity is an important part in any public relations campaign, but it is by no means the whole concern of public relations.

A favourable impression of a company and its products may also with advantage be created among the shareholders of the company, with the object of keeping up share prices and encouraging new investors. In these days investment is also made by people from other countries, and hence the value of the company image among investors on a worldwide scale. In addition to the shareholders, the company's suppliers may be influenced to think well of the company with advantage, because in times of short supplies, for example, suppliers will naturally tend to favour those customers with whom they are on the best terms, and of whom they think the most highly.

A fourth public of major importance today are the company's employees, because companies are no better than the people in them, while good industrial relations are imperative. Regrettably, many companies treat their employees, both senior and junior, badly, and many still deny those who work in the company any say in the running of its affairs. You cannot run a successful exporting company, or one which works on a truly international basis, without paying great attention to the needs and wants of all your staff, and the wider the company's interests the more necessary this becomes. You have already seen how important it is to treat your intermediaries as part of the company, and you must treat your own people at least as well. After all, the whole standing of your company in the international market-place will depend on the acceptance of it by the various 'publics' in both your domestic and overseas market, so that you should devote a part of any promotion budget to international public relations.

To carry out this work effectively, you may do a number of things:

(*a*) When anyone from the company travels overseas, they should be encouraged to make speeches and appear on local television and radio stations whenever possible, as a means of publicising the company and its activities. Local Rotary and other business associations welcome visitors at their meetings, and you may obtain an immense amount of valuable publicity for your company free by being prepared and willing to do this kind of work.

(*b*) As much information as possible should be channelled to the Press and other forms of media overseas. In this respect the COI can be a most valuable source of help because of its close connections with the media around the world.

(*c*) You can use advertising to promote a good image of the company, putting it in those publications which influence what are called the 'opinion-moulders' of the world—that is, people who are followed and imitated by others. These people almost form another 'public', and will include prominent business people, government officials, pop stars, film stars, famous sportsmen and women, and so on. You will appreciate the importance of being on good terms with foreign rulers and officials, especially when you wish to obtain permission to start local selling or manufacturing operations.

(*d*) You may help to publicise your company and its products in the export field by taking an interest in export clubs and by joining and taking an active part in such bodies as the Institute of Export and similar organisations.

(*e*) Making use of government-sponsored inward and outward missions is another effective means of publicity, and is good for export business. One of the largest contracts I have ever obtained began because someone remembered in one of the African countries that I had met them, and that I was in their line of business. It was at a lunch, and I had spoken about British exports. As a result I was asked to quote and obtained business I would otherwise probably have missed.

(*f*) Having visitors come to your factory or offices is another valuable way of obtaining publicity, and you should be prepared to encourage such visits. It is also a means of interesting your own people in export and showing them the results of their work, particularly when they meet the customers whom they supply in the flesh rather than only know them as unpronounceable names from unknown countries.

(*g*) The social responsibilities of any company operating internationally are becoming increasingly important, and you should, as an exporter, take an active interest in problems of pollution, ecology, labour relations, and the lessening of the gap between the richer and poorer nations.

Handling public relations on a worldwide scale presents many problems, because while adequate facilities in the form of public relations agencies and consultants exist in the more developed countries, such facilities are scarce in the developing ones. There are only a few agencies or consultants able to handle public relations on an international scale, and you may have to resort to using local facilities in most cases. But keep these firmly under your control and make sure the image you seek to promote is a uniform one throughout the world. Your most important tools will, however, always be the people you send around the world, because they have a unique opportunity of influencing people to think well of you, and that should be your prime object.

All your promotion efforts must be integrated into your export marketing plans. They form an integral part of your sales work and they are the means by which you obtain the business you have equipped yourself to handle.

Revision

Cover the page with a sheet of paper and uncover one question at a time.

Answers	*Questions*
	1. What are the two essential ingredients of all forms of promotion?
1. Information and persuasion.	2. What is the COI?
2. The Central Office of Information.	3. What are the three basic elements in a sales message?
3. The theme, the words and the illustrations.	4. What is direct marketing?
4. A development of direct mail.	5. What is the most commonly used paper size for promotion material?
5. A4.	6. By whom is advertising usually handled?
6. Advertising agencies.	7. How are space rates usually quoted in newspapers?
7. At so much a column-inch, centimetre or line.	8. What is a better word for translating?
8. Re-writing.	9. With whom is public relations concerned?
9. The company's various 'publics'.	10. Which seems the best method of arriving at a promotion budget?
10. Basing it on the marketing tasks to be accomplished.	

Exercises

1. Why might you hesitate to leave all your export promotion to the local people?
2. Discuss the merits and demerits of the various ways by which a promotion budget may be calculated.
3. What do you understand by non-advertising media, and what use can be made of them?
4. Look at a number of advertising campaigns currently running in your own country, and consider how far they would be suitable for other countries, and how far they might have to be amended.
5. What would be the main ingredients of a public relations campaign directed at export markets?
6. What help can the British government give exporters to promote their products?

16

MARKETING PLANS

The preceding chapters in this book have been designed to enable you to put into practice the principles of exporting. But before you can prepare a plan of action you must first decide on a strategy, whether you are starting to export for the first time, or trying to increase an already existing export business. Every company must of course develop its own export strategy, but if it does not, its export business is likely to drift along without any clear sense of direction.

An export strategy must have clear objectives to give it a sense of purpose and direction. It is a moot point whether objectives are produced as a result of deciding on strategies, or vice-versa. From practical experience I suggest it is generally easier, and often more satisfactory, if the objectives emerge as a result of decisions taken regarding strategy, because this allows you to base your objectives on what you know to be possible, rather than on what may be theoretically desirable but impossible to carry out in practice.

Having become clear about your export strategies and objectives, you must next prepare the export marketing plans to carry them out. This means you need to take all the elements of a modern marketing-mix, and weld them into meaningful and practical plans. You will need to consider the implementation of these plans, and then to evaluate them in the light of the results achieved. Successful exporters have found that the best results come when efforts are concentrated in a few directions, because diversifying efforts over too wide a scale in the world market-place usually results in insufficient attention being paid to the individual marketing operations.

Since the primary purpose of this book is to help you to become a professional exporter, you will have to consider what practical use you can now make of its contents. And if you do this, instead of remaining a shipping clerk, or staying in charge of export administration, you can progress towards becoming an export manager. You now manage, instead of merely carrying out strategies and plans prepared by someone else. The professional export manager produces the strategies and the plans, and is then responsible for seeing they are carried out. This book has been designed to enable you to do just this, and in due course to progress to becoming an export director.

Because export consists of so many closely related but seemingly diverse subjects, you will need, finally, to draw all the elements of export practice and marketing together. This is especially important for more junior staff, who are often unable to relate what they do, or know, to what goes on elsewhere in the export organisation. Hence this chapter has been divided into the following sections:

1. Export strategies
2. Export objectives
3. Export marketing plans

4. The export manager
5. The complete export transaction.

Export Strategies

You could well take the following principle as a basis for determining an export strategy: 'Don't do anything unless you know the export markets well and reckon you can get a good share of some of them, which is to say that you must have potential demand markets overseas.'

Hence you must initially recognise there is a need or a want for your product or the results of your skills, in other parts of the world. Your strategy will then determine how you satisfy those needs and wants by exporting. You must accordingly work out a manufacturing and selling strategy for your company, as it may be applied to the export side of the business. In this respect you have four basic options.

1. Manufacturing and Selling from a Domestic Base

You may decide to manufacture all your products for export in your own country and to sell them in overseas demand markets by supplying from your domestic base. You may either sell direct to the users, or use some form of intermediary to sell for you locally. For example, you make hand tools, perhaps a range of some twenty items. You may make them in the domestic factory and export them to as many demand markets overseas as you can find, or wish to develop.

2. Manufacturing and Selling from Overseas Bases

You may decide to decentralise both your manufacturing and selling activities, establishing local factories overseas and setting up your own sales organisations. You are in effect exporting your skills, but you are at the same time controlling the whole operation yourself, without the intervention of outside people. For example, you make soft drinks. As you do not wish to export bottles, tins or water, you establish local bottling plants, and set up local sales companies to market the drinks produced there. In this case you are in effect turning your company into a multi-national one, because you have established subsidiaries in other parts of the world.

3. Supplying Skills for Others to Export

You may prefer to sell the know-how, or the skills, you possess rather than the actual results of those skills, and leave others to turn these into products and sell them locally. Here your involvement with export will be minimal, but you may well add to your domestic earnings a substantial sum from overseas, as a result of selling your skills. For example, you sell high-technology electronic components, but you do not wish to enlarge your own domestic production capacity, either domestically or overseas. So you license others to manufacture and sell for you and collect royalties on the sales made, as well as on the sale of the local manufacturing rights.

4. Manufacturing but not Selling for Export

You may elect to remain a manufacturer of products suitable for export, but not actually to export them yourself, leaving this work to be handled by experts in export marketing. For example, you produce a wide range of computer peripherals, and your main skill lies in your ability to produce a continuous stream of new ones. You concentrate on this side, and leave others to export them for you. Hence your sales are to companies in your own country.

So far so good. But nothing is ever quite as clearcut as this, because your demand markets are, as you have seen, affected by world political factors, which means there is no true international free trade. Hence you can seldom adopt the same strategy for all your demand markets, and you may have to adopt more than one according to where in the world your demand markets exist. So you might have to manufacture locally in demand markets where direct imports are forbidden for some reason, although you could supply to other demand markets where imports of your products were freely allowed. You might have to license others to make and sell your product where there was no other means of supplying that demand market. Hence you must decide, not only on your basic export strategies, but which you will use in each of your major demand markets.

You will in addition have to consider the following variations in these strategies.

Same Product, Same Marketing

As you have seen, while your product may have to be varied, it is possible to export the same product, for much the same reasons, in overseas demand markets. Pepsi Cola is a good example of this form of strategy.

Same Product, Different Marketing

While you may not need to vary your product to any major degree, you may have to alter the way it is sold. For example, outboard motors are sold in developed markets for recreational use. In less developed markets they will probably have to be sold for more commercial reasons, such as fishing or transport.

Different Product, Same Marketing

As you saw in Chapter 12, product modifications are often essential for overseas markets. But you may still sell in basically the same way, because it is only the outward appearance of the product which changes. For example, if you sell instant coffee, you might use the same appeal, merely altering the blend to suit local tastes.

Different Product, Different Marketing

In addition to modifying your product for demand markets overseas, you may also have to change your methods of marketing. For example, when exporting pottery you may have to alter the lead content, as well as produce different designs to suit local tastes. You might also have to consider selling the pottery as a useful household article in some markets but as a status symbol in others.

You will recall here that you might, in extreme circumstances, have to adopt an entirely different manufacturing strategy in export markets from that used domestically. But these are extreme cases, and rarely adopted by exporters because of the immense problems involved in having one product for export and an entirely different one for the home market.

In addition to the above you should also consider the following points.

Prices and Profit

When you price for export, will you aim to sell a high volume in return for a modest profit on each unit, or a smaller volume but obtaining a much higher margin of profit per unit?

Finance of Exports

When you consider the finances needed to operate your export trade, you must decide whether these shall come from the company's resources or whether you will seek them outside, and if so, from which source.

Personnel Required

To export in any way you require people. Will you try to obtain them from outside the company or use company personnel and provide them with the necessary training and experience?

To decide on export strategies you normally begin by studying your export demand markets, and work backwards through the various options until you arrive at what seems to you the best set of options. At this stage you will be concerned with your company's export objectives, and you will need at the same time to decide on these objectives in the light of the various options open to you as regards strategy.

Export Objectives

You must start with your company's overall objectives, which you may find difficult to define in anything other than vague and meaningless terms. But you must be more specific when considering export objectives, and you might begin by considering why you wish to become involved with export at all, or why you wish to expand your existing export business. You might come up with any or all the following reasons.

Your Domestic Market is Saturated

Your product's life cycle may be diminishing, and the domestic market be saturated with newer and better competitive products. Hence export may provide the best outlet for your products.

Greater Profitability

You may decide that increased profitability of the company can only come from a larger output, and that export provides the best means of increasing your output.

Better Use of Existing Resources

You may be under-using your resources, and feel that export can provide the best means of increasing the use of your existing resources, in terms of money, production, marketing and personnel capacities.

Spreading the Risk

You may feel your domestic market's ups and downs could be evened out if you were less dependent on it, and that your export markets would not be subject to such uneven trading conditions.

None of these is, of course, an entirely satisfactory objective for exporting or increasing your involvement with export. Hence you might expand your thinking towards deciding to what extent you wish to be involved with export trade, and you might well express this in terms of the percentage of the effort and resources you wish to devote to export. Thus you might arrive at an objective which stated that of your total company's business, your wish is to have 60 per cent provided from overseas and 40 per cent from the domestic market. This will enable you also to determine the ratio of effort to be devoted to each side of the business, and to apply this ratio to the use of the company's total resources.

If you apply this kind of thinking to formulating your company's export objectives, you will need to consider the various strategies you can adopt, and you might then come up with something like the following.

The Growth Rate Expected of Export

You could set a precise figure on the rate of growth expected from the export side of the business, and the length of time you feel will be required to achieve that rate.

The Means of Achieving this Growth

This could be expressed in terms of the products or skills to be exported, the finance required, and the possibility of growth through acquiring other companies, at home or overseas. After all, you can buy local manufacturing and/or selling companies as well as setting them up yourself.

The Profits Required

You can then decide on the amount of profit export is expected to produce, and assess this in relation to the company's overall profitability.

What you must not do is to come up with objectives which are vague. For example, you should not merely say that you wish to obtain from export the maximum profits possible, because this tends to induce you to dissipate your efforts, merely in an attempt to grab any business that happens to be going in another part of the world. It also tends to induce you to spend as little as possible on developing your exports, and to take as much profit as you can at the time.

What you must do is to be precise, both as to the strategies which are within your means and the objectives which you expect them to produce for the company. To illustrate this, consider the examples quoted earlier. In the case of the company selling hand tools, its objectives might be to have 50 per cent of its business overseas and 50 per cent at home, with a growth rate on each of say 10 per cent and a profit figure of 15 per cent gross, representing a return on capital of 20 per cent. The company selling soft drinks might decide that 80 per cent of its total business should come from overseas, and that the same percentage of its overall profits should come from its non-domestic business, thereby allowing it to allocate up to that amount of its overall resources to developing its export business. The company selling high-technology electronic components might, however, opt for a contribution to the company's profits of no more than 7½ per cent, the investment and resources needed to achieve this being minimal. Finally, the company selling computer peripherals might expect no more than a 5 per cent return for supplying others in the domestic market with the peripherals, and have virtually no outlay at all other than supplying the products, since the entire export business would be someone else's concern.

You will appreciate that these examples are greatly oversimplified, but they serve to show the manner in which export objectives may be expressed, and how these may be determined. If you add together the strategies you propose to employ, you should be able to come up with a set of simple, yet worthwhile objectives, and these will show you the direction in which you should make your export efforts.

Export Marketing Plans

You will need to prepare, execute and evaluate export marketing plans to carry out your export strategies and objectives. You will also need to adapt basic marketing principles to suit the environmental conditions of your overseas demand markets. But you should, as far as possible, concentrate on those demand markets which are most similar to your domestic market. And you should concentrate your efforts on a few overseas demand markets; you will find in fact that you cannot as a rule do justice to more than a third to a half of them. This means using what has been described as the commonsense of concentration.

Preparing an Export Marketing Plan

This will involve you in a consideration of the following points.

The Product

What you propose to offer an overseas demand market must be evaluated in terms of the modifications it may need, and the way it is to be presented. It must, as nearly as possible, meet the needs of the demand market in question. It must have some comparative advantages over its competitors. For example, if you offer tractors, they must suit the local soil conditions; the local labour to operate them; and the means of the buyers to pay for them. If you offer some form of packaged food, this must be manufactured, packaged and labelled to suit local conditions, both social and legal. In both cases there must be genuine advantages in your product over competing products. You must not adopt the attitude that what you make is best for the buyers; it is for them to decide, not you.

The Distribution

To ensure that supplies are available, in addition to arranging this with your factory or outside suppliers, you must consider first the transport of your goods to the demand in question. You must include in any plan a consideration of which method of transport is to be used; what documentary procedures have to be followed; what insurance will be necessary; what method of payment will be acceptable to the buyers; and if any legal problems require to be settled.

Second, you must consider what method of selling you will adopt: that is, whether you go direct to the final users; use intermediaries to sell for you; or to stock and supply for you and so on. For example, selling tractors you might decide to ship by sea and supply from stocks held locally, but to use local selling agents to carry out the actual selling on your behalf, at the same time providing an after-sales service.

The Promotion

No marketing plan is complete without some consideration of which methods of promotion you will use. For example, you might decide that the spearhead of your promotion for tractors would be to show them at special agricultural trade fairs held overseas; to advertise the tractors in the farming magazines; and to provide small presents for the farmers in the shape of special hats or caps with the tractor's name on them. You must consider how much is to be spent on promotion, and how the campaign is to be handled.

The Price

As you have seen, you have so far been unable to fix a final price for your exports because you did not know all your costs. At this stage you are in a position to do so, because you know your transport and distribution costs; you know how much documentation will cost; what insurance will be required; what payment terms and all their implications in regard to credit, etc., will cost you; you will have discovered what price the market will bear; and you now can say what your costs of obtaining the business are likely to be in terms of selling and promotion. So an essential feature of an export marketing plan is the price and terms to be charged, together with the method you will use to quote the customer. You cannot possibly know the price you should charge, in order to obtain the required profit, until you have finally made up your marketing plan.

The Strength of the Demand Market

In order to arrive at a precise estimation of the sales you aim to achieve, you will need to examine your demand markets, and then to compare the returns which seem likely with the expenditure you feel is necessary to achieve them. In practice you will have to do these sums a good many times in order to arrive at the optimum result.

If all this sounds like a great deal of hard work for each demand market, remember that in practice export marketing plans for the same product are seldom so dissimilar to each other as they may sound. Moreover, they usually follow a similar pattern from one year to another, provided they are successful. Thus you can usually build on what has already been done, either in that demand market or elsewhere, and only make minor amendments from time to time. But you must have a marketing plan for each demand market, otherwise your export trade with it will suffer from lack of direction and you will not be able to exploit its possibilities to the full. Nor will you know what returns to expect, or even be able to say whether the operation was financially successful or not.

Implementing an Export Marketing Plan

Having prepared a plan you must see it is effectively carried out. This involves you in many things, but basically you must:

(*a*) Ensure that supplies of the product are available in the right quantities at the right time, which will involve you in using all the resources of the export office, as set out in Part 2 of this book.

(*b*) Ensure that all the channels of distribution are able and willing to handle the supplies, so that every potential customer is able to purchase your product when required.

(*c*) Arrange to have the promotion and selling carried out in the agreed way and at the correct time, in the manner most suited to the local environmental conditions.

Both the above will involve you in using all the principles and practices set out in Part 3 of this book.

(*d*) See that everyone involved knows well in advance what part they are to play in the execution of the plan, and how this fits in with the tasks of the other people concerned. The success of any marketing plan is in direct proportion to the ability of the export manager in charge to communicate with the rest of the people concerned.

(*e*) Keep a strict control over the whole operation, whether this is being handled by company personnel or people from outside.

Evaluating an Export Marketing Plan

Having set the targets which you expect your plan to achieve, you must monitor the results in order to be able to assess them in terms of the effort and expenditure involved and to enable you to amend the plan if it does not produce the desired results. To do this you should:

(*a*) Have a system for checking the results at frequent intervals. Normally it has been found that quarterly figures are sufficient, unless it is a major operation when weekly or monthly results will be needed.

(*b*) Have a series of options available if the plan appears not to be succeeding. This is necessary because while you may be able to stop the plan, you should also be able to alter it without a complete stoppage of the operation.

(*c*) Make sure everyone concerned knows what results are expected, and what they should do if things are not going according to the plan. Moreover, make sure everyone is informed as soon as any alterations have to be made.

(*d*) Decide in advance what you consider is to be a success or failure, and how you will view the results.

Should you feel that the whole process of preparing, implementing and evaluating an export marketing plan sounds like a series of spasmodic operations, remember that in practice the development of demand markets is a continuing process, and that you will be largely contributing to that process.

The Export Manager

By now you will appreciate that to be a successful export manager requires you to be far more than one who runs an export office. It means more than setting off on an endless round of selling trips overseas. It means more than becoming immersed in the routine of documentation and payment problems. As an export manager you will be expected to know how to carry out all these functions, but you need to be able to do a great deal more. You must, for example, be able to put into practice management principles as applied to export. You must be able to prepare and have agreed export strategies and objectives. You must be able to initiate and control export marketing plans. And you must be able to handle all the export personnel, as well as see that they are the right people for the work, training them whenever necessary.

You might then define the role of the professional export manager as follows.

1. *Evaluating export demand markets.* A great deal of an export manager's time will be taken up in assessing his export demand markets, especially as these are constantly changing and requiring fresh evaluation.
2. *Preparing export marketing plans.* These will present a continuing challenge in order to take into account opportunities as they occur or disappear. One day, for example, your market in Angola disappears because of internal wars; the next day an opportunity presents itself in Cyprus because internal strife comes to an end.
3. *Evaluating the competition.* As soon as you succeed in a demand market someone will try to take the business away from you, so that you must always aim to keep one step ahead of your competitors.
4. *Delegating responsibilities.* Since most of your time will be taken up with planning and supervising the export activities of the company, you will need to be able to delegate responsibility. You will need to be able to communicate easily, and above all motivate other people, both at home and overseas, of any nationality.
5. *Controlling complex operations.* Because export is concerned with such a wide range of complex operations you will need at all times to be firmly in control, and able to take decisions, often at short notice.

What particular additional qualities should an export manager possess? There are four which are of especial importance:

1. You must have a liking for all aspects of export practice, and the mechanics of export trade.
2. You should be anxious to use modern marketing methods, and have an interest in adapting them to widely differing local environments overseas.
3. You should possess special abilities for handling financial matters, because an export manager will be more concerned with finance than almost any other side of the business. Products may not be all that different overseas, but the way they are priced and the manner in which you arrange the financial details are what make all the difference between successful and profitable exporting and unprofitable export business.
4. You should be able to put into practice modern management techniques, and apply them to markets which often use dissimilar ones, by adapting them to suit local conditions.

How can the necessary knowledge be obtained to fit the export manager for what is an exacting, yet immensely rewarding career? There are many ways, but in particular the following:

1. You must take the National Foundation Course in Export, sponsored by the BOTB and now available at many colleges of higher education in Britain.
2. You must take the Final Part II examination of the Institute of Export syllabus, and thus earn the right to put M.I.Ex.(Grad.) after your name.
3. You should complete some form of Diploma in Management Studies, preferably one with an emphasis on international trade.
4. You should take every opportunity of travelling overseas, in order to learn local conditions at first hand.
5. You should cultivate the art of diplomacy, and a liking for, as well as an understanding of, people of all colours, races and creeds.
6. You should learn at least one other language, and be able to speak it reasonably fluently. You should also learn to say a few words in any language you are likely to encounter.
7. You should have a natural love of travel; and you should aim to travel well, anywhere in the world, whatever the conditions.
8. You should possess or develop a strong entrepreneurial spirit, because export lends itself to the art of the entrepreneur.
9. You should always be ready to continue learning, because you will never know enough about the world or the art of export. Hence you might, having read this book, study the comprehensive book list in Appendix 2 and read those books in the areas of the greatest interest to you.

You may not be paid in material wealth as much as your opposite number on the domestic side. But remember that in job satisfaction you will gain immeasurably, and that the top positions in business increasingly go to those with international experience.

The Complete Export Transaction

It is to some degree inevitable that when a subject as complex as export is divided up into easily assimilated sections, the overall pattern tends to disappear. But you should always try to view any export transaction as a whole, and this you may do under the following headings:

1. *The company's skills.* You should be aware of these as they are expressed in the products or services produced by the company, and be able to place them in the context of present-day international trade.
2. *The company's export objectives.* You will have to define and work to the company's export objectives, and in particular relate these to the resources the company is prepared to devote to the export side of the business.
3. *Overseas demand markets.* You must be fully aware of the possibilities and extent of your demand markets overseas and how far these are affected by local environmental conditions, thus being enabled to assess your ability to satisfy the needs and wants of those markets.
4. *Information.* You must know where and how to obtain all the information you need about your demand markets.
5. *The legal side of export.* You must understand the legal requirements in

international trade, and how to avoid becoming entangled with the law anywhere in the world.

6. *Product requirements.* You must be able to assess and make any necessary modifications to a product, so that it exactly matches the needs and wants of each demand market, and in addition possesses some advantages over its competitors.

7. *Export practice.* You will have to decide the conditions under which your goods will be offered for sale in terms of delivery, payment, prices and conditions of sale, as well as how they will be transported overseas and the documentation required to effect this.

8. *Insurance.* You will need to insure your goods against loss or damage; and you will have to take out insurance against risks of non-payment by your customers, especially those due to causes beyond their control.

9. *Payment.* You must be able to agree terms of payment with your customers, and use them as an essential means of obtaining the business.

10. *Distribution.* You must ensure the smooth distribution of your goods to the end user, and be able to sell or motivate others to sell for you.

11. *Promotion.* You should be able to use all the means of promotion in a highly competitive world, and thus ensure the sale of your products.

All the above are closely interrelated, and the practice and marketing of export are in fact part of the whole transaction. Since your demand markets are largely fashioned by the state of international trade, you must examine your export business and evaluate it against a background of world trading conditions, as shown in Part 1 of this book. Hence you might liken export to a circle, so that you finish more or less where you begin, because the process of exporting is never-ending, but revolves endlessly, spurred on by the activities of the export manager in a highly professional way. You should by now see how you personally can keep that circle turning, to both your own and your company's advantage.

Revision

Cover the page with a sheet of paper and uncover one question at a time.

Answers	*Questions*
	1. How are a company's export objectives often decided?
1. As a result of determining its export strategies.	2. What is an export manager?
2. One who manages the exports of a company instead of carrying out other people's plans.	3. When you establish local manufacturing and selling companies overseas what are you in effect doing?
3. Setting up a multi-national company.	4. Give an example of a product with the same marketing strategy everywhere.

Answers	*Questions*
4. Pepsi Cola.	5. How might you sell household pottery, other than as a useful article?
5. As a status symbol.	6. Who sponsors the National Foundation Course in Export?
6. The BOTB.	7. How could you define a company's export objectives?
7. As a percentage of the company's business overall.	8. How many other languages should an export manager be able to speak?
8. At least one.	9. What must you do to increase your knowledge of export matters?
9. Read widely and travel.	10. Why should you use insurance in export?
10. To protect goods against loss or damage, and the exporter against non-payment.	

Exercises

1. Make an evaluation of the qualities, knowledge and experience that you feel an export manager should possess.
2. What are the four main export strategies?
3. How could you arrive at a company's export objectives, and how might they be expressed?
4. What would you do to ensure the successful completion of an export marketing plan?
5. How would you define the main elements in any export transaction?
6. Set down briefly what you have learned from this book.

APPENDIX 1

EXPORT DOCUMENTATION

This Appendix contains specimen copies of the main documents and forms currently used in the export trade in the United Kingdom. These have been shown blank, since indications of how they should be filled in are given in appropriate places in the text.

FOR OFFICIAL USE

No........ /.................. /......

DEPARTMENT OF TRADE — Export Licensing Branch

Application for Export Licence

FORM A - PART 1

A Applicant's Reference........ .... Telephone No......................(Ext. ....: .. ..)

1. (a) Name of consignor ....

(b) Address..

....

(c) Telephone No. .... (Ext...................................)

2. Enter the official reference number of any previous application made in respect of these goods or any part of them. If no such application has been made, enter "None". ....

3. Give any relevant information in support of your application, e.g. details of Import Licence or Certificate of Essentiality; Government Department's reference number where the application has official approval. ....

4. Name and address of consignee

....

....

5. Proposed date of shipment

....

SPECIMEN

I HEREBY DECLARE that to the best of my knowledge and belief all the particulars in Part I and Part II of this application (including any accompanying schedules) are correctly stated, and I undertake that if a licence is granted to me, it shall be used solely for the export of goods being my own property or the property of a person, firm or company named above as consignor for whom I am authorised to act in this transaction as the sole responsible representative. I am aware that the exporter or shipper of the exported goods, if so required by the Commissioners of Her Majesty's Customs and Excise, must produce to them, within such time as they may allow, proof to their satisfaction that the said goods were duly delivered at the destination named in the licence.

Date.. *Signature* ....

Status ....

B Official No. of signatory specially authorised to sign applications for export licences (see Note 4 on page 1)

WARNING: Penalties may be imposed in respect of false statements in applications for export licences.

Page 2

Fig. 1. Form A: Application for Export Licence.
(courtesy Department of Trade)

FOR OFFICIAL USE

No........../......................../19.....

DEPARTMENT OF TRADE — Export Licensing Branch

A

Applicant's Reference	Telephone No	(Ext)

FORM A - PART II

(Before completion please read instructions on page 1)

C *Insert in this address box the name and address of the person or company to whom the licence, when validated, is to be sent do not use for the transmission of the application to the Export Licensing Branch.*

THIS DOCUMENT WILL BE EFFECTIVE AS AN EXPORT LICENCE ONLY WHEN IT HAS BEEN VALIDATED BY THE DEPARTMENT OF TRADE

For the purposes of any Order made under the Import, Export and Customs Powers (Defence) Act 1939, prohibiting without licence the export of goods from the United Kingdom, the Secretary of State hereby authorises and permits

D Consignor's name..

Address..

Telephone No. .... (Ext. ....)

to export by post (see Note 5, page 4) or from any port in the United Kingdom *(see Note 6, page 4)* within a period of twelve months from the date of this Licence, to

Port and Country overseas..

consigned to

Consignee's name..

Address..

the following goods, namely:

SPECIMEN

Quantity *(see Instructions)*	Full description of the goods (Not more than one item should appear on each line)	F.O.B. Value £
	If the above space is insufficient, please continue on a separate sheet in triplicate	
	TOTAL F.O.B. VALUE	

.... *Authorised on behalf of the Secretary of State for Trade*

Page 3

Fig. 1 (contd)

ORIGINAL

C.273(1)

Exporter (name and address)

Customs assigned number **CAN**

Air WB or B/L No.

Exporter's ref.

Tariff Heading No. (first 4 digits)

F/Agent's ref.

H.M. CUSTOMS AND EXCISE

*SPECIFICATION/PRE-SHIPMENT ENTRY FOR EXPORTS

THIS FORM MAY BE USED FOR ONE ITEM ONLY. For consignments of more than one item, attach a form C.273 (SCHEDULE) or use Form C.273(4).

FOR OFFICIAL USE

Forwarding agent (name and address)

NOT to be used for goods on which U.K. duty relief is claimed or for which an export licence, other than a CAP export licence is required.

Country of destination | Code

Date of clearance

Dock/Wharf/Station

DIRECTIONS FOR COMPLETING THESE BOXES ARE AT NOTE 4 BELOW

ICD | Container | (a) RO/RO (b)

Ship/Flight etc. | Code | Port/Airport of export | Code

Port/Airport of discharge

WARNING
There are heavy penalties for making false declarations

NOTES

1. Further instructions on the completion of this form will be found in the Customs and Excise Tariff and on its use in Notice No. 275.
2. If return of the duplicate by post is required the box on reverse thereof should be completed.
3. The Code should be inserted after Country of destination, Ship/Flight, etc. (Nationality of ship) and Port/Airport of export. The Codes are listed in the Tariff.
4. *See below.*

Marks and numbers | Number and kind of packages; description of goods | Tariff/Trade code number

Quantity 2 | Quantity 1 (Net wt.) | Value (f.o.b.) (nearest £)

Quantity 3

For goods consigned to or via the EEC or to Greece or Turkey, insert X in appropriate box and complete or delete the items as appropriate.

CT form type........../ AG1/ATR1 attached ☐   CT form type........../AG1/ATR1 already lodged Customs No. .... ☐   CT form, AG1 or ATR1 not required ☐

The above quantities (nearest unit in each case) are as required for the appropriate code number in the Tariff.

NOTES *(Continued)*

4. **ICD Box.** For goods exported through an Inland Clearance Depot or Inland Rail Depot, enter Code of Depot (see list in Tariff).

Container Box. If goods are exported in a container enter "2" in this box.

RO/RO Box (Roll on/Roll off Road Traffic).

Under (a). If goods are exported by this method enter "1", if not enter "8".

Under (b). *If applicable and when known enter code:*

"2" for U.K. registered powered vehicle
"4" for foreign registered powered vehicle } with or without trailer
"5" for unaccompanied trailer

DECLARATION I, the undersigned, declare that:—

(a) all the particulars set forth above are correctly stated;
(b) the *exporter/agent is the holder of the Customs assigned number quoted;
(c) the export of the goods specified does not contravene export control restrictions on account of the description, ultimate destination or other reason.

Name of firm *Exporter/Agent

Signature

Date

C.273 (1)   *Delete as necessary   F 3690 (Dec. 1973)   52-9038 8/74 HPB

Fig. 2. H.M. Customs Entry Form C.273(1).
(reproduced by permission of the Controller, HMSO)

C. 63A (1)

Customs assigned number CAN		Air WB or B/L No.
	Exporter's ref.	Tariff Heading No. (first 4 digits)
Entry No.	F/Agents ref.	

Exporter (name and address)

H.M. CUSTOMS AND EXCISE

Shipping Bill for Merchandise required to be entered before shipment solely by reason of Export Licensing requirements

FOR OFFICIAL USE

Passed ....

Port of first lodgement if other than Port of shipment ....

Forwarding agent (name and address)

Export Licence No.

Country of destination | Code

Date of clearance | Dock/Wharf/Station

DIRECTIONS FOR COMPLETING THESE BOXES ARE AT NOTE 3 BELOW | ICD | Container | (a) RO/RO (b)

Ship/Flight etc. | Code | Port/Airport of export | Code

Port/Airport of discharge | Final destination

WARNING

There are heavy penalties for making false declarations

NOTES

1. Further instructions on the completion of this form will be found in the Customs and Excise Tariff.
2. The Code should be inserted after Country of destination Ship/Flight etc. (Nationality of ship) and Port/Airport of export. The Codes are listed in the Tariff.
3. *See below*

Marks and numbers | Number and kind of packages; description of goods | Tariff/Trade code number

THIS FORM MAY BE USED FOR ONE ITEM ONLY

Consignments of more than one item may be entered on a Form C. 63A (4)

Quantity 2 | Quantity 1 (Net wt.) | Value (f.o.b.) (nearest £)

Quantity 3

Note—These goods must not be shipped without the authority of the officer of Customs and Excise and must be produced to him at the time of shipment if so required.

For goods consigned to or via the EEC or to Greece or Turkey, insert X in the appropriate box and complete the first item, or delete, as appropriate.

CT form type ..../ AG1/ATR1 attached ☐ | CT form, AG1 or ATR1 not required ☐

The above quantities (nearest unit in each case) are as required for the appropriate code number in the Tariff.

NOTES (*Continued*)

3. ICD Box. For goods exported through an Inland Clearance Depot or Inland Rail Depot, enter Code of Depot (see list in Tariff).

Container Box. If goods are exported in a container enter "2" in this box.

RO/RO Box (roll on/Roll off Road Traffic).

Under (a). If goods are exported by this method enter "1", if not enter "9".

Under (b). *If applicable and when known* enter code:
"2" for U.K. registered powered vehicle } with or
"4" for foreign registered powered vehicle } without trailer.
"5" for unaccompanied trailer.

DECLARATION I, the undersigned, declare that :—
(a) all the particulars set forth above are correctly stated;
(b) the * *exporter/agent* is the holder of the Customs assigned number quoted;
(c) the export of the goods specified does not contravene export control restrictions on account of the description, ultimate destination or other reason.

Name of Firm
*Exporter/Agent

Signature

Date

C63A (1) *Delete as necessary F.509 (Nov. 1973) 2836/2404L D365575 150M 3/74 TP 52-00

Fig. 3. H.M. Customs Entry Form C.63A(1).
(reproduced by permission of the Controller, HMSO)

T3 INTERNAL COMMUNITY TRANSIT

Declaration

E.C. E.F. E.G. C.E.

1. Guarantee

Statistical No.

ORIGINAL

COPY FOR THE OFFICE OF DEPARTURE 1

Please see Notice No. 751 before completing this form

Office of departure

2. Appended documents

5. Customs assigned number CAN

Document issued on under No.

3. Prev. customs procedure

4. Number of Forms T.3. bis

6. Exporter's reference No.

7. Agent's reference No.

Stamp

Signature

10. DECLARATION.......................................
represented by.......................................
hereby undertakes to produce the goods described below intact and within the prescribed time limit at the office of destination
at.......................................
At............................on............................
(place of signature) (date)

Signature.......................................

11. Consignee

25. Country of destination

30. Number, kind, marks and numbers of packages

31. Description of goods

32.

35. Country of consignment

36. Gross weight

37. Price

30. Number, kind, marks and numbers of packages

31. Description of goods

32.

35. Country of consignment

36. Gross weight

37. Price

45. Offices of transit intended (and countries)

46. Offices of transit used (and countries)

50	Place	Mode of transport	CHR	Identity of vehicle	C	Nationality/Flag	51. Previous country of consignment
Entry into the Community							
Loading/ Transhipment							
Transhipment							
Transhipment Unloading							52. First country of destination
Exit from the Community							

C117 Sec. F3813 (Nov. 1972) MLC 56-7541 9/72

Fig. 4. T3 Movement Certificate.
(reproduced by permission of the Controller, HMSO)

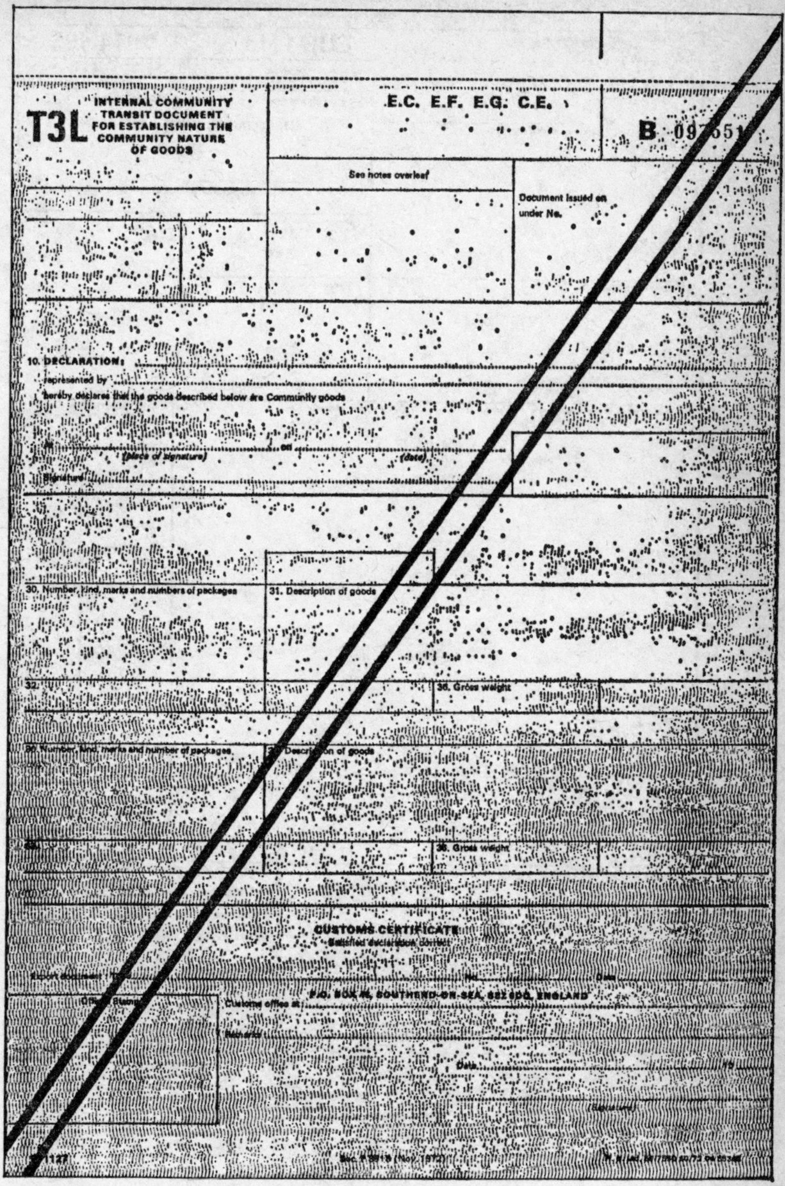
T3L INTERNAL COMMUNITY TRANSIT DOCUMENT FOR ESTABLISHING THE COMMUNITY NATURE OF GOODS

E.C. E.F. E.G. C.E.

See notes overleaf

Document issued on

under No.

10. DECLARATION:

represented by

hereby declares that the goods described below are Community goods

(place of signature) on (date)

Signature

30. Number, kind, marks and numbers of packages

31. Description of goods

32.

36. Gross weight

30. Number, kind, marks and number of packages

31. Description of goods

32.

36. Gross weight

CUSTOMS CERTIFICATE

Satisfied declaration correct

Export document No. Date

Official Stamp

Customs office at

Remarks

Date 19

(Signature)

Fig. 5. T3L Movement Certificate.
(reproduced by permission of the Controller, HMSO)

MOVEMENT CERTIFICATE

1 Exporter (Name, full address, country)

EUR 1 No. D074 495

See notes overleaf before completing this form

2 Certificate used in preferential trade between

THE EUROPEAN ECONOMIC COMMUNITY

and

(Insert appropriate countries or groups of countries or territories)

3 Consignee (Name, full address, country) (Optional)

4 Country, group of countries or territory of exportation

EEC

5 Country, group of countries or territory of destination

6 Transport details (Optional)

7 Remarks

8 Item number: marks and numbers	Number and kind of packages (1): description of goods	9 Gross weight (kg) or other measure (litres, cu.m, etc.)	10 Invoices (Optional)

(1) If goods are not packed, indicate number of articles, or state "in bulk" as appropriate.

11 CUSTOMS ENDORSEMENT

Declaration certified.

Export document (2):

Form .... No ....

Customs office ....

Issuing country or territory:

UNITED KINGDOM

Date ....

(Signature)

Stamp

(2) Complete only where the regulations of the exporting country or territory require.

12 DECLARATION BY THE EXPORTER

I, the undersigned, declare that the goods described above meet the conditions required for the issue of this certificate.

(Place and date)

(Signature)

C.1299

F.4265 (Dec. 1973)

Fig. 6. EUR 1 Movement Certificate.
(reproduced by permission of the Controller, HMSO)

FORM **EUR. 2** B 678040

(Copy 1)

Before completing this form read the instructions overleaf carefully.

1. Name and address of exporter

2. Declaration by the exporter

I, THE UNDERSIGNED, the exporter of the goods described below contained in this postal packet,

— DECLARE that the goods are situated in the United Kingdom and fulfill the conditions required for the completion of this form in accordance with the provisions governing trade between the European Economic Community and the country of destination(1) and that the goods are originating products within the meaning of these provisions;

— UNDERTAKE to furnish to the appropriate authorities any supporting evidence which they may require, and to allow them to inspect my accounts and verify the circumstances of manufacture of the goods described below.

3. Name and address of consignee

4. Place and date

5. Remarks (2)

6. Signature of exporter

7.

8. Country of destination

9. Gross weight

10. Description of goods

11. Authority in the exporting country responsible for verification of the declaration by the exporter.

International Division,
H.M. Customs & Excise,
King's Beam House,
Mark Lane,
London EC3R 7HE,
England.

(For notes see reverse)
C.1297

Notes (see reverse)

(1) Indicate the contracting parties to the agreement under which this form has been completed.

(2) Give particulars of any verification already undertaken by the appropriate authorities.

Instructions for completing form EUR. 2

A. This form may only be completed in respect of goods in the exporting country which fulfill the conditions specified in box 2 overleaf. These conditions should be studied carefully before the form is completed.

B. The reference "EUR. 2" and serial number of the form should be stated on the Customs green label declaration C1 or on the Customs declaration C2/CP3, as appropriate.

C. After completing and signing the two copies of the form, the exporter should,
— for goods sent by parcel post attach both copies to the despatch note,
— for goods sent by letter post attach copy 1 firmly to the packet and place copy 2 inside the packet.

This form is for use for exports by post to Austria, Portugal, Sweden or Switzerland of a value not exceeding 1,000 Units of Account under the Free Trade Agreements between these countries and the EEC. For further information see Notice 810, obtainable from any Custom House or office of a Collector of Customs & Excise in the United Kingdom or from GSD Unit 4, H.M. Customs & Excise, King's Beam House, Mark Lane, London EC3R 7HE. Special attention is drawn to paragraph 72 of Notice 810 relating to the endorsement for ex-EFTA treatment:

While at the time of printing, Free Trade Agreements with Finland, Iceland and Norway were not in force, this form may be used for exports to those countries. Further information will be published in a supplement to Notice 810.

Dd 148489 5/73 W(B)L 52-7784

Fig. 7. EUR 2 Movement Certificate.
(reproduced by permission of the Controller, HMSO)

Johnson ScanStar

JOINT SERVICE: JOHNSON LINE STOCKHOLM
THE EAST ASIATIC COMPANY LTD. COPENHAGEN
BLUE STAR LINE LTD. LONDON

WESTBOUND SAILING SCHEDULE

No. 47 April, 1978

UNITED KINGDOM TO PACIFIC COAST OF U.S.A. AND CANADA

VESSEL	Voy.	LONDON			LIVERPOOL			GLASGOW			ARRIVES					
		FCL/LCL	RECEIVING	SAILS	FCL/LCL	RECEIVING	SAILS	FCL/LCL	RECEIVING	SAILS	LOS ANGELES	OAKLAND	VANCOUVER	SEATTLE	PORTLAND	HONOLULU
AXEL JOHNSON	38W	FCL LCL	29/3 - 9/4 25/3 - 7/4	12/4	FCL LCL	8/4 - 12/4 6/4 - 9/4	14/4†	FCL LCL	7/4 - 13/4 6/4 - 12/4	14/4	1/5	3/5	5/5	7/5	9/5	★
FALSTRIA	27W	FCL LCL	12/4 - 15/4 8/4 - 14/4	18/4	FCL LCL	13/4 - 19/4 12/4 - 16/4	20/4	FCL LCL	14/4 - 20/4 13/4 - 19/4	21/4	8/5	10/5	12/5	14/5	—	★
CALIFORNIA STAR	28W	FCL LCL	18/4 - 23/4 15/4 - 21/4	26/4	FCL LCL	20/4 - 26/4 19/4 - 23/4	28/4†	FCL LCL	21/4 - 27/4 20/4 - 26/4	28/4	15/5	17/5	19/5	21/5	23/5	★
ANTONIA JOHNSON	25W	FCL LCL	28/4 - 30/4 22/4 - 28/4	2/5	FCL LCL	27/4 - 3/5 26/4 - 30/4	4/5	FCL LCL	28/4 - 4/5 27/4 - 3/5	5/5	22/5	24/5	26/5	28/5	—	★
SAN FRANCISCO	32W	FCL LCL	3/5 - 7/5 29/4 - 5/5	10/5	FCL LCL	4/5 - 10/5 3/5 - 7/5	12/5†	FCL LCL	5/5 - 11/5 4/5 - 10/5	12/5	29/5	31/5	2/6	4/6	6/6	★
MEONIA	24W	FCL LCL	10/5 - 14/5 6/5 - 12/5	16/5	FCL LCL	11/5 - 17/5 10/5 - 14/5	18/5	FCL LCL	12/5 - 18/5 11/5 - 17/5	19/5	5/6	7/6	9/6	11/6	—	★
COLUMBIA STAR	27W	FCL LCL	17/5 - 21/5 13/5 - 19/5	24/5	FCL LCL	18/5 - 24/5 17/5 - 21/5	26/5†	FCL LCL	19/5 - 25/5 18/5 - 24/5	26/5	12/6	14/6	16/6	18/6	20/6	★
ANNIE JOHNSON	36W	FCL LCL	24/5 - 28/5 20/5 - 26/5	30/5	FCL LCL	25/5 - 31/5 24/5 - 28/5	1/6	FCL LCL	26/5 - 1/6 25/5 - 31/5	2/6	19/6	21/6	23/6	25/6	—	★

LONDON: FCL CARGO RECEIVED AT 41/43 BERTH, TILBURY
LCL CARGO RECEIVED AT 23/24 SHED, TILBURY

†From Glasgow

LIVERPOOL: FCL CARGO RECEIVED AT SEAFORTH CONTAINER TERMINAL
LCL CARGO RECEIVED AT SEAFORTH CONTAINER TERMINAL

GLASGOW: FCL CARGO RECEIVED AT CLYDEPORT CONTAINER TERMINAL, GREENOCK
LCL CARGO RECEIVED AT BRAEHEAD DEPOT, RENFREW

★Through Bills of Lading with transhipment at Los Angeles (LCL cargo accepted by arrangement only).

All cargo is accepted subject to the terms, conditions and exceptions of the Joint Service Bill of Lading.

All sailings are subject to alteration or cancellation with or without notice.

Printed by Wilkinson Bros. Ltd., 12-16 Laystall Street, London EC1R 4PB

Fig. 8. A typical shipping card.
(courtesy Johnson ScanStar)

EXPORT CARGO SHIPPING INSTRUCTIONS (GENERAL CARGO) ALL TRADES

OCL Booking Reference Number to be entered here and quoted in all communications.

Shipper's Name & Address (in whose Name Bill of Lading to be drawn) ①

Containerbase

Shipper's Reference (if any)

Please indicate if Conference Signatory | YES | NO

Customs Assigned Number | CAN or Pre Entry No.

Consignee's Name & Address (if Order state "ORDER" and give Name & Address of Notify Party) ②

OCL

OVERSEAS CONTAINERS LIMITED will appreciate early advice of your intentions to make a shipment

All the information indicated on this form will be required before cargo can be packed into a container or a container accepted for transportation.

If nos. of packages & wt./measurement are unknown, estimated details must be given and so stated. Individual packages exceeding 1,814 kg. gross must be separately declared.

This form must not be used for refrigerated, hazardous or obnoxious cargo, for which please use the Special Cargo Form.

Shippers are reminded that FCL Packing Details, completed either on the Shipper's own packing list or on Carriers form, are the Customs Control Documents and must be presented to OCL as follows:–

(i) FCL's being collected by OCL Transport: packing details must be given to the driver on collection

(ii) FCL's being delivered to Containerbase or Terminal by the Shipper: packing details must accompany the Container and be presented to the OCL Movements Office on delivery

Forwarding Agent's Name & Address (if applicable) ③

Place of acceptance of cargo by OCL (Please state Full Name & Address or Container base) ④

Place of delivery of cargo in country of destination (Please state Full Name & Address or Depot Name) ⑤

CUSTOMS STATUS: Indicate X — Free ☐ Drawback ☐ Bonded ☐ Licensed ☐

No. of Containers Required by Shipper: ☐

TYPE OF SERVICE REQUIRED: Indicate X below

Container packed by	OCL (LCL)		Container unpacked by	OCL (LCL)	
	Shipper/Supplier (FCL)			Consignee (FCL)	

Marks & Numbers	Number & Type of packages: Description of Goods Please list different commodities separately	B.T.N.	Gross Weight (Kilos)	Cube (Cbms)
		Quantity	Net Weight	F.O.B. Value

Total Number of Packages

FREIGHT AND CHARGES to be paid by: Indicate party to pay ① ② ③ ④ ⑤ in appropriate box(es) below:

		Or other party:
UK/Europe zone transport charge		
UK/Europe zone service charge (Far East only)		
Sea Freight/Basic Service Freight		
Destination zone service charge (Far East only)		
Destination zone transport charge		

BILL OF LADING to be posted to: ① ② ③ ④ ⑤ indicate Party ☐

Or other party:

Or collected at:

QUARANTINE REGULATIONS – *AUSTRALIA ONLY*

For containers which are to be unpacked by Consignees in Australia, Shippers must make the following declaration to the Carrier:–

FOR GUIDANCE COMMONWEALTH OF AUSTRALIA, DEPARTMENT OF HEALTH

1. Wooden crates, cases . . . . not used ☐
2. " " " . . . . used, not treated ☐
3. " " " . . . . used, treated ☐
4. Wooden pallets, dunnage . . . . not used ☐
5. " " " . . . . used, not treated ☐
6. " " " . . . . used, treated ☐
7. Straw packing and/or rice hulls and/or similar packing material . . . not used ☐
8. " " " " " " " " . . . . used ☐

Place X in appropriate box(es).

SUPPLEMENTARY SERVICES REQUIRED (charges on application) Indicate Party to Pay: ① ② ③ ④ ⑤

	A. Preparing & lodging Customs Entry in United Kingdom
	B. Lodging prepared Customs Entry in United Kingdom
	C. Cargo insurance: – State value: £ – Risks:

Certificates and/or Declaration for treatment will be forwarded by Shipper to Consignee with invoices or Shipping Documents.

This declaration may be completed above, or where an FCL is presented to the Carrier, be completed either on the Shipper's own Packing List or on Carriers form to be given to the driver on collection or presented to OCL on delivery of the container.

FAILURE TO MAKE THIS DECLARATION CAN RESULT IN DELAY AND EXTRA EXPENSE TO CARGO

We require Overseas Containers Limited to arrange through transport of the cargo detailed above between the place of acceptance and the place of delivery shown above. We warrant that the details of cargo declared above are correct as known to us. We undertake to advise OCL of any subsequent alterations.

Signature of Representative   Date   Shipper's Name
Tel. No.
Ext. No. or Dept.

Goods are accepted for transportation on the terms of OCL Tariff, Rules and Conditions.

Fig. 9. OCL booking form (by sea).
(courtesy Overseas Containers Ltd)

This Note must be lodged WITH the vehicle at the receiving point OR at the Receiving Authority's designated office BEFORE arrival of the goods, according to local port practice. Only goods for shipment to one port of discharge on one sailing may be grouped on one Shipping Note. For multi-vehicle deliveries or any further information contact the Receiving Authority.

◄ Enter Scale (if required)

© SITPRO 1976

STANDARD SHIPPING NOTE

Exporter/Shipper (Name and Address) [1]

Vehicle Bkg Ref. [2]

CAN/Pre-Entry No./Other Customs Ref. [3]

Exporter's Ref.

Port Handling charges to be paid by*
☐ Exporter ☐ Agent
Other (Name and Address)

F/Agent's Ref.

S.S. Co. Bkg. No. [4]

[5]

Name of Shipping Line or CTO (if required) [6]

Port Account No.

Forwarding Agent/Merchant (Name and Address) [7]

For use of Receiving Authority only

Receiving Date(s)

Berth&Dock/Container Base Etc. [8]

Ship

Port of Loading [9]

This six part set is printed on Baron self-copy paper and is suitable for use with reprographic equipment. The sixth sheet is the shippers' file copy. The fifth sheet is to be returned to the haulier by the Receiving Authority.

TO THE RECEIVING AUTHORITY
Please receive for shipment the goods described below subject to your published Regulations and Conditions (including those as to liability.)

Port of Discharge

Destination Depot (LCL only) [10]

Name of Receiving Authority (if required) [11]

[12] Marks and Numbers; No. and Kind of Packages; Description of Goods; Package dimensions in cm (if required) [13]

For Receiving Authorities Use.

Gross Weight (Kg) [14]

Cube (M^3) [15]

Cargo Status* | Customs Free Status | Customs Pre-Entry | Special Stowage [16]

Reserved for Shipping Company's Use

Total Gross Wt.

Total Cube

For Use of Receiving Authority Only

Carrier.................................Vehicle Reg. No.................................

Number of Packages Received.................................

....

Condition.................................

....

Signature and Date

Name of Company preparing this Note [17]

Date

(Indicate Name and Telephone Number of Contact)

*Mark 'X' as appropriate.

Printer's/Licensee's Name

4119E OZALID (U.K) LTD

Fig. 10. The Standard Shipping Note.
(courtesy SITPRO)

SPECIAL STOWAGE ORDER FOR DANGEROUS GOODS AND GOODS REQUIRING SPECIAL STOWAGE

To: EASTERN LINER SERVICES LTD.
ENTRANCE THREE, BEAUFORT HOUSE,
15 ST. BOTOLPH STREET,
LONDON, EC3 7EA.
01-247 5498

U.K. FREIGHT BROKERS FOR:-
P & O and B.I. CUNARD BROCKLEBANK
JOINT SERVICE TO
INDIA PAKISTAN SRI LANKA BANGLADASH
and RED SEA

SHIPPER/FORWARDING AGENT, and POSTAL ADDRESS TO WHOM STOWAGE ORDER SHOULD BE SENT.

TELEPHONE NUMBER:

REFRIGERATED CARGO

Refrigerated cargo is only accepted for shipment on the understanding that the temperature or range of temperatures agreed by shippers is suitable for the carriage and landing in good condition of the goods concerned, and no liability can be accepted if the agreed temperatures are subsequently found to have been unsuitable.

Every effort is made to operate refrigerated Chambers continuously at the temperature or within the range of temperatures agreed, but liberty is reserved to open Chambers at intermediate ports of call for loading and/or discharging other refrigerated cargo.

Cargo delivered for shipment in refrigerated Chambers should arrive at a temperature consistant with the maintenance of the agreed operating temperature in the Chamber concerned, and while every effort will be made to accept cargo as delivered for shipment, liberty is reserved to reject cargo if delivered at a temperature which would serve to raise the temperature of the Chamber and deleteriously affect other cargo.

FOR SHIPMENT BY (or first available)	FROM
PORT OF DISCHARGE	FINAL DESTINATION

"All quotations of freight or other rates, offers of space, acceptance of bookings, engagements and contracts of affreightment are subject to the terms and conditions of:

(a) the carrier's Bill of Lading and (b) the Tarriff of the relevant Conference provided that in case of any inconsistency the terms and conditions of the Bill of Lading shall prevail".

MARKS & NUMBERS	NUMBERS AND KIND OF PACKAGES	CONTENTS:—CORRECT CHEMICAL NAME	CLASS	FLASH POINT	GROSS WEIGHT WEIGHT KILOS	MEASUREMENT CUBIC METRES

DECLARATION BY SHIPPERS

We hereby certify that all the packages (and/or containers) enumerated above and the substances contained in them, together with the method of packing and labelling, comply in every respect with the provisions of the Merchant Shipping (Dangerous Goods) Rules, 1965, and the Report of the Standing Advisory Committee of Transport, 1966, and any additions or amendments thereto.

Where packages containing dangerous chemicals in limited quantities are concerned, we also certify that each of the above packages is declared under Class 10 of the Merchant Shipping (Dangerous Goods) Rules, 1965, and complies with the method of preparing such packages recommended in Class 10 of the BLUE BOOK (Second Edition 1971).

(1) No package exceeds 125 kg. (2½ cwt.) gross weight.
(2) No substance prohibited by the terms of Class 10 is included in any of these packages.
(3) No two or more substances which are not recommended under the terms of Class 10 to be included in the same package, are so packed.
(4) The packing material, absorbent material, or insulating material used for packing each package is suitable and in accordance with the terms of Class 10.
(5) Where any substance is restricted in any way as to quantity by the terms of Class 10 the quantities packed so conform.

NOTE: Where agreement with the Department of Trade and Industry has been reached for packages not complying with the provisions of Class 10, a copy of the Board's letter of agreement should be forwarded with this Declaration.
Cargo presented by Shippers in containers or on pallets must also conform to the appropriate Conference rules.

Signature________________ Date__________ This declaration must be signed by a duly authorised person.
(Shippers or Shippers' Agent)

Fig. 11. A typical Stowage Order.
(courtesy Eastern Liner Services Ltd)

†No claim shall under any circumstances be attached to the vessel or her owners by reason of the absence of notification.
*Applicable only when document used as a Through B/L

B/L No.

Shippers Ref.

F/Agent's Ref.

HARRISON LINE

WEST INDIES SERVICE WESTBOUND

Shipper		
Consignee (If "Order" state Notify Party)		
†Notify Party (ONLY if not stated above: otherwise leave blank)		
*Local vessel	*From (Local port of Loading)	
Ocean vessel	Port of Loading	
Port of Discharge	*Final destination (if on-carriage)	Freight payable at

Number of Bs/L signed

Marks and Numbers	Number and kind of packages; description of goods	Gross weight T C Q L	Measurement
	PARTICULARS OF GOODS ARE THOSE DECLARED BY SHIPPER		

SHIPPED in apparent good order and condition (unless otherwise stated herein) on board (the Local vessel subject to clause 19 hereof, if such a vessel be named above, but otherwise on board) the Ocean vessel at the Port of loading thereof, the pieces and/or packages said to contain goods (herein called " the goods ") above specified, warranted lawful merchandise at the Port of loading, throughout the voyage, and at the Port of discharge and Final destination, to be carried by the Ocean vessel from the Port of loading thereof bound on a voyage, as described and agreed by clauses 8, 9, 10, 11 and 12 hereof, and/or to be forwarded by any other vessel or vessels and/or other method or methods of conveyance as agreed under clause 20 hereof, and to be delivered (such carriage and delivery being subject to the exceptions, limitations, conditions and liberties herein agreed) in the like order and condition at the Port of discharge or Final destination (as the case may be) named above or so near thereto as the carrying vessel may safely get always afloat unto the Consignee or his or their assigns.

IN WITNESS whereof the Master or Agent of the ocean vessel has signed the number of Bills of Lading stated above, all of this tenor and date, one of which being accomplished, the others shall stand void

Number of Pieces or Packages (in words)

Dated IN____LONDON________________

____________________________ of ____

SEE CONDITIONS OF CARRIAGE AND OTHER CONDITIONS ON REVERSE

COPY — NOT NEGOTIABLE

For the MASTER.

Printed for and sold by F. C. Richardson & Co., Ltd., 4 Whittington Avenue, London, E.C.3 6/74

Fig. 12(a). A typical Bill of Lading.
(courtesy Thos. & Jas. Harrison Ltd)

PAGE 2

COMBINED TRANSPORT BILL OF LADING

SHIPPER CODE

B/L-No.

SHIPPERS REFERENCE

Carol - Caribbean Overseas Lines

CONSIGNEE OR ORDER CODE

☐ Cie Gle Maritime ☐ Harrison Line

☐ Hapag-Lloyd AG ☐ KNSM

Please indicate carrier by "X"

NOTIFY ADDRESS CODE

PLACE OF RECEIPT

PLACE OF DELIVERY

MOVEMENT

OCEAN VESSEL/VOYAGE No. PORT OF LOADING

PORT OF DISCHARGE

Freight & Charges Appropriate columns to be marked by shipper with "X"

Seafreight		Origin - Land Freight - Destination				Origin - LCL Service Charge - Destination			
TO BE		TO BE		TO BE		TO BE		TO BE	
Prepaid	Collect	Prepaid	Collect	Prepaid	Collect	Prepaid	Collect	Prepaid	Collect

CARRIER'S CONTAINER NUMBER MARKS AND NUMBERS | QUANTITY AND TYPES OF PACKAGES, DESCRIPTION OF GOODS | GROSS WEIGHT (KGS) | MEASUREMENT

PARTICULARS (EXCEPT FREIGHT & CHARGES) AS DECLARED BY SHIPPER

FREIGHT AND CHARGES | RATE | PER | TO BE PREPAID | TO BE COLLECTED

TOTAL NUMBER OF CONTAINERS OR OTHER PACKAGES OR UNITS RECEIVED BY THE CARRIER*

NUMBER OF ORIGINAL BS/L:

PLACE AND DATE OF ISSUE

RECEIVED in apparent good order and condition except as otherwise noted the total number of containers or other packages or units enumerated above for transportation from the place of receipt to the place of delivery subject to the terms hereof. [illegible]

IN WITNESS WHEREOF the number of original Bills of Lading stated above all of this tenor and date has been signed, one of which being accomplished the others to stand void.

FOR THE CARRIER

ORIGINAL

Fig. 12(b). A combined Bill of Lading.
(courtesy Thos. & Jas. Harrison Ltd)

MSAS
McGREGOR SWIRE AIR SERVICES LTD.

AIR FREIGHT FORWARDING INSTRUCTIONS.

COLLECT/RECEIVE FROM: ____________

TEL.: ____________

SHIPPERS REFERENCE: ____________

DESPATCH TO: ____________

ALSO NOTIFY: ____________

DESTINATION AIRPORT: ____________

No. AND NATURE OF PACKAGES	NATURE AND QUANTITY OF GOODS	WEIGHT SPECIFY LBS or KG.	DIMENSIONS

Value for Carriage ________ Value for Customs ________ Value for Insurance ________

Country of Origin ________ Consignees Order No. ________

SERVICE REQUIRED: All Shipments will be sent via MSAS Consolidation unless otherwise indicated.

ECONOMY ☐ AIRLINE DIRECT ☐ AIR/SEA ☐ CHARTER ☐ OTHER ☐

CHARGES PAYABLE BY:

SERVICE	PREPAID	COLLECT	SERVICE	PREPAID	COLLECT
Air Freight			Duty on Arrival		
F.O.B. Charges			Foreign Customs Clearance		
Insurance			C.O.D. (Airline only)		

DOCUMENTATION ATTACHED:

HAZARDOUS CERTIFICATE ☐ INVOICES ☐ EXPORT LICENCE ☐

CERT. of ORIGIN ☐ MOVEMENT CERT. ☐ LETTER OF CREDIT ☐ OTHER ☐

DOCUMENTATION TO BE PREPARED BY MSAS AS AGENT:

CONSULAR FORMALITIES ☐ CERTIFICATE OF INSURANCE ☐ INVOICE LEGALISATION ☐

NB. FOR SHIPMENTS TO E.E.C. COUNTRIES THE FOLLOWING DECLARATION MUST BE COMPLETED:-

☐ GOODS ARE/ARE NOT OF T3L STATUS.

☐ GOODS ARE OF T3L STATUS AND WE HEREBY AUTHORISE MSAS TO COMPLETE T3L ON OUR BEHALF.

SPECIAL INSTRUCTIONS: 1. ____________

2. ____________

3. ____________

SIGNED ____________ DATE ____________

All goods carried in accordance with MSAS Conditions of Contract (MSAS consolidation only) or MSAS Standard Trading Conditions copies of which are available on request.

OP 13

Fig. 13. MSAS booking form (by air).
(courtesy McGregor Swire Air Services Ltd)

Set your tabulator stops here

STAPLE DOCUMENTS ABOVE PERFORATION

Line-up here

125- 0001 1480

Airport of Departure | Execution Date Day/Month/Year | TC | Chge Code | Currency Code | For Carrier use only | Flight/Day | Flight/Day

125- 0001 1480

Airport of Departure (Address of First Carrier) and Requested Routing | Airport of Destination | Flight/Day | Flight/Day | Booked

Routing and Destination: To | By First Carrier | To | By | To | By

Consignee's Account Number | Consignee's Name and Address

Shipper's Account Number | Shipper's Name and Address

Issuing Carrier's Agent, Account No. | Issuing Carrier's Agent, Name and City

Agent's IATA Code

British airways

Issued by British Airways, London
Member of International Air Transport Association

Air Waybill
(Air Consignment note)
Not negotiable

If the carriage involves an ultimate destination or stop in a country other than the country of departure, the Warsaw Convention may be applicable and the Convention governs, and in most cases limits the liability of carriers in respect of loss of or damage to cargo.
Agreed stopping places are those places (other than the places of departure and destination) shown under requested routing and/or those places shown in carrier's timetables as scheduled stopping places for the route. Address of first carrier is the airport of departure.
SEE CONDITIONS ON REVERSE HEREOF.

The shipper certifies that the particulars on the face hereof are correct, agrees to the CONDITIONS ON REVERSE HEREOF, accepts that the carrier's liability is limited as stated in 4(c) on the reverse hereof and accepts such value unless a higher value for carriage is declared on the face hereof subject to an additional charge.

....
Signature of Shipper or his Agent)

Carrier certifies goods described below were received for carriage subject to the CONDITIONS ON REVERSE HEREOF, the goods then being in apparent good order and condition except as noted hereon.

Executed on .... at ....
(Date) (Place)

....
Signature of Issuing Carrier or its Agent

Copies 1, 2 and 3 of this Air Waybill are originals and have the same validity.

Currency | Declared Value for Carriage | Declared Value for Customs

Weight Charge and Valuation Charge: Prepaid | Collect
All Other Charges at Origin: Prepaid | Collect
Accounting Information

No. of Packages RCP	Actual Gross Weight	kg lb	Rate Class Commodity Item No.	Chargeable Weight	Rate/Charge	Total	Nature and Quantity of Goods (incl. Dimensions or Volume)

PREPAID: Prepaid Weight Charge | Prepaid Valuation Charge | Due Carrier | Total other Prepaid Charges | Due Agent | Total Prepaid | For Carrier's Use Only at Destination

AWB Fee and Code | Clearance and Handling | Cartage | Other Charges (except Weight Charge and Valuation Charge) → | Collect Charges in Destination Currency

COD Amount

Disbursements | COD and/or Disb. Fee | Total Charges

COLLECT: Collect Weight Charge | Collect Valuation Charge | Due Carrier | Total Other Collect Charges | Due Agent | COD Amount | Total Collect

CA Number | Attached EEC Transit Documents | Type | Customs Reference Number | In Envelope: Yes / No

Handling Information

T.327 (12th)

Original 3 - (For Shipper)

125- 0001 1480

Fig. 14. An Air Waybill.
(courtesy British Airways)

BAIN DAWES (INTERNATIONAL) LIMITED | **871 BDL**

POLICY NO.	REF. NO.		
REGISTRATION	V.A.T.	T.O.C. TRIBUNAL	
B.O.T CODE	REGISTRATION CATEGORY	YEAR	MONTH
ASSURED/ACCOUNT		ADJUST SCHEME	YES / NO
COUNTRY OF ORIGIN	MARINE	NON-MARINE	AVIATION
	OVERSEAS BROKER		
CURRENCY	SIGNED LINE %	GROSS PREMIUM INC. WAR	GROSS PREMIUM WAR ONLY
TOTAL			
LLOYD'S			
ILU			
COMPANIES			
CRA YES / NO	SERIAL NO.	CERTIFICATE NOS.	
BUREAU SCHEME NO.	BROKERS COVER NO.		

SIGNED LINE %

Type: Cargo Voyage Risk.

Form: S.G.

Assured: The United Kingdom Exporting Company Ltd.

Conveyances: Steamer (to be named - subject to Institute Classification Clause) & connecting conveyances to and from.

Voyage: From interior of United Kingdom via London to Bombay, India thence to Delhi.

Interest: 6 Cases of tool making machinery, valued £10,000 (based on cost, insurance & freight plus 15%).

Conditions: Institute Cargo Clauses (All Risks).
Including war risks as per current Institute War Clauses and including strikes etc. risks as per current Institute Strikes Riots & Civil Commotions Clauses.
Institute Replacement Clause.

Rate: 0.375% plus War S.R. & C.C. risks @ 0.0375%

Security: Lloyd's Underwriters.

ALL DEDUCTIONS INCLUDING BROKERAGE

WRITTEN LINES % PART OF ORDER WHOLE	ORDER	CLOSED FOR

BDI General Agreement and L/U Clause

81-66

Fig. 15. Example of a Lloyd's Slip.
(courtesy Bain Dawes Ltd)

BAIN DAWES (INTERNATIONAL) LIMITED,
P.O. BOX 115,
BAIN DAWES HOUSE,
HAYWARDS HEATH,
SUSSEX RH16 1GA
Tel: 0444-51691 or 01-283 4611
Telex: 87477

21001

Please insure *provisionally / *definitely under Cover No.__________ Reference__________

STEAMER OR CONVEYANCE	VOYAGE		GOODS (Deck cargo must be specially declared)	INSURED VALUE
	FROM	TO		

Certificate *not required
*required

FIRM__________
(Please write clearly)

*Delete as not applicable.

Dated __________ 01-156

Fig. 16. A Marine Cargo Insurance Declaration Form.
(courtesy Bain Dawes Ltd)

LLOYD'S

THIS CERTIFICATE REQUIRES ENDORSEMENT

Lloyd's Agent at ....
is authorised to adjust and settle on behalf of the Underwriters and to purchase on behalf of the Corporation of Lloyd's in accordance with Lloyd's Standing Regulations for the Settlement of Claims Abroad any claim which may arise on this Certificate.

Certificate of Insurance No. C 000/

This is to Certify that there has been deposited with the Committee of Lloyd's an Open Cover effected by *J. O. B. Long & Co., Ltd.* of Lloyd's, acting on behalf of *The Herne Bay Supply Company* with Underwriters at Lloyd's, dated the *First* day of *January, 1971*, and that the said Underwriters have undertaken to issue to *J. O. B. Long & Co., Ltd.* Policy/Policies of Marine Insurance at Lloyd's to cover, up to *£10,000 (or equivalent in other currencies)* in all by any one steamer *or sending by air and/or parcel post, Golf Equipment, other interests held covered* to be shipped on or before the *Thirty-first* day of *December, 1971*, from any port or ports, place or places in *the United Kingdom* to any port or ports, place or places in *the World*; and that *The Herne Bay Supply Company* are entitled to declare against the said Open Cover the shipments attaching thereto.

Dated at Lloyd's, London, 1st January, 1971.

Conveyance   From   INSURED VALUE ....

(in words) ....

Via/To   To   Currency: Figs:

Marks and Numbers   Interest

SPECIMEN

We hereby declare for Insurance under the said cover interest as specified above so valued subject to terms of the Standard Form of Lloyd's Marine Policy providing for the settlement of claims abroad and to the special conditions stated below and on the back hereof.

Institute Cargo Clauses (All Risks) (1.1.63) excluding rust, oxidisation, discolouration, twisting and bending.
Subject to Institute Replacement Clause (1.1.34).
Institute War Clauses (1.1.71) or Institute War Clauses (including on-carriage by Air) (1.1.71) or Institute War Clauses (Air) (excluding sendings by Post) (1.1.71) or Institute War Clauses for the insurance of sendings by Post (1.1.71) as applicable.
Institute Strikes Riots and Civil Commotions Clauses (1.1.63).

Underwriters agree losses, if any, shall be payable to the order of HERNE BAY SUPPLY COMPANY on surrender of this Certificate.

This Certificate not valid unless the Declaration be signed by
THE HERNE BAY SUPPLY COMPANY.

Dated at Herne Bay.

Signed

In the event of loss or damage which may result in a claim under this Insurance, immediate notice should be given to the Lloyd's Agent at the port or place where the loss or damage is discovered in order that he may examine the goods and issue a survey report.

Brokers: J. O. B. Long & Co., Ltd.,
999, Lloyd's Street, Insurance Avenue, London, E.C.0.   213/001

Printed at Lloyd's, London, England.

Fig. 17. A Marine Certificate of Insurance.
(courtesy Bain Dawes Ltd and Lloyd's of London)

General Accident

GENERAL ACCIDENT FIRE AND LIFE ASSURANCE CORPORATION LIMITED
THE YORKSHIRE INSURANCE COMPANY LIMITED

MARINE DEPARTMENT

Lloyd's Building Lime Street London EC3M 7DX

Telephone: 01 606 1030

Survey Report

1 Name of (i) Consignees (ii) Applicants for Survey	1 (i)...... (ii)......
2 Name of vessel by which goods arrived	2
3 Name of original vessel, if goods transhipped	3
4 Port of (i) shipment; (ii) transhipment	4 (i)...... (ii)......
5 (i) Port of Discharge; (ii) Date of arrival of vessel	5 (i)...... (ii)......
6 Date on which goods discharged into lighters (if so discharged)	6
7 Date on which goods were landed	7
8 (i) Date of entry into Custom House and (ii) External condition of goods on arrival there	8 (i)...... (ii)......
9 (i) Place where survey held and (ii) Date of delivery there	9 (i)...... (ii)......
10 Date of request for survey	10
11 Date(s) on which survey held. Reason for delay, if any, in requesting or holding survey	11
12 Description of packing used	12
13 External condition of goods at time of survey	13
14 Nature and cause of loss and/or damage	14

MAR. CL/2. M. & S. 1M—8/73.

Continued overleaf

Fig. 18. A Marine Survey Report.
(courtesy General Accident Assurance Corp. Ltd)

NEW ZEALAND.—FORM 57.

Combined Certificate of Value and of Origin and Invoice of Goods (the Produce or Manufacture of Countries being part of the British Commonwealth) for Exportation to New Zealand.

I, ______________________ the undersigned being the seller of the goods enumerated in this invoice amounting to ______________________ (or manager, chief clerk or other responsible person in the sole employ of and authorised by the seller to make and sign this certificate) have the means of knowing and hereby certify as follows:—

VALUE.

1. That this invoice is in all respects correct and contains a true and full statement of the price actually paid or to be paid for the said goods, and of the actual quantity and description thereof.

2. That no different invoice of the goods mentioned in the said invoice has been or will be furnished to anyone: and that no arrangement or understanding affecting the purchase-price of the said goods has been or will be made or entered into between the seller and purchaser, or by anyone on behalf of either of them, either by way of discount, rebate, compensation, or in any manner whatever other than as fully shown on this invoice, or as follows (1) ______________________

(1) Here insert particulars of any special arrangement.

3. That the said invoice exhibits, in the column headed "Current Domestic Values in Currency of Exporting Country", the current domestic value of identically similar goods when sold for home consumption for cash in equal quantities in the ordinary course of business in the principal markets of the country from which the said goods are exported to New Zealand at the time when they are so exported.

4. That the said current domestic value includes import or excise duty amounting to (2) ______________________

*(a) Which has been paid on any parts, materials, or ingredients used in making the goods, and in respect of which drawback has been or will be paid or allowed by the revenue authorities in the country of exportation; and/or

*(b) Which has actually been paid on the goods in the country from which they are exported, or would have been payable on the goods in that country if they had there been entered for home consumption instead of being exported therefrom.

(2) The actual amount in currency of exporting country to be shown.

*Delete and initial as applicable.

ORIGIN.

(Paragraphs which do not apply should be deleted and initialled.)

5. That every article mentioned in the said invoice has been—

(a) Wholly produced in (3) ______________________ or

(b) Wholly manufactured [see note (1)] in (3) ______________________ and that all the manufacturing processes involved in making the articles from unmanufactured raw materials [see note (2)] and/or from one or more of the following imported partly manufactured materials have been performed in that part of the British Commonwealth:—

(3) Insert United Kingdom or name of other part of British Commonwealth.

Abrasive materials, including corundum, alundum, carborundum, emery and similar materials; Argols; Asbestos, fibre; Asphalt, bitumen, tar and pitch; Barium Carbonate; Barium Sulphate; Bromine and iodine; Camphor, laurel, crude; Carbon-black or gas-black; Cellulose acetate film base; Cherries in brine; Coir yarn; Cork strip for tipping cigarettes; Dyes and vegetable substances used in making dyes; Earth colours, dry ground; Fibres, natural, animal or vegetable, even though sorted, dressed, scoured or similarly treated, including raw silk, organzine, tram silk, grege, boil, crepe, grenadine, and single spun schappe yarn; Graphite, natural or artificial, in powder form; Greenstone and precious stones cut and/or polished; Gums and resins, refined; Hides and skins, with or without wool or hair, salted or pickled; Isinglass; Lemon or orange rinds in brine; Liquorice extract: in bulk, Magnesite, calcined; Meats and fish, fresh, chilled, or frozen, Metals in the form of pigs or ingots or in cruder forms (e.g. mattes, concentrates, regulus); mercury; copper or zinc in bars, blocks, cakes, and slabs; iron or steel blooms, billets, or slabs; iron bars (Swedish) made from iron puddled with charcoal; ferro-silicon; metal scrap, suitable for remelting; Nitrocellulose film base; Oils essential natural, oil of turpentine; Oils—viz., whale-oils and fish oils, crude; Chinese wood-oil, palm-oil, olive oil, crude or refined; Potassium, chloride and sulphate of; Rags, or waste, cotton or linen, for respinning or for paper and pulp making; Rags, woollen, for respinning or for making flocks; Rubber—viz., crepe rubber, guttapercha and balata, crude; Sodium nitrate; Sponges, unbleached; Strawboard (of Dutch type); Sugar, unrefined, and molasses; Sulphur, in blocks; Tanning extracts, vegetable; Tanning materials, vegetable—viz., barks, sumach, gambier, and similar materials, ground or powdered; Timber, hewn or rough sawn; also brier-root or similar blocks, rough shaped for making tobacco pipes; Titanium oxide; Waxes, animal, mineral, or vegetable, refined or unrefined; Wood-pulp, chemical or mechanical; or

(c) Partially manufactured in (3) ______________________ and

(i) That the final process of manufacture of each article has been performed in that part of the British Commonwealth; and

(ii) That, in respect of each article, the expenditure in material the produce of (4) ______________________ and/or in other items of factory or works cost [see note (3)] incurred in (4) ______________________ is not less than half (or where the goods are for exportation to Niue, not less than one-quarter) of the factory or works cost of the article in its finished state; and

(iii) That in the calculation of that proportion of expenditure in material the produce of, and/or in other items of factory or works cost incurred in, (4) ______________________ none of the following items have been included or considered, viz:—

Manufacturer's profit, or the profit or remuneration of any trader, agent, broker, or other person dealing in the articles in their finished condition; royalties payable in respect of the finished goods; cost of outside packages or any cost of packing the goods into them; administrative and general office expenses; any cost of conveying, insuring, or shipping the goods or any other charge incurred after their manufacture.

(4) Insert United Kingdom and/or name(s) of other part(s) of British Commonwealth.

Dated at ______________ this ______________ day of ______________ 19__

______________________ Signature and status

NOTES.—(1) Goods shall be deemed to be wholly manufactured in a country being part of the British Commonwealth if they are wholly manufactured in that country from unmanufactured raw materials and/or from one or more of the partly manufactured raw materials enumerated in paragraph 5 (b) of this certificate imported into that country.

(2) The following are regarded as examples of unmanufactured raw materials for the purposes of this certificate:

Natural products (e.g., minerals; animals; plants, shrubs, trees, vegetables, or parts thereof such as leaves, barks, fruits pods, nuts, nut-kernels or roots) which have not been subjected to any industrial process or processes except (a) those primary processes whereby natural products are ordinarily obtained from the farm, mine, forest, fisheries, &c., and (b) the processes of cleaning, separating, sorting, and drying, and of the killing of animals. For example—Bones, hoofs, and horns; tusks (ivory); cork, unmanufactured; grain or seeds, cleaned or graded, but otherwise unmanufactured; logs, unwrought; ores, metallic; petroleum, crude; salt, rock; skins, raw or sun-dried; wool, greasy, washed, or scoured.

(3) Calculation of factory or works cost. (Customs regulation 73 (1) provides as follows):—

The factory or works cost of any article shall be the sum of the following items: (a) Cost of materials as received into factory excluding Customs or excise or other duty paid or payable in respect of those materials; (b) Manufacturing wages; (c) Factory overhead expenses, namely: (i) All expenses directly or indirectly connected with manufacture, for example, rent, rates, and taxes in respect of factory; (ii) Motive power, gas, fuel, water, lighting, and heating of factory; (iii) Expenses of factory supervision, for example, wages and salaries of manager, foreman, timekeepers, and watchmen; (iv) Repairs, renewals, and depreciation of plant, machinery, and tools; (v) Interest on capital outlay on plant, machinery, tools, and factory buildings; and (vi) Royalties payable in respect of patented machines or processes used in the manufacture of the goods; (d) Cost of containers other than the outside package.

No 728 (1968) (SPIRIT DUPLICATOR) Printed in England by Waterlow (London) Ltd., Forms Department, Holywell House, Worship Street, London EC2A 2EN

Fig. 19. A Commonwealth invoice form.

________________________ 19____
(Place and Date)

*State here general nature or class of goods.

*INVOICE of supplied

by of

to of

to be shipped per

Order Number____________________

COUNTRY OF ORIGIN.	MARKS AND NUMBERS ON PACKAGES.	QUANTITY AND DESCRIPTION OF GOODS.	CURRENT DOMESTIC VALUES, IN CURRENCY OF EXPORTING COUNTRY. (See pars. 3 and 4 of certificate.)		SELLING PRICE TO PURCHASER.	
			●	AMOUNT.	●	AMOUNT.

If all the goods shown on the invoice have the same country of origin, that country need not be shown in a separate column, provided that it is clearly indicated in a conspicuous place on the invoice, e.g., "Country of origin: England."

Goods of British origin admissible in New Zealand under the British Preferential Tariff must not be shown on the same invoice as goods not so admissible. Likewise goods the produce or manufacture of countries other than British Commonwealth and admissible under any Act or other authority free of duty (when otherwise liable to duty under the General Tariff), or at rates lower than those set out in the General Tariff, must not be shown on the same invoice as goods not so admissible. (See section 150 of the Customs Act, 1966.)

The current domestic values shown above should be the *duty-paid* current domestic values. (See paragraph 3 of certificate.) The trade and cash discounts allowed in the domestic market should be shown on the face of the invoice and deducted from the gross values set forth thereon.

When drawback or remission of duty is allowable (see paragraph 4 of certificate) the invoice, if containing more than one item, should indicate to which items such drawback or remission relates, and also the amount allowable in respect of each item.

DECLARATION AS TO PACKING MATERIALS USED.

N.B. No declaration is required in respect of woodwool which may be freely used for packing.

I hereby certify:—

1. That no packing material of any kind is used for the goods on this invoice.
2. That the material(s) used as packing for the goods on this invoice is (are)

3. That no hay, straw, chaff, flax rug or rice husks has been used as packing for the goods on this invoice.
4. That all timber used for the packing of goods on this invoice has been inspected and was, to the best of my knowledge free from bark and visible signs of insects and fungal attack when the goods were shipped to New Zealand.

________________________ Signed. ________________________ 19____

Fig. 19 (contd)

Consignor: (Expéditeur:)

Consignee: (Destinataire:)

Consignment by: (Expédition prévue par:)

C 153572

COPY

EUROPEAN COMMUNITIES
(Communautes Europeennes)

CERTIFICATE OF ORIGIN
(Certificat d'origine)

THE LONDON CHAMBER OF COMMERCE AND INDUSTRY

THE UNDERSIGNED AUTHORITY certifies that the goods shown below
(L'AUTORITE SOUSSIGNEE certifie que les marchandises désignées ci-dessous)

Serial No.	Packages: Number and kind	Packages: Marks and numbers	Description of goods	Weight (1): gross	Weight (1): net

originated in:
(sont originaires de:)

The London Chamber of Commerce and Industry

(Place and date of issue)

(Name, signature and stamp of competent authority)

(1) This entry may, where appropriate, be replaced by others allowing identification of the goods.
DTI/XP/1302.

Netherton and Worth Limited, Truro, Cornwall.

Fig. 20. A Chamber of Commerce Certificate of Origin.
(courtesy London Chamber of Commerce and Industry)

FORM SPE **SPE 374652**

EXCHANGE CONTROL ACT 1947

APPLICATION FOR SPECIAL PERMISSION TO EXPORT GOODS FROM THE UNITED KINGDOM

This form should be completed where special permission is required for exports from the United Kingdom to destinations outside the Scheduled Territories. The Notice to Exporters sets out the circumstances in which such permission is required and exporters are advised to read the Notice carefully before completing this form. The Notice also contains the full text of H.M. Treasury's general permission for exports. Where special permission is required for a particular consignment, it should be obtained before exportation of the goods. The exporter should retain this form after it has been authorised as H.M. Customs may require to see it at a later date.

---

1. Name and address of the bank to whom application is made ______________________

2. Name and business address of exporter ______________________

3. Description and value of the goods ______________________

4. Country of ultimate destination ______________________

5. Amount to be received in settlement, with the approximate date. If the amount to be entered differs from the value stated in Section 3, an explanation should be given. (If necessary the reverse of this form may be used.) ______________________

6. Any other relevant information (see paragraph 9 of the Notice to Exporters), e.g., where goods are to be exported on hire, the period of hire and amount of hire charges; where goods are to be exported on extended credit, the terms of payment, etc.; where payment is not being made in the prescribed manner, the method of payment should be stated and the reason therefor. (If necessary the reverse of this form may be used.) ______________________

Signature of exporter ______________________

Date ______________________

For use by Bank of England or Authorised Bank

Fig. 21. Form SPE: Application for Special Permission to Export Goods from the United Kingdom.

Please affix stamp of firm here →

To SWISS BANK CORPORATION,
Commercial Credit Dept.
P.O. BOX 114,
99, GRESHAM STREET,
LONDON, EC2P 2BR

Date..

My/Our Ref. No..............................

Dear Sirs,

By order of Messrs..

I/we request you to open an Irrevocable / a Revocable Letter of Credit, by airmail / cable at cheap rate. in favour of

Messrs..

for £.............................. say..

valid for presentation in (place).............................. until and including (date)..............................

available { at sight (no draft). / by draft at sight. / by draft at .... days after sight.

relating to shipment of..

Price.............................. Terms (F.O.B., C. & F., C.I.F., etc.)..............................

Shipment from.............................. to..............................

Time of shipment..

Import Licence (if applicable) No.............................. valid until..............................

Part shipments are allowed. / not allowed.

Please honour drawing(s) under this Credit to my/our debit against surrender of the following documents:—

Invoice,

Certificate of Origin,

Weight Note,

*Insurance Policy or Certificate including War Risks,

Bill(s) of Lading, full set "on board" to "order" endorsed in blank,

Further Instructions

Documents to be presented within .... days from date of Bill of Lading.

It is understood that you are not to be held responsible as to the quantity, quality or value of goods, nor as to the validity, accuracy or sufficiency of the documents, provided the documents tendered appear to be in order.

This Credit is subject to Uniform Customs and Practice for Documentary Credits (1974 Revision), International Chamber of Commerce Brochure No. [redacted] 290.

Yours faithfully,

258 * If Insurance Policy or Certificate is not required, please state who covers insurance.

Fig. 22. Application to open a letter of credit.
(courtesy Swiss Bank Corporation)

Newtown Bank Limited

International Division
PO Box 999 60 Aldminster Street London EC3R 7DB
Telephone 01-123 4567 Telex 987654 Telegrams Newbankco London EC3

7

Original

Except so far as otherwise expressly stated, this documentary credit is subject to the "Uniform Customs and Practice for Documentary Credits" (1974 Revision) International Chamber of Commerce (Publication No. 290).
This Document conforms with the standard Form No. 1 of the I.C.C.

IRREVOCABLE DOCUMENTARY CREDIT	Date — Credit number — of issuing bank / of advising bank
Advising bank	Applicant
Beneficiary	Amount
	Expiry Date In for negotiation

Dear Sir(s)

We hereby issue in your favour this documentary credit which is available by negotiation of your draft at

drawn on Newtown Bank Ltd. Overseas Branch, PO Box 999, 60 Aldminster St., London EC3R 7DB

bearing the clause: "Drawn under documentary credit No. of Newtown Bank Ltd."

accompanied by the following documents:

SPECIMEN.

Covering

SPECIMEN.

Despatch/Shipment from to	Partial shipments	Transhipments

Special conditions:

We hereby engage with drawers and/or bona fide holders that drafts drawn and negotiated in conformity with the terms of this credit will be duly honoured on presentation and that drafts accepted within the terms of this credit will be duly honoured at maturity.

The amount of each draft must be endorsed on the reverse of this credit by the negotiating bank.

Yours faithfully,

Newtown Bank Limited International Division
PO Box 999, 60 Aldminster Street London EC3R 7DB

Countersigned

Advising bank's notification

Place, date, name and signature of the advising bank

9A

Fig. 23. Advice of a letter of credit.
(courtesy Midland Bank Ltd)

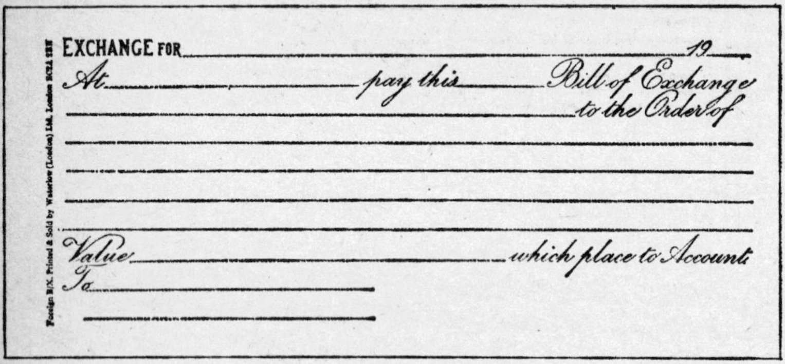
EXCHANGE FOR ______ 19__

At ______ pay this ______ Bill of Exchange ______ to the Order of

Value ______ which place to Account

To ______

Foreign B/X. Printed & Sold by Waterlow (London) Ltd. London EC2A 2BE

Fig. 24. A Bill of Exchange.
(courtesy Waterlow (London) Ltd)

Newtown Bank Limited

International Division
PO Box 999 60 Aldminster Street London EC3R 7DB
Telephone 01-123 4567 Telex 987654 Telegrams Newbankco London EC3

Please quote this number in all correspondence. 53/ / and date

Newtown Bank encloses the undermentioned bill for collection. Please acknowledge on the attached form. Please follow the instructions marked X below.

To

Drawer's No. and Rem. Date	Date of Bill	Due Date/Tenor	Amount	Drawee

Documents	Draft	Statement	Invoices Com.	Invoices Cert.	Invoices Cons.	Cert. of Origin	Cert. or Policy	Bills of Lading	AirCon. Note	Parcel Post Receipt		Drawer
Enclosed												
By next mail												

SPECIMEN.

Relating to:

Release Documents/Goods against ☐ Acceptance ☐ Payment

☐ Acceptance/Payment may be deferred pending arrival of the goods.

☐ If Unaccepted/Unpaid protest.

☐ If Unaccepted/Unpaid do not protest.

☐ Collect all charges from drawees including ours of ....

These may not be waived/may be waived if refused.

☐ If documents are not duly taken up on arrival of goods, store goods (If possible in customs or bonded warehouse) and insure against: (a) fire only (b) all available risks Claim from drawees, all expenses thus incurred; if refused by them, they are for our account.

☐ Advise acceptance and due date by airmail/cable.

☐ Remit proceeds by airmail/cable.

☐ Advise non-acceptance by airmail/cable.
☐ Advise non-payment by airmail/cable.
} Stating reasons

SPECIMEN.

In case of need refer to

....

....

☐ Follow their instructions without reserve. ☐ For assistance only.

☐ It is most important that we receive an immediate advice of acceptance.

Other instructions:

Please account for proceeds as marked X below.	
☐	Remit us first class Bankers' Cheque on London in Sterling or, if applicable, authorise us to debit your account, settlement to be made without loss of exchange to us only when definitely paid.
☐	Credit our account under airmail/cable advice. Please forward your credit advice to us only after the item is definitely paid.
☐	Please remit proceeds by airmail/cable without loss in exchange to: for the credit of our account with them under advice to us and request them to advise us by airmail/cable of the amount placed to our credit quoting our reference....................

Fig. 25. A typical Bills for Collection form.
(courtesy Midland Bank Ltd)

CREDIT LIMIT APPLICATION

PLEASE SEND THIS APPLICATION TO YOUR ECGD REGIONAL OFFICE

R O CODE

In respect of firm business or a current enquiry in excess of the discretionary limit

FOR USE IN DEPARTMENT

Received in Regional Office

ECG 3377/A

Checked in Regional Office (initials and date)

Submitted to U/W

39 911 914 issued.

Name and full address of INSURED in Block letters (for use in window envelope)

Guarantee No.	ECGD Buyer Ref. No. (if known)	Date of application	OBTAIN F/I AWAIT	ECGD Buyer Ref. No. if not as opposite

Full name and address of Buyer (including street, town, country) in BLOCK LETTERS

Name and/or address of approved buyer if different from opposite

Name and address of Buyer's Bankers (omission may delay a decision)

£ — Approved on the terms of payment stated opposite/below/overleaf and subject to Credit Limit Condition —

Goods

Limit applied for (i.e. amount likely to be owing at any one time) £	Amount of firm order or current enquiry £	Amount of Current Credit Limit (if any) £
Precise Terms of Payment	Is the buyer a subsidiary of or associated with your company?	Have you previously applied for a Credit Limit on this buyer?

U.W.	Date

Country Code	Terms Code	Status D.P. Records noted	R.O. Position Sheet noted

CREDIT LIMIT DECISION - CONFIDENTIAL

ANY COMMUNICATION ABOUT THIS DECISION SHOULD BE ADDRESSED TO YOUR ECGD REGIONAL OFFICE

R O CODE

This Decision supersedes any previous Credit Limit Decision given on this buyer; it is subject to the Terms and Conditions of the Guarantee including any special conditions of cover notified in Schedule 2 to the Guarantee or in any notice given to the INSURED.

If different from that stated by you Name and/or Address of the buyer on whom this decision has been given. You should verify that this is the buyer with whom you intend trading

ECG 3377/B

Guarantee No.	ECGD Buyer Ref. No. (if known)	Date of application	ECGD Buyer Ref. No.	Please ensure that this number is quoted on all communications you may have with ECGD about this buyer.

Full name and address of Buyer (including street, town, country) in Block Letters

CREDIT LIMIT

£ — Approved on the terms of payment stated opposite/below/overleaf and subject to the terms and conditions of the Guarantee and Credit Limit conditions .... overleaf and/or attached

Name and address of Buyer's Bankers

Goods

Limit applied for (i.e. amount likely to be owing at any one time) £	Amount of firm order or current enquiry £	Amount of current Credit Limit (if any) £
Precise Terms of Payment	Is the buyer a subsidiary of or associated with your company?	Have you previously applied for a Credit Limit on this buyer

Unless otherwise agreed by the Insurer in writing, it is a breach of the terms of the Guarantee to inform any person of this Credit Limit Decision other than your bank and or broker in confidence.

Initialled .... for the Insurer

Date ....

Fig. 26. Credit limit application (top) and decision (bottom) forms.
(courtesy Export Credits Guarantee Department)

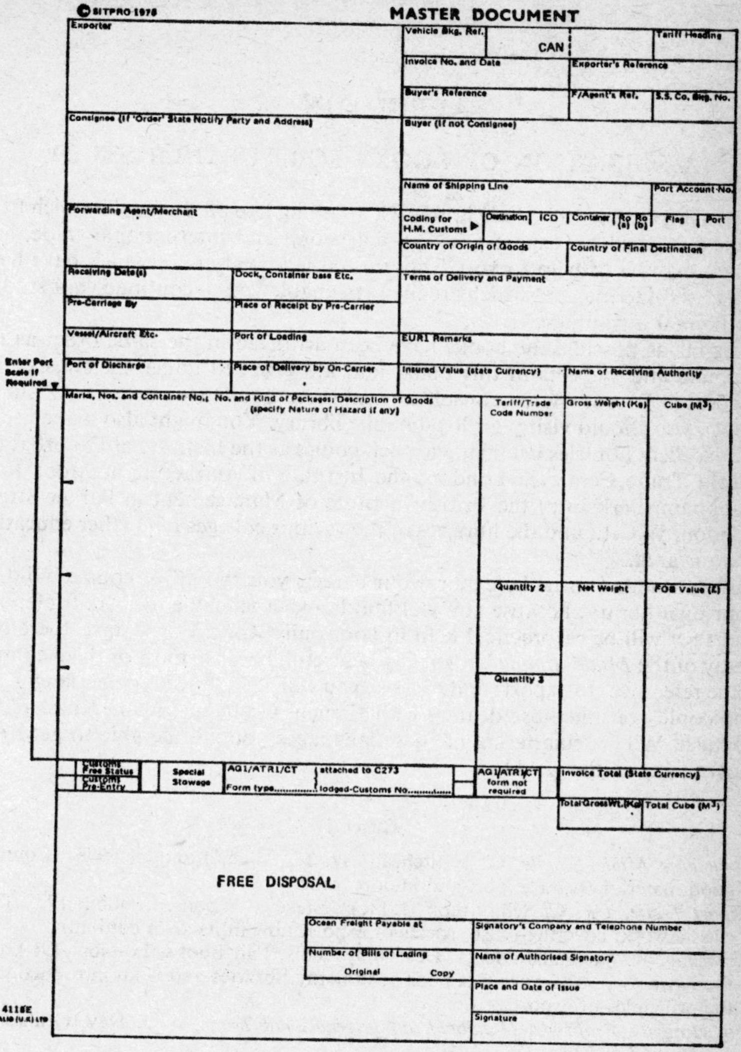
© SITPRO 1978

MASTER DOCUMENT

Exporter

Vehicle Bkg. Ref.

CAN

Tariff Heading

Invoice No. and Date

Exporter's Reference

Buyer's Reference

F/Agent's Ref.

S.S. Co. Bkg. No.

Consignee (If 'Order' State Notify Party and Address)

Buyer (If not Consignee)

Name of Shipping Line

Port Account No.

Forwarding Agent/Merchant

Coding for H.M. Customs ▶

Destination | ICD | Container | No (a) | No (b) | Flag | Port

Country of Origin of Goods

Country of Final Destination

Receiving Date(s)

Dock, Container base Etc.

Terms of Delivery and Payment

Pre-Carriage By

Place of Receipt by Pre-Carrier

Vessel/Aircraft Etc.

Port of Loading

EUR1 Remarks

Enter Port Scale if Required ▼

Port of Discharge

Place of Delivery by On-Carrier

Insured Value (state Currency)

Name of Receiving Authority

Marks, Nos. and Container No.; No. and Kind of Packages; Description of Goods (specify Nature of Hazard if any)

Tariff/Trade Code Number

Gross Weight (Kg)

Cube (M^3)

Quantity 2

Net Weight

FOB Value (£)

Quantity 3

Customs Free Status

Customs Pre-Entry

Special Stowage

AGI/ATR1/CT Form type............ attached to C273 lodged-Customs No...........

AGI/ATR1/CT form not required

Invoice Total (State Currency)

Total Gross Wt. (Kg)

Total Cube (M^3)

FREE DISPOSAL

Ocean Freight Payable at

Signatory's Company and Telephone Number

Number of Bills of Lading

Original Copy

Name of Authorised Signatory

Place and Date of Issue

Signature

4118E GEALIS (U.K.) LTD

Fig. 27. The Master Document of an Aligned Series.
(courtesy SITPRO)

APPENDIX 2

A SELECTION OF BOOKS FOR FURTHER STUDY

It is impossible to include in this list anything like all the books which have been published on export practice, marketing and international trade, and which may be of help to you. Those listed below are ones which have been most useful to me, and which are likely to enable you to continue your studies to the best advantage.

As far as possible the books have been arranged in the same order as the chapters and subjects in this book, and are grouped under their respective headings. To borrow or consult any of these books (some are now out of print), you should visit your local public library. You might also make use of the excellent libraries belonging to such bodies as the Institute of Export at the World Trade Centre in London; the Institute of Marketing at Moor Hall, Cookham, Berkshire; the British Institute of Management in Parker Street, London, W.C.1., and the libraries of the various colleges of further education in your area.

If you intend to make export your career, you should of course build up your own library, because you will find books a valuable means of reference and they will be of practical help in your daily work. For a start, therefore, many of the *Made Simple* books may be useful, because most of them contain some references to export; and because you will need to study other languages, you could consult those dealing with French, German, Italian, Russian and Spanish. With a smattering of these languages you will be able to get by in most places in the world.

General

Commerce Made Simple, G. Whitehead, W. H. Allen, London, 1976. (Contains good material on the export and import trade.)

Export Trade, The, C. Schmitthoff (Editor), Stevens & Sons, London, 1975. (The classic work, covering most aspects of export, now in its sixth edition.)

Exporting, R. Neillands and H. Deschampsneufs, Pan Books, London, 1969. (Although now out of print this book is in many libraries and is an introduction to the principles of export.)

Exporting for Profit—A Handbook on International Trade, A. J. Day, Graham & Trotman, London, 1976.

Harmonization of Business Practice in the Common Market, D. Tookey, Gower Press, Epping, 1973. (A useful work dealing with the conduct of business between Britain and the EEC.)

International Marketing Management, J. M. Livingstone, Macmillan Press, London, 1976. (An excellent background to the practice and marketing of exports.)

Marketing Overseas, H. Deschampsneufs, Pergamon Press, Oxford, 1967. (A helpful summary of the main elements of exporting.)

World Trade

International Trade

And Tomorrow the World—Inside IBM, R. Malik, Millington, London, 1976. (An interesting account of one of the world's largest multi-national corporations.)
Applied Economics Made Simple, D. T. Lobley, W. H. Allen, London, 1976. (Contains material on international trade and the underdeveloped nations.)
Economic History Made Simple, B. J. Smales, W. H. Allen, London, 1975.
Economics for Managers, P. Crowther and B. A. Richards, Edward Arnold, London, 1975. (Contains much helpful information about national and international trade, as well as details regarding costs and prices.)
Economics Made Simple, G. Whitehead, W. H. Allen, London, 1977. (Contains excellent material on the working of international trade.)
International Business, R. M. Blough, McGraw-Hill, Maidenhead, 1966. (An excellent introduction to international trade.)
Modern World System, The, I. Wallerstein, Academic Press, London, 1976. (A good economic history of the Western European nations.)
US Power and the Multi-national Corporation, R. Gilpin, Macmillan, London, 1976. (A useful study of American multi-national companies.)

Geography

Economic and Social Geography Made Simple, R. Knowles and J. Wareing, W. H. Allen, London, 1976. (A comprehensive survey of world economic geography.)
Economic Geography, H. Robinson, Macdonald & Evans, London, 1968. (A concise summary of the main elements of world economic geography.)
Economic Geography for Professional Students, J. Inch, Pitman, London, 1973. (A most useful introduction to economic geography in simple terms.)
Lloyd's Maritime Atlas, Lloyds Corporation, London, 1971.
Oxford Economic Atlas of the World, Oxford University Press, Oxford, 1972.
Reader's Digest Great World Atlas, Reader's Digest, London, 1972.

Statistics

On Thinking Statistically, M. B. Brodie, Pelican, Harmondsworth, 1974. (An excellent introductory text about statistics.)
Profit from Figures, C. J. Anson, McGraw-Hill, Maidenhead, 1971. (One of the most up-to-date books on managerial statistics.)
Statistics Made Simple, H. T. Hayslett, W. H. Allen, London, 1976. (An excellent introduction to statistics in commerce.)

Dictionaries

Dictionary of Shipping Terms and Phrases, E. F. Stevens, Pitman, London, 1971.

Export Practice

General

Elements of Overseas Trade, G. Whitehead, Croner Publications, New Malden, 1976.
Export Data, L. A. Rocker, Benn Brothers, Tonbridge. (A guide to documentation and local requirements for shipping, updated every month.)
Export Practice and Documentation, A. G. Walker, Butterworth, London, 1970. (Although this book is out of print it can still be found in libraries, and is the most comprehensive book on export practice.)
Exporting, D. F. Taylor and E. A. Rutland, Teach Yourself Books, London, 1971. (A short summary of the main ways in which an export order may be handled.)
Practice of Exporting, P. Allen, Macdonald & Evans, London, 1975. (A concise summary of the main elements in an export transaction.)

Reference Book for Exporters, R. K. Bridges (Editor), Croner Publications, New Malden. (A standard work, updated monthly, Croner's is especially useful for the details of documents and procedures for every overseas market.)

Transportation and Distribution for European Markets, J. Frain, Butterworth, London, 1970. (Contains invaluable details of transport facilities and distribution options for European countries.)

Orders and Customs Entries

Documentation of Exports for Statistical Purposes, H.M. Customs & Excise, 1975. (Available through any HMSO branch. Explains how to complete Customs entries correctly.)

Incoterms 1953, British National Committee, 52 High Holborn, London, W.C.1. (The international rules for the interpretation of trade terms of delivery as set out by the ICC.)

Office Practice Made Simple, G. Whitehead, W. H. Allen, London, 1977. (Contains excellent material on the export office and procedures.)

European Economic Community Preferences, Notice No. 810.

Notes on Completing Community Transit Terms, Notice No. 751. H.M. Customs & Excise. (Available from HMSO.)

Transport and Documentation

Aligned Documents for Export, D. Smith, Gower Press, Epping, 1974. (A practical book on how to introduce a system of aligned documentation into a company.)

Containerisation and Other Unit Transport, G. Van Den Burg, Hutchinson, London, 1972. (A valuable study of the use of containers and other unit loads.)

Elements of Shipping, A. E. Branch, Chapman & Hall, London, 1970. (A useful book for anyone concerned with the shipping industry.)

Freight Forwarders, D. J. Hill, Stevens & Sons, London, 1972. (A useful book about the work of the freight forwarder.)

Systematic Export Documentation, SITPRO, 11/12 Waterloo Place, London S.W.1., 1976.

Transport and Distribution Made Simple, D. Benson and G. Whitehead, W. H. Allen, London, 1975. (A comprehensive book covering all aspects of transport and the documents used in domestic and foreign trade.)

Finance of Exports

Finance of Foreign Trade and Foreign Exchange, D. F. Whiting, Macdonald & Evans, London, 1969. (A most useful outline of methods of payment for exports and the finance of international trade.)

Market the World, ECGD, Aldermanbury House, Aldermanbury, London, E.C.2., 1976. (This and other leaflets explain the terms under which ECGD will insure exporters against loss of payment.)

Sources and Management of Export Finance, W. W. Syrett and R. F. Pither, Gower Press, Epping, 1972. (An up-to-date study of how to finance export business.)

Uniform Customs and Practice for Documentary Credits.

Uniform Rules for the Collection of Commercial Paper.

(Both the above, published by the International Chamber of Commerce, British National Committee, 52 High Holborn, London, W.C.1., are necessary since they contain the rules for Documentary Credits and Bills of Exchange as agreed by most countries.)

Cargo Insurance

Handbook to Marine Insurance, V. Dover, H. F. & G. W. Witherby, London, 1971. (A valuable book containing the elements of marine insurance practice.)

Marine Insurance, Volume 2: *Cargo Practice*, R. H. Brown, Witherby, London, 1970. (An authoritative work on cargo insurance.)

Principles of Marine Insurance, H. A. Turner, Stone & Cox, London, 1971. (An excellent summary of the basis of marine insurance.)

Legal Aspects of Export

Introduction to English Law, P. S. James, Butterworth, London, 1972. (Contains the essential elements of English Law.)
Law Made Simple, C. Padfield, W. H. Allen, London, 1976. (An introduction to the English legal system and English law.)
Law of the Carriage of Goods by Land, Sea and Air, J. Ridley, edited by G. Whitehead, Stevens, 1970. (An excellent book on the legal aspects of these forms of transportation.)
Legal Aspects of Export Sales, C. Schmitthoff, Institute of Export, World Trade Centre, London, E.1, 1969. (An excellent summary of the laws governing export sales contracts.)
Principles of Mercantile Law, E. W. Chance, edited by J. Westwood, Cassell, London, 1970. (An authoritative book on all aspects of mercantile law.)

Export Marketing

General

International Marketing, P. Cateora and L. Hess, Irwin, New York, 1972.
International Marketing, V. Terpstra, Holt, Rinehart and Winston, New York, 1972. (Both the above books are American, but explain the operation and principles of international marketing fully.)
International Marketing, J. Fayerweather, Prentice-Hall, Englewood Cliffs, N.J., 1970. (A concise account of international marketing in the series *Foundations of Marketing*.)
International Marketing Text and Cases, D. Leighton, McGraw-Hill, Maidenhead, 1966. (Excellent case histories on all aspects of international marketing.)
Marketing Made Simple, B. Howard Elvy, W. H. Allen, London, 1975. (A clear presentation of the principles of marketing, including export marketing.)
Overseas Marketing and Selling, D. Weller, Pitman, London, 1971. (A useful book on the principles of selling overseas.)

Overseas Markets

Business in Japan, Norbury and Bownas, Macmillan, London, 1974. (A penetrating analysis of how to sell to the Japanese.)
Guide to Europe, Institute of Directors, Thornton Cox, London, 1970. (Contains a wealth of valuable information about all the major European markets.)
Hints to Businessmen Booklets, BOTB, published continuously and obtainable from Export Series Division, Export House, 50 Ludgate Hill, London, E.C.4. (This series of booklets covers almost every overseas market, and each contains the essential facts of each country.)
Marketing in the Common Market, H. Deschampsneufs, Pan Books, London, 1973. (A concise view of marketing conditions as they affect British companies in the EEC.)
Overseas Trade Statistics of the United Kingdom, Department of Trade, HMSO, London. (Published monthly and annually, here is a list of the complete exports and imports of the United Kingdom.)
Selling to the Americans, P. Possess, Business Books, London, 1971. (A most helpful book showing how to sell to the Americans.)
The New Europeans, Anthony Sampson, Hodder & Stoughton, Sevenoaks, 1968. (An account of the new race of 'Europeans' who are emerging in Europe.)

Trade Contacts in Eastern Europe.
Trading with the USSR
(Two useful books with names of contacts in these areas, published by the London Chamber of Commerce.)
Year Book of the Commonwealth, HMSO, London. (Published annually, this contains essential information about Commonwealth countries.)
Note: Every public library contains a wealth of interesting and helpful travel books which will increase your knowledge of individual overseas markets.

Research

Assessing Export Potential, M. T. Slijper, Gower Press, Epping, 1972. (Explains how to explore overseas market possibilities.)
Compilation of Basic Information on Export Markets, International Trade Centre, Palais de Nations, Geneva, Switzerland, 1972. (A useful guide to assembling all the necessary information about export markets.)
Industrial Marketing Research, G. Wills, Pergamon, Oxford, 1972. (A valuable book on research as applied to industrial products.)
Leading Cases in Market Research, M. Adler, Business Books, London, 1971. (Good examples of market research, and how they were carried out.)
Short Guide to Market Research in Europe, M. Adler, Crosby Lockwood, London. (Explains how you may carry out research in European markets.)

Production

Economics of Multi-Plant Operation, F. M. Scherer, Harvard University Press, Harvard, 1975. (The handling of local plants in six countries, including setting them up.)
Exporting Know-how, BOTB, Export Series Division, Export House, 50 Ludgate Hill, London, E.C.4, 1974. (A concise guide to local licensing practices and how to arrange them.)
Fundamentals of Packaging, F. A. Paine (Editor), Institute of Packaging, Blackie, Glasgow, 1962. (An excellent guide to all aspects of packaging.)

Distribution

Export Agents, C. McMilland and S. Paulden, Gower Press, Epping, 1972. (A book dealing specifically with the use of agents in overseas markets.)
Physical Distribution for Export, D. Tookey, Gower Press, Epping, 1971. (A valuable book on the principles and practice of export distribution.)
Specimen Agency Agreements, Institute of Export, World Trade Centre, London, E.1, 1969. (A simple and clear explanation on how to draw up local agency agreements.)

Promotion

Advertising Made Simple, F. Jefkins, W. H. Allen, London, 1977. (A concise and clear account of how advertising works and how to do it.)
Advertising Today and Tomorrow, W. A. Evans, Allen & Unwin, London, 1968. (An excellent book on the principles and practice of advertising.)
International Direct Marketing, J. Dillon, McGraw-Hill, Maidenhead, 1976. (Almost the only book which covers direct mail and its use as a marketing weapon.)
Public Relations in World Marketing, F. Jefkins, Crosby Lockwood, London, 1966. (An excellent guide to the practice of public relations.)
Sales Literature for Industry, R. Stock, McGraw-Hill, Maidenhead, 1976. (Although not specifically on export, this is one of the few books dealing with sales literature of all kinds.)

Strategy and Management

Export Marketing Decisions, D. Tookey, Penguin Books, Harmondsworth, 1976. (Shows you how to develop your export business.)

International Business Management, J. Fayerweather, McGraw-Hill, Maidenhead, 1969. (A study in depth of international management problems.)

International Marketing Strategy, I. Thorelli, Penguin Books, Harmondsworth, 1973. (A valuable set of case histories about the various aspects of export marketing and management.)

Managing for Results, P. Drucker, Pan Books, London, 1967. (An excellent account of how managers have to take decisions and the ways in which they can do this.)

Thinking Managerially about Exports, G. H. Sharman, Institute of Export, World Trade Centre, London, E.1, 1971. (Deals in an easy-to-read form with the elements of management accounting and export management.)

Index